INFORMATION SYSTEMS
AND PUBLIC MANAGEMENT

INFORMATION SYSTEMS AND PUBLIC MANAGEMENT

John M. Stevens
Robert P. McGowan

PRAEGER SPECIAL STUDIES • PRAEGER SCIENTIFIC

New York • Philadelphia • Eastbourne, UK
Toronto • Hong Kong • Tokyo • Sydney

350
S 844

Library of Congress Cataloging in Publication Data
Stevens, John M.
  Information systems and public management.

  Bibliography: p.
  Includes index.
  1. Public administration—Data processing.
  2. Administrative agencies—Data processing.
  3. Management information systems.   I. Title.
  JF1525.A8S88   1985   350'.00028'54   85-6472
  ISBN 0-03-004447-2 (alk. paper)

Published in 1985 by Praeger Publishers
CBS Educational and Professional Publishing, a Division of CBS Inc.
521 Fifth Avenue, New York, NY 10175 USA

© 1985 by Praeger Publishers

56789 052 987654321

Printed in the United States of America on acid-free paper

INTERNATIONAL OFFICES

Orders from outside the United States should be sent to the appropriate address listed below. Orders from areas not listed below should be placed through CBS International Publishing. 383 Madison Ave., New York, NY 10175 USA

Australia, New Zealand
Holt Saunders, Pty, Ltd., 9 Waltham St., Artarmon, N.S.W. 2064, Sydney, Australia

Canada
Holt, Rinehart & Winston of Canada, 55 Horner Ave., Toronto, Ontario, Canada M8Z 4X6

Europe, the Middle East, & Africa
Holt Saunders, Ltd., 1 St. Anne's Road, Eastbourne, East Sussex, England BN21 3UN

Japan
Holt Saunders, Ltd., Ichibancho Central Building, 22-1 Ichibancho, 3rd Floor, Chiyodaku, Tokyo, Japan

Hong Kong, Southeast Asia
Holt Saunders Asia, Ltd., 10 Fl, Intercontinental Plaza, 94 Granville Road, Tsim Sha Tsui East, Kowloon, Hong Kong

Manuscript submissions should be sent to the Editorial Director, Praeger Publishers, 521 Fifth Avenue, New York, NY 10175 USA

Preface

The purpose of this book is to provide a means for students of public organizations and management to understand the relationships between information systems and public management concepts. Students of public management and organizations have typically relied on diverse readings on information systems concepts used in private sector management or individual case studies. These approaches are useful and not invalid in themselves, but they do not provide the integrated perspective that is needed to address the unique and many times more complex operating requirements of public sector managers.

This book is written for advanced undergraduate or graduate students of public management/administration, public policy, or other disciplines that focus on the public sector. This book is for those students who are in need of understanding information management as managers or those who wish to become more specialized in computer-based information systems. It is designed for individuals who have had some grounding in organization and management theory and are interested in information systems management in government or in other public or nonprofit organizations. Any exposure to programming or research methods would be useful; however, this background is not required for the student to benefit from the material on systems design and public management.

Public sector managers today are being asked to make critical and costly decisions in an environment of increased demands for accountability coupled with shrinking resources. These conditions, unfortunately, are expected to continue; therefore, every resource, especially information, must be more economically and effectively managed. In the future, many public sector managers will be confronted with resource allocation decisions that will probably involve personnel and information systems trade-offs. As public sector organizations and society become more information intensive, public managers will have to master key information issues that support the decisions and objectives of those organizations.

This book is based on the experiences of the authors, who have taught public administration courses in information management at Pennsylvania State University and Syracuse University, researched public management and information issues, and have developed information concepts based on work with various government officials on information systems matters. Various approaches have been used to present the material—integration of management and information systems issues, case analyses, discussion of an overall systems framework, and analysis of existing systems. Also, information management principles are discussed in relation to policy issues and to such substantive areas as human service, local government, federal agencies, public safety (police, fire), and computerized welfare functions.

The outline for the book follows a conceptual framework that has essentially three major elements. Part I provides an overview of management and a systems-contingency model of a public sector organization in which the information management and control process is embedded. It also presents an overview of computer fundamentals, as well as information and control process issues in various levels of government that will be used to structure the remaining chapters.

Part II presents the systems development, analysis, implementation, and evaluation phases of the design cycle that will be applied to the federal, state, and local levels of government. Part III presents organizational, policy, and privacy considerations, as well as prospects for the future.

An implicit assumption throughout is that public managers require a systematic framework for understanding the complexity and massive amounts of information in the context of decisions and management. Managers will become more effective if computer-aided information and decision support systems are understood, designed effectively, and used in the service of the public. Of course, the major emphasis is on the public sector management process and the explicit supporting role of information management.

Acknowledgments

This book reflects the help and support of many people to whom we are sincerely grateful. Because there are so many, it is not possible to thank here all of those individually who have influenced our thinking, so these acknowledgments are by no means considered complete. We are indebted not only to the individuals or groups mentioned here, but also to those who helped and are not explicitly recognized. Our thinking has profited immeasurably from the friends, colleagues, other scholars and practitioners cited and not cited who we hope will recognize their part. Especially, we thank the federal, state and local practitioners from whom we have drawn directly such as the Pennsylvania State Government managers and analysts in the Office of Budget and Administration who are responsible for the design and implementation of the Integrated Central System. This also includes the leadership in the Pennsylvania State Bureau of EDP Policy and Planning. Others in the Federal ADP Reorganization Study complemented our approach with their important analyses and insights.

Carol Kottmeier, Scott Kutz and Mike O'Neill, the authors of the three cases, are long time supporters whose valuable contributions to our effort to anchor information system concepts in the realities of Federal, state and local government are appreciated. We also want to give our thanks to the many members of the Public Sector Division of the Academy Management and the Management Science and Policy Analysis Section of the American Society of Public Administration for their ongoing help, advice, professional appraisals of our work and friendship. The contributions of our colleagues in the Institute of Public Administration, other departments and the Capitol Campus of The Pennsylvania State University and the Department of Management at the University of Denver were central to the development and completion of this book.

Though many others have helped greatly, we owe special thanks to Marilyn Ehrlich and Stephanie Grant of Praeger Publishers who provided critical, positive guidance, timely support and expert editorial assistance throughout the publication process. Our typists over the haul, Jan Smith initially, then Carol Coppolino deserve our gratitude because the work continued coherently even when nobody could remember which draft was being placed in their queue or which was being typed. Because of the necessary revisions and reductions we could not include every idea that was once in draft form; however, we do accept the responsibility for the final substance and structure of the end product and any deficiencies that exist. We have learned and hope that we can transmit the lessons here and in the future.

Finally, but not least, we cannot, in many respects, acknowledge the many tangible and intangible contributions and opportunity costs provided by our families, but we believe that they will recognize their valuable roles in supporting this project and consider the benefits worthwhile.

Contents

PART I:

INFORMATION SYSTEMS AND PUBLIC MANAGEMENT

1

Overview of Information Systems and Management Issues in Public Sector Organizations

BACKGROUND AND PURPOSE

One societal litany being recited with increased frequency and volume is that government is not keeping its promises to cure economic and social ills, and is now itself a major part of the problems facing the United States. An opposing argument is that government's ability to collect, store, process, analyze, and use information to deal with complex problems has never been greater. Even with hundreds of mainframes, thousands of minicomputers, millions of microprocessors, massive use of micro or personal computers inside the executive, legislative, and judicial branches of government, and the capability to use satellites with worldwide computers, the sources of and demands for accountability from managers in government are accelerating along with the problems. One critical question in this dilemma of increased demands and resources is whether the ability and understanding of government managers to use information systems and the related technology have accelerated as rapidly as the problems. Some would argue that the capability of government brainware and information management structures have fallen behind the technological capacity of information system hardware and software.

If there was ever a technological trend that was linked to managerial processes and had significant long- and short-term implications for public management, it is the development of computerized information systems. This development includes the recent emphasis on personal or microcomputers, intelligent terminals, work stations, networking, integration, word processing, and telecommunications, combined with the use of large mainframes in government agencies such as those that store defense information, spew the checks for the Social Security Administration, or provide for early warning ballistic missile systems. However, a major deficiency in the growth of computerized information systems is not their basic or advanced technology, but rather their interdependence with and application to managerial processes in government.

This growth of computer technology does not mean that existing manual filing techniques, information retrieval, or decision systems are obsolete or inadequate. It does suggest that the complex tasks and functions of government can be more effectively performed if the supporting information systems correspond to information requirements and are understood and controlled by their managers. Different government programs and levels of government must address some of the most difficult and intractable problems a modern society can generate. If not managed properly, the information resource can exacerbate the complexity and ambiguity of the managerial task in government. The most recent evaluations of government information systems and their components by the General Accounting Office, congressional, and executive reports demonstrate that substantial improvements are still required in their management (see, for example, Public Law 96–511, 1980).

The purpose of this book is to provide a systematic approach to the complex problem of understanding the role of information systems in public management. This is a conceptually difficult problem because the roles of information systems in public management are not totally prescribed or understood. Many books on public administration and management emphasize internal, administrative, or functional operations, whereas others address information-related functions or focus on a specific level of government (Danziger et al. 1982). These approaches have their individual strengths and limitations. Yet an approach that attempts to integrate these basic concepts has to take a broader view of the use and design of information systems by public managers.

The approach taken here views the public organization as the basic foundation, with the managers as the primary controllers of the organization. This perspective does not discount the influence of external factors or exclude the influence of behavioral variables such as clients or citizens; rather, it attempts to place each factor in the context of other, many times competing, influences. Public sector managers have external as well as internal demands to deal with and often do not have the luxury of choosing their tasks. Though there are many kinds of public organizations that provide services, the focus in this book is on general government management.

NEED FOR IMPROVED INFORMATION SYSTEMS MANAGEMENT

Public managers have the authority for and are responsible for such processes as policy formulation, planning, implementation, decision making, and control. Some short-term questions for operational managers may deal with budgetary, personnel, inventory problems, or resource efficiency, whereas top-level managers in government organizations normally have to allocate resources over many programs as well as plan for achieving strategic and statutory goals or objectives. Each of these managerial functions can be performed more effectively if the organizational information system supports the relevant decision-making requirements.

An information system should provide support for monitoring and controlling internal operations across the varied functions of the agency or government level. Policy, planning, implementation, decision making, and control processes have to be applied to such substantive areas as public safety, welfare, transportation, and education, as well as to such administrative functions as personnel management and budgeting. Though the information technology is available to support the needs of these administrative processes, specification of objectives and measures of performance for the public sector do not yet correspond to the level of sophistication in state-of-the-art technology. For example, though revenue forecasting models have been available for many years, most government units do not have reliable methods that are used consistently. One critical need for public sector managers is the development of measures and processes for improving the efficiency and effectiveness of daily operations. These specifications can be aided by an effective information system.

Another important level of responsibility for government managers is the strategic or policy-planning function. Each requires valid information about external influences that affect the internal management of the organization. Uncertainty reduction and policy formula-

lation concerning the organizational objectives require information that supports both internal efficiency and external effectiveness. An examination of the success of efforts such as program evaluation for government programs would illustrate that measures of effectiveness for these internal and external efforts are usually inadequate both in terms of formulating standards and assessing performance in most government service functions. These points will be pursued in subsequent chapters, but the point here is that public managers need improved information systems to support their strategic and top-level decision-making and evaluation functions.

With the problems of developing internal performance criteria and measuring effectiveness to meet external objectives or demand, public sector managers need a management-based perspective on information systems and their uses (Horton and Marchand 1982). Monitoring ongoing operations, integrating internal functions, and dealing with political, economic, and technological factors in the environment require that managers use and control every possible resource, especially information, that could make the difference between effective and ineffective decisions. Because information is a vital resource in managing public functions, the management of information must also be effective.

INFORMATION THEORY, CONCEPTS, AND DEFINITIONS

The usual definition of information theory includes mathematical formulations of the communication process, sometimes with both mechanical or electronic components. The transmission of information starts with a source and progresses through a channel to a receiver or destination. The information is encoded by the source and decoded by the receiver and is subject to distortion and/or noise through the process. Noise may take the form of overload, condensation, or loss. Senders may distort information intentionally or unintentionally by introducing noise. There may be breaks in the communication chain, the recipient may misinterpret the message, or external factors such as time constraints on the sender or receiver may inhibit full communication of information.

Information theory can be analyzed mathematically or behaviorally, but the important issue here is how information can be used in the managerial decision process. If there are potential distortions emanating from the sender (Is the information or data valid?), the channel or medium (Was reduction, truncation, or other form of noise introduced during transmission?), or the recipient (Does the manager understand the data or information that was collected or used in an evaluation?), the manager must deal with the uncertainty or problems associated with the specific part of the information-communication process. Information systems are only as effective as the managers who design and use the data or information that is processed by them.

INFORMATION SYSTEM CONCEPTS AND DEFINITIONS

A primary ingredient of the communication system to be discussed is information. The terms "information," "data," and "knowledge" are commonly intermingled and substituted one for the other. Therefore it is helpful to define our terms before examining the process by which they are interrelated.

Data can be thought of as the building blocks of information. Data are manipulated in some manner, and the way in which they are handled leads us to the second element: *information.* The term "information" involves the concept of utility attached to the data.

> Information utility may be realized only when information is transmitted from one data-processing or information-generating system to another. Information when transmitted assumes an economic value because it can modify the behavior of the second system. (Knight and McDaniel 1979, p. 13)

Finally, *knowledge,* the third element, involves the collection of information into an organized body of thought or guiding principles. It allows us to comprehend theoretical frameworks and interpret differences.

As components of a system, these elements build on one another. Data that are faulty or subject to distortion will, in turn, bias information, limit our available knowledge of a particular set of events or potential outcomes, and adversely affect decisions. Conversely, data that have been carefully acquired, scrutinized, and disseminated as information will contribute to effective decision making.

INFORMATION AND DECISION MAKING

Before looking at information systems as they operate within government agencies, it is useful to explore the concept of information as it relates to decision making. Today's managers in government organizations and students of management no doubt have been exposed to the variety of terms associated with the use of information. Often a source of confusion and bewilderment to the novice, terms such as "ADP," "EDP," "MIS," "data base management," "information resource management," "software," and "CRT" no longer elicit more than a flinch from experienced managers (Dutton 1982). Today's managers assume that information systems, in whatever form, are here to stay and will continue to have a growing influence in our society (Senn 1982; Danziger et al. 1982). One possible explanation for the growing acceptance of these new systems has been the transition from large mainframe computers to smaller units and hand-held devices that the user can understand and manipulate without the help of a professional staff. Use of the devices in the organization is no longer based solely on availability and cost considerations. Equipment costs have steadily declined over the past ten years with the advent of large scale integration technology. Thus management must determine if ongoing programs and activities can be refashioned to take advantage of available information storage and processing technologies.

INFORMATION ACTIVITIES

In a government agency, such factors as organizational mission, departmental size, and history (the amount of time that the agency has been in existence or responsible for delivery of particular programs and activities) will determine the extent to which one element of the information system is emphasized over the other. Information storage and retrieval, record keeping, statistical data collection and reporting, and providing management information are some of the major information systems activities. Two of these activities, information storage and retrieval and record keeping, are dominant in many government agencies. Emphasis at this stage is on routines, and data are often transferred from manual to automated form to facilitate speed and accuracy of processing (McGowan and Loveless 1982).

The collection of statistical data has, in many instances, involved the development and use of a databank approach to managing information. Referring to the collection and long-term storage of large amounts of data that serve many purposes, databanks have been successfully established and used in areas such as law enforcement, for example, the FBI files. A limitation of this approach has been that databank activities are viewed as secondary to the agency's primary service functions and therefore are not integrated into the day-to-day management of the organization (Kraemer and King 1977).

Two other activities, reporting and providing management information, are areas that have not until recently been extensively used by government managers. Now there are indications that they will be used to provide more integrated and comprehensive approaches to the use of information. Coupled with the necessity for government agencies to measure and assess program *outcomes* as opposed to *outputs*, efforts are being made to increase staff competence in analyzing information for program management purposes. Information that is presently being collected and stored for routine functions is also being scrutinized and updated to serve multiple purposes.

INFORMATION SYSTEMS, DECISION MAKING, AND PUBLIC MANAGEMENT

Figure 1.1 represents a general view of the linkage between information systems and public management. Data have to be interpreted and processed by the manager to become information that is relevant for analysis/evaluation and decisions. For the manager to manage well and to make effective decisions, the information system must be composed of well-integrated components and processes. Such current problems as demands for accountability have added new levels of complexity to the decision-making process and the role of information systems in that process. Managers should be able to understand the technology associated with the information process as well as its organizational impact.

Because the activities of government organizations are becoming more extended, demands for accountability from wider sectors of society are increasing. With the role of government being scrutinized more regularly, computerized information systems must conform to the needs of managers. Internal data are collected for budgeting, per-

FIGURE 1.1. General Information Systems Process for Public Managers

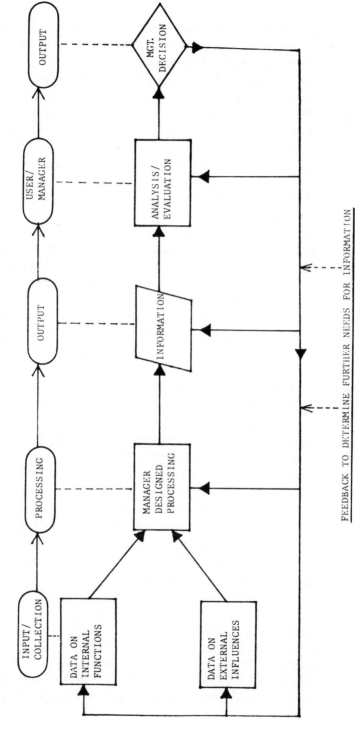

Source: Compiled by the author.

sonnel planning, or related information-based activities such as filing of records. The manager must decide whether the benefits, costs, or size of organization require automated data collection, storage, processing, or filing procedures. A municipality of 5,000 people with public safety, public works, water billing, and taxing functions primarily handled by a larger jurisdiction or working with a joint agreement may not require its own computerized record keeping; but a similar local government responsible for handling these same functions may benefit greatly from automated taxing, billing, and data collection.

Data for intergovernmental transfers and related accounting or statutory requirements may require sophisticated record keeping and online review capability in both large and small local governments. The key element in the information system is the manager who must specify what data are collected for what reasons, in addition to justifying the costs and benefits both financially and in terms of impact on the organization.

The manager dictates how data are processed—that is, how they are produced, formatted, and disseminated. The data then become information when they are used in the decision-making process by the manager or other users. Also, the information may be used for further analysis or evaluation. For example, forecasting the expected rate of automobile accidents when switching from twice-a-year to once-a-year inspections is an exercise that is heavily dependent on a reliable information base. Specific elements of the information system for public managers outlined in Figure 1.1 will be discussed in later chapters; however, each of the steps in the process, including how feedback is used to improve the system, has to be viewed in a managerial framework to understand the broader linkages of information systems with the organizational functions. Each of these elements has implications for the usual planning, organizing, controlling, staffing, and reporting processes for the top, mid, and operational levels of management in government organizations.

DECISION TYPES

While the information system, as previously defined, involves a series of integrated steps, the decision process often operates in a less defined manner. A distinction that managers and theorists have drawn to a great extent is that between *routine* and *nonroutine* decisions. Simon (1973b), defining the two types as "programmed" and "ill-structured", views routine decisions as those that can be made in a prescribed manner. Often of an administrative or procedural nature, these decisions are governed by the traditional mores of the organization: The public agency has historically operated in a particular manner, the clients or constituent groups have grown to expect a fixed pattern of behavior, or the agency is governed by established rules and legislative mandates that circumscribe its activities.

Conversely, nonroutine or ill-structured decisions involve complex problems and issues for which no precedent or pattern exists. Radford (1977) has described some of their primary characteristics. As he points out, one of the distinctions between programmed and nonprogrammed decisions is the amount of information that is available to assist the decision maker. For routine administrative decisions, information is processed to the extent that it matches the required input format. In a social service agency, for example, the caseworker frequently enters the relevant information about a client on forms that, in turn, are entered into a reporting system. Based on these data, levels of eligibility and availability of service are determined. Information that does not fall within the preset reporting categories is not used. Benefits of a system of this kind are that decision criteria are unambiguous and applied to cases by class of problem, an increased number of clients are serviced, and caseworkers do not reach decisions on a case-by-case or idiosyncratic basis. There are limitations as well. There is little or no room left for including additional information that the client feels is important to his or her case. The caseworker often becomes frustrated by the process—performing a processing role as opposed to a professional service activity.

At the opposite extreme, individuals in a public agency may be required to make decisions based on limited information. Returning to the social service agency example, we see problems that arise for which no procedures or documentation exist. A program to establish counseling for unwed mothers is one example of this decision situation. Although the funding for the program comes from the federal level, state and local social service agencies must often operate on limited or nonexistent information in establishing standards and monitoring progress. Should the program be relatively passive in nature, that is, providing service only to those individuals who contact the agency? Or should an active search program be enacted by contacting recipients through school districts and community groups? What, in fact, are the estimated number of individuals who would participate, and over what period of time? These questions illustrate the nature of a nonprogrammed or ill-structured decision situation.

MANAGEMENT CONTROL ISSUES IN PUBLIC/GOVERNMENT ORGANIZATIONS: BASES FOR MORE PRECISE ROLE OF MANAGEMENT IN DEFINING INFORMATION SYSTEMS NEEDS

Historically, public organizations have been more difficult to control than private organizations because their objectives have been more oriented toward such intractable problems as welfare, defense, transportation, public safety, or education. It may be easier to assess the performance of police departments in their apprehension than their prevention functions, but there is more need for consensus on what constitutes adequate performance in both of these activities. There is continuing debate on what constitutes appropriate levels of education, defense, welfare/poverty reduction, or even such mundane operations as parking garages. Characteristics of nonprofit and, by extension, government organizations that influence management control have been presented by Anthony and Herzlinger (1980): absence of a profit measure, tendency to be service organizations, constraints on goals and strategies, less dependence on clients for financial support, dominance by professionals, differences in governance, and differences in top management controls. These characteristics set up imperatives for managers who have to deal with and control these ambiguities to achieve their organizational objectives.

A powerful impetus for seeking and having a valid, timely information system is to acquire managerial control. Control is not being used here in the personalized, manipulative, or overly rationalistic sense, but rather as a critical component of the managerial process with its attendant ambiguities, uncertainties, and behavioral influences. The basic assumption is that management at all levels is in the most central position to identify, understand, and interpret organizational objectives in the context of multiple, sometimes competing, influences. Therefore the control process is most effectively centered at the nexus where operational requirements, relevant information, the corresponding resources, and authority converge.

The overarching information systems design issue is that if managers are to control organizations, they must understand critical information variables.

ORGANIZATIONAL ISSUES RELATED TO INFORMATION SYSTEMS

Because many problems confronting government organizations originate in their diffuse missions, there is a tendency to centralize decision making and remove responsibility from lower levels in the organization. In addition, the intangible products of government, such as ajudication and regulation of service, require different measures and sources of accountability. The manager becomes subject to influences other than the more rational or precise criteria of effectiveness measures, quality, and quantity.

Most government organizations have a functional structure with more or less standardized functions to perform. For example, an urban or municipal government includes divisions of housing, public safety, health, education, social/welfare services, utilities, recreation public works, property, financial, and personnel functions. Each of these functions has unique outputs and processes but also are supported by common revenue generating, personnel, and administrative processes. These functions, along with intergovernmental coordination, comprise the major tasks and activities that have to be performed and efficiently managed. The managers must provide for integrated control of each of these functions both separately and together using proper informational and evaluation support. Neither control nor evaluation can be performed effectively if the information system does not support the subsystems of the government organization.

OVERVIEW OF MANAGEMENT APPROACH

Because the major purpose of this book is to present an approach to understanding and designing information systems for public managers, it is assuming a systematic management view rather than simply a rational, behavioral, or political posture. This does not imply that public management is a predominantly rational enterprise; rather, our approach chooses to emphasize what is possible to understand and accomplish. Public managers have accepted the responsibility for delivering public services with public resources and should therefore be accountable for doing it effectively with a minimum of costs. The basic argument here is that a systematic management-based approach to designing and using computerized information systems will contribute to solving many complex problems, only if managers play a central role in deciding how the systems will be used.

OUTLINE OF USES AND NEEDS FOR INFORMATION SYSTEMS IN PUBLIC MANAGEMENT

Management functions have been viewed as the processes by which strategic plans are made and decisions are translated into operational activities or outcomes. Many times managerial decisions focus on allocation of financial, authority, and personnel resources. Relevant information used to support these activities is usually related to implementing objectives. It is more structured than external information and usually more detailed. Operational control is normally focused on routine or more prescribed processes that emphasize precision, quantity and quality standards, division of authority, and responsibility for specific tasks. Operational control is more likely to emphasize material, service, or technological objectives. The common requirements across managerial levels is that information be accurate, complete, usable, timely, and supportive of the various managerial requirements.

Table 1.1 presents a general outline that can be used to define and examine the needs at different levels in the organization for information systems in government organizations. The table shows that the management levels of public organizations have different sources of information, responsibilities, needs, decisions, and objectives. The information needs correspond to levels of authority and responsibility.

Strategic management is associated with top-level goals or decisions. Broad organizational strategies are derived to achieve overall goals or objectives. The information used to support these actions and decisions is usually derived from the external environment and often lacks precision. In public sector organizations, strategic control or decisions may focus on the controllers (grantors of authority or

TABLE 1.1. Information Systems Needs for Public Managers

Management Level	Type of Information Needed	Primary Sources	Decisions Supported	Control Objective
Organizational–institutional–agency strategic level	Statutory authority, charter, long-term economic and budget resources, forecasting information on political uncertainty, social and technological trends	Executive, legislative, and judicial controllers Charter/laws Economic forecasts Technology forecasts Political environment Constituencies	Overall objectives Budgetary allocations Authority allocation Overall organization structure Level of differentiation and integration External coordination Intergovernmental relations	Acquire statutory authority Acquire budgets Achieve goals, support organization stability and survival Ensure overall organizational interdependence
Management—mid-level or coordinating	Control objectives, resources available, long-term needs, operational capability, resource potential	Internal resources Top level management Operational environment Past performance Financial sources	Allocate financial and personnel resources Ensure alignment of strategy and operations Reallocation of tasks	Resolve organizational conflict Achieve organizational objectives Align goals and set standards
Operational task/supervisory	Task technology, process requirements, resource availability, performance data, financial support, standards development, service impact	Technology requirements Past performance Personnel resources Budget forecasts Clients/recipients Top-level information	Evaluate and monitor operations Task design Procedures Measures need for evaluation Efficiency determination Cost reduction	Support objectives Efficient operations Low cost Meet standards Align top, mid, and operational level objectives

Source: Compiled by the author.

resources) either in the executive, legislative, or judicial area. For example, appropriations may carry specific riders, executive orders may impose additional reporting requirements, or court orders may require further compliance procedures. For the organization to meet its objectives, a critical level of authority and resources is therefore required from legislative and executive bodies. Top-level managers must produce a satisfactory service to further goal attainment and survival. It is the responsibility of the strategic managers to meet the strategic external contingencies with relevant information that favorably influences the external legislative or executive controllers.

Mid-level managers have the responsibility for implementing strategies developed by the top-level managers and aligning more global goals and objectives with operational and organizational realities. Most of the information needed by managers in this co-ordinating role will be derived from authority further up in the hierarchy or from lower levels where such information as costs, efficiency, and service problems or issues may be found. A manager serving in a senior civil service position in the federal government may be responsible for coordinating state or local government imple-mentation of a federal program, whereas a state level department head or regional director may have different political and financial factors to consider in meeting constituency needs. A municipal gov-ernment manager in a department of public safety or public works will have still different operational issues to manage in order to meet shorter term citizen, mayoral, or council objectives.

Though many managers will have to deal with information from sources outside the organization, the coordinating or mid-level man-ager has a key role. His or her primary task is acquiring essential information and meeting expectations from the top and operational levels inside the organization where financial and personnel resource allocation decisions are implemented.

Supervisory or operational level managers are also influenced by top and mid-level management, but their major task is to monitor and control specific behavior. The operational level manager requires more specific process-related information than the upper or mid-level manager.

Supervisors have to understand and translate statutory and func-tional requirements into operational concerns. Personnel require-ments, evaluation systems, and budgetary constraints converge on the front-line supervisor, who is responsible for actually meeting the imperatives specified in the law or regulation. Creating cleaner environments, reducing poverty, increasing public safety, developing educational standards, fixing potholes, or improving health have broad objectives that become difficult to define when they are operationalized. The task supervisor has to develop procedures to meet the standards of mid- and top-level management, as well as environmental pressures (client or constituency demands or political influence).

Table 1.1 outlines some of the information systems needs for public managers—from the top level, where organizational legitimation is an issue, to the operational level, where the rubber meets the road. There are different demands and needs that the information system must meet. Data collection on welfare clients meets higher level needs to compile agency program information and operational requirements for setting performance standards or work load requirements. Mid-level managers may use the same data to allocate departmental financial and personnel resources.

The value of an information system will be directly dependent on how well the public manager understands the organizational context, designs the supporting information system, and uses it to meet and maintain control. The interaction of multiple objectives, conflicting priorities, and internal-external demands requires a public manager who can best design tools to meet the real needs. With the evolving economic, technological, and political environment, a computerized information system is only as powerful as the manager's understanding of how to use it to meet public objectives.

APPROACH AND ORGANIZATION OF THIS BOOK

The organization of this book is based on a general approach that attempts to provide a structured and systematic view of information systems and their role in public management. Chapter 2 presents an overview of public organizations and the tasks of their managers. The major breakdown for the framework is based on external and internal information systems needs. The hardware, software, database, and filing components of an information system are presented in Chapter 3. Chapter 4 outlines the major federal, state, and local government information systems and management issues to provide a basis for further development of the systems design approach.

The information systems analysis and design process is presented in Chapter 5, building on the preceding conceptual, substantive, and analytical foundation. Chapter 6 examines issues in and approaches to the evaluation of information systems. Chapter 7 relates the use of information systems to the public sector policy process, and Chapter 8 views the societal, security, and privacy implications of government information systems. Finally, Chapter 9 addresses the future needs and effects of information systems on government and society.

Three cases are provided to supplement the material presented in the text. These appendixes act as practical mechanisms for integrating the conceptual and operational issues associated with certain managerial functions at the federal (Veterans Administration Insurance Management Information System), state (Programmed Project Management in Pennsylvania), and local (Comprehensive Employment and Training Act program in a county) levels.

2

Information Systems and Public Management Framework

It is being stated with increasing frequency that the ability to produce, store, process, and use information has extended in geometric proportions the capabilities of humans more than any technology since the advent of writing or printing. It has been estimated that in 1980 there were as many as 18,000 central processors in the federal government, more than 4,576 data systems, and at least 3.4 billion records on individuals who receive social security or medicare payments or who are suspects, taxpayers, motorists, government employees, service personnel, businesspeople, and others related to various government functions. This network of computers and data systems has the potential to reach from telephones to satellites and either directly or indirectly influence the lives of practically every person in the United States and many beyond the national borders. This widespread information network is significant for most citizens and especially important for people with organizational and management responsibilities in public organizations where the potential impact of their actions can affect delivery of the mail, human services, or ballistic missiles.

Madnick (1977) stated that "the complexity, interdependence, and rapidity of events in modern society have accelerated demands for more effective ways to store, process and manage information" (p. 1191). Others argue that the contribution of the human element to the effectiveness of information systems hardware has been outstripped by software and computer capability and that "brainware" has fallen woefully behind. The gap between human and technological capabilities has had an increasingly visible effect on public managers, who must routinely deal with the increasing complexity, demands, and costs of providing a multitude of services and products that must satisfy requirements of diverse publics and controllers.

BASIC PUBLIC MANAGEMENT FUNCTIONS

With the increasing demands for accountability, the skeptical attitude toward government effectiveness, the implications of the new federalism, and the general cutback management approach to most government functions, public managers at all levels must be able to meet their objectives and fulfill their responsibilities. Usually this means that more, better, and/or faster delivery of public services is needed; the capability and productivity of the public work force must be improved; the size of the work force must be reduced; program and agency management must be improved; waste and fraud must be eliminated; costs of services must be reduced; financial and operational functions have to be controlled and made efficient; public managers have to be controlled and made efficient; and public managers have to upgrade their knowledge to acquire control by establishing standards. All of these public managerial functions require significant improvements at all levels of government.

The traditional or classical approaches to public management can best be summarized with the well-known acronym *POSDCRB*, which addresses the common processes or functions that managers typically perform.

Planning is the pivotal managerial function because it is supposed to be based on organizational analysis and forecasts that precede and structure the other managerial activities. A plan should consist of the development and selection of alternatives to achieve objectives. For example, if a public organization is assigned through statutory, judicial, or executive authority certain responsibilities in welfare, fiscal, public safety, transportation, or personnel matters, the manager must gather information on organizational capabilities and the most likely future in order to derive alternatives and choose the best plan for meeting the public needs in the defined area of responsibility. This plan then becomes the basis for structuring the remaining actions.

Organizing is based on the definition of actions and tasks derived from the plan. It involves the selection of organizational forms in terms of centralization or decentralization of authority and responsibility among subordinates or functions within the agency, program, or organization. This means that the manager has to aggregate functions or operations into similar departmental groupings or levels and provide for coordination among them. The organizing function of management is a distribution of tasks, authority, and responsibilities to achieve the goals and objectives that were assigned or required by the plan.

Staffing is the managerial activity that follows and implements the plan and operationalizes the distribution of authority and responsibility by defining personnel requirements. The personnel functions of developing position classifications, job descriptions, recruiting, selecting, evaluating, training, and compensating are subparts of the staffing function that complement or fill the positions designed into the organization structure. The systematic approach to staffing includes forecasting, planning, and what is currently labeled human resource management.

Directing is the vehicle by which instructions, regulations, guidelines, and orders are formalized into organizational procedures and operations. It is an essential function that translates managerial requirements and authority into human behavior that corresponds to the accomplishment of organizational objectives. Direction can be formal, informal, or both, but the common thread is that the directives are linked to managerial and organizational/statutory objectives. Most standard operating procedures, regulations, directives, reporting requirements, and instructions used at all levels of government to implement laws are examples of the directing function.

Coordinating/controlling are the managerial functions that bring the plans and objectives of the manager to fruition. They affect all parts of the organization and require the manager to set standards for performance that correspond to the objectives, evaluate actual performance in terms of the standards, and take action to deal with the discrepancy between standards and performance across all organizational functions. Control is the most pervasive and coordination the most interdependent function of public managers because they have linkages backward to the plan and forward to the actual and future behavior of individuals and their contributions to the objectives of the organization.

Reporting integrates information and performance, and its purpose is to inform management about critical operations. Annual reports, status reports, budget estimates, expenditure levels, operational statistics, inventory status, input/output measures that inform managers, and executive, judicial, or legislative authorities are elements of the reporting process. The classical school of management saw reports as powerful means of control if used properly.

Budgeting, which is probably the most visible aspect of public management, is supposed to match resources with objectives through a plan of programs, activities, and expenditures for a given time period. If used correctly, the budget becomes a key method of implementing and integrating plans and programs with the current allocation of revenues or resources.

The traditional approach to management characterized by POSDCRB is probably the most common and easily understood model of public management. It has a long history and many current adherents, in addition to providing a comprehensive framework for the practical aspects of management. However, the classical model has undergone severe criticism and review because it offers what most critics call a "closed-system" perspective. That is, it provides a normative model of the managerial process with little or no appreciation of the complex information processing capabilities of humans and of the conflicting motivational, behavioral, and environmental variables associated with managing. Current models of management still observe the utility of the traditional processes associated with the classical approaches; however, the focus has shifted to more comprehensive views that incorporate not only internal focal points but also the more complex interactions with the critical components of the environment.

Because the dominant mechanism for providing public services, implementing public policy and regulations, adjudicating conflicting societal demands, and/or controlling internal government operations is the public organization, a systematic approach to ordering the managerial process is needed. Whether the organization is an agency of the federal executive branch, a state's department of transportation, a municipality, or a federal installation in a state or foreign country, the most feasible management strategy for achieving objectives and acquiring control toward these ends is to derive a realistic model of how the organization can or should be operated. This understanding should in turn provide the basis for designing organizational structures, determining information needs, and establishing control mechanisms that correspond to achieving public functions.

DECISION MAKING AND NEED FOR INFORMATION BY PUBLIC MANAGERS

One consistent activity that differentiates managers from other workers in an organization is that they have the authority and responsibility to make decisions regarding policies, objectives, structures, budgets, personnel, information, and controls within the organization. Strategic or top-level managers have different decision-making requirements and information needs than do operational managers, upon whom personal, organizational, and environmental factors have varying impacts. Managers require the capability to identify issues and/or problems that affect them and the ability to take some corrective action or deal with the cause of the problem by making a decision.

When the central problem is understood, alternative solutions should be formulated if there is sufficient time and resources. These solutions are not generated spontaneously, based on yes-no considerations, but are usually determined by assessing relative costs and benefits or effectiveness measures across the alternatives. Any type of analysis requires valid information, and the more critical, costly, or strategic the decision, the more attention is needed for the information-gathering process. If new federal programs or reporting requirements are dictated to state and local governments for meeting welfare, education, or transportation objectives, how can managers best evaluate the effectiveness or cost efficiency of alternative modes of meeting the regulations except with relevant information?

AN INFORMATION SYSTEMS AND DECISION-BASED PERSPECTIVE ON THE CLASSICAL AND SYSTEMS APPROACH TO PUBLIC ORGANIZATIONS AND MANAGEMENT

Current thinking in organization and management theory emphasizes a systems model that views the organization and managerial task as an open system that integrates the traditional and the environment-transaction processes. The systems model focuses more on the *interdependence* of functions and structure within the organization and the internal subsystems in the organization, with the relevant parts of the environment or task environment outside the boundary (Katz and Kahn 1966; Lawrence and Lorsch 1967). Figure 2.1 presents a

FIGURE 2.1. Systems and Contingency Perspective on Public Sector Organizations

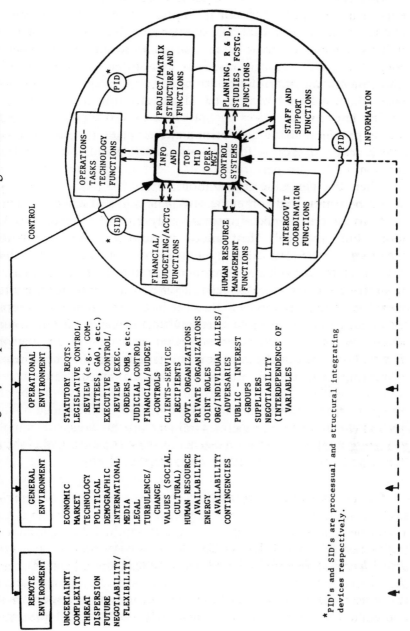

REMOTE ENVIRONMENT	GENERAL ENVIRONMENT	OPERATIONAL ENVIRONMENT
UNCERTAINTY	ECONOMIC	STATUTORY REQTS.
COMPLEXITY	MARKET	LEGISLATIVE CONTROL/
THREAT	TECHNOLOGY	REVIEW (e.g., COM-
DISPERSION	POLITICAL	MITTEES, GAO, etc.)
FUTURE	DEMOGRAPHIC	EXECUTIVE CONTROL/
NEGOTIABILITY/	INTERNATIONAL	REVIEW (EXEC.
FLEXIBILITY	MEDIA	ORDERS, OMB, etc.)
	LEGAL	JUDICIAL CONTROL
	TURBULENCE/	FINANCIAL/BUDGET
	CHANGE	CONTROLS
	VALUES (SOCIAL,	CLIENTS-SERVICE
	CULTURAL)	RECIPIENTS
	HUMAN RESOURCE	GOVT. ORGANIZATIONS
	AVAILABILITY	PRIVATE ORGANIZATIONS
	ENERGY	JOINT ROLES
	AVAILABILITY	ORG/INDIVIDUAL ALLIES/
	CONTINGENCIES	ADVERSARIES
		PUBLIC - INTEREST
		GROUPS
		SUPPLIERS
		NEGOTIABILITY
		(INTERDEPENDENCE OF
		VARIABLES)

*PID's and SID's are processual and structural integrating devices respectively.

Source: Compiled by the author.

25

general overview of this model and incorporates the managerial functions that require information and resources from both outside and inside the organization—the essence of the argument being that public organizations do not exist in a vacuum because their management requires resources to perform the functions and arrive at decisions that are linked to organizational or statutory objectives. Information, then, is both a resource, because it has an acquisition cost and is required to make effective decisions, and an essential element of the managerial process. Without information, plans cannot be achieved, nor can performance be assessed. Managerial processes and decisions are not ends in themselves but, rather, means to public ends. Information is required for the decision and evaluation of the decision's effectiveness to provide feedback or a steering and correction function to adjust the performance of the top, mid, and operational managers who guide the organization.

A systematic and comprehensive perspective of a public management context is needed to provide a structure for designing public information systems. Most public organizations are functionally structured in the classical or pyramidal form, but many also exhibit project, staff, research and development, and interorganizational subsystems that correspond or relate to the various functions imposed from various controllers or influences in the environment. Complex environments make complex and multiple demands on public managers. This situation does not mean that behavioral or interpersonal factors do not enter the equation but, rather, that they become part of the intricate set of interrelationships that must be understood and managed by public administrators. The managers must be able to meet organizational and statutory objectives in the milieu of competing, many times conflicting, influences. This arena of complex demands requires a resolution mechanism that considers and evaluates the impact of individual and social variables; it does not set behavioral processes as organizational ends but, rather, is part of how the manager achieves legitimate public goals.

SYSTEMS AND CONTINGENCY PERSPECTIVE OF PUBLIC SECTOR ORGANIZATIONS AND MANAGEMENT

Figure 2.1 presents a systems and contingency perspective of a public sector organization and managerial functions. It is composed of internal and external elements and arrays the assorted influences that provide and/or require information and managerial attention. The figure illustrates that there is an interdependence among the organization, its management, and the environment(s) (for example, task-operational for specific organizational objectives and general as applied to many organizational functions). A systems-contingency approach is particularly useful for managers to use in their approach to information systems because it emphasizes multivariate interrelationships between the organization and its environment, as well as those within and among subsystems. The purpose of a comprehensive view is to understand and provide a structure for explaining how various parts of organizations operate, given varying general and specific conditions, so that managerial actions can be derived (Kast and Rosenzweig 1979).

There is no inherent explanatory power in the approach, but it does provide the manager with a contextual mapping tool that permits an analytical observation of the major variables acting on a given organization. If external resources or budget pressures are affecting personnel or task effectiveness, the relationship can be made explicit and become the focus of managerial action. If behavioral, union, or productivity factors or other government agencies are the sources of problems, or if their effects require action, their impact, in the context of the other influences, can be evaluated. The systems-contingency, or, more recently, ecological model (Aldrich 1979), emphasizes the broad view of organizations and managerial functions.

ENVIRONMENTAL INFLUENCES ON PUBLIC
MANAGEMENT AND INFORMATION SYSTEMS

The most recent and comprehensive analyses of public organizations examine the relative lack of practical application and explanatory power of traditional models because they have no comprehensive concept of the reality of public or general management. Current management analysts argue for more realistic and systematic or dynamic perspectives, or political-economic models. The overriding practical consideration is that those issues or variables determined to be important by the public manager should provide the foundation for the design of information systems that support the reality of the organization and the decision structure as closely as possible. Anything less permits untested or unidentified ambiguities or intangibles to influence the operational processes in the organization and make them less effective. The management and information model implicit in the relationships in Figure 2.1 is not provided to be all-inclusive in the sense that certain public organizations may have to deal with all elements of the remote, general, and operational-task environment. Rather, it suggests a framework for key influences that should be considered.

Total organizational information systems can be designed but the eventual organizational structure for the information system should be derived systematically and embedded in the managerial decision structure that supports the central organizational objectives. Further, it is not profitable in the design stage to focus on which means are the most important or to argue about how much information is enough if the public manager and the levels of management are capable of defining overall and related specific organizational objectives, which are usually statutorily based.

For example, a federal agency dealing with health and human services or welfare payments, such as aid to families with dependent children, has macro-environmental forces, such as interest groups and clients and a turbulent political-economic context; but a state welfare or social services department or a county-level human services department has a finite set of key influences to evaluate because reporting requirements to federal or state funding agencies filter and focus many diffuse pressures. However, even at the state and county levels, adequate client information systems do not exist for the majority of governments. That is, recent estimates have shown that computer-reporting networks with common eligibility and automatic eligibility determination mechanisms can save as much as $21 million a year by eliminating payments to ineligibles and reducing overpayments (Chi 1982).

The systems-contingency perspective aids the structuring of the information design process in terms of management's ability to understand the primary forces affecting the organization. For example, supercomputers have the capability to perform 2 billion transactions a second and a memory of 256 million words, but, without an understanding of the decision requirements in a department of state, a national security agency, or a state legislature, this technological capability is superfluous. The U.S. Department of State faces a highly uncertain, widely dispersed, complex, high-risk, and many times threatening environment, at present and for the foreseeable future. Uncertainty, dispersion, economics, and budgeting variables in the environment are more complex and influence internal planning and control functions in more extreme ways than these same variables would for a state department of transportation.

EXTERNAL INFORMATION REQUIREMENTS AND MANAGERIAL STRATEGY

Public managers perform many functions that can be classified as decision making or, when planning for the future, may be called strategy or strategic planning. The role of information in this strategic process is to provide support for decisions or policies that provide guidance over the long- and mid-range periods that exceed most short-term purposes or budgets, which emphasize short-term thinking. According to Steiner and Miner (1982) managers are subjected to expectations of major outside and inside interests. Databases, information systems, evaluations, and strategies have to address the expectations of outside interests that have controlling authority or financial influence over the organization and its functions. The evaluation of these external or environmental factors is performed using an analysis of strengths and weaknesses of the organization and opportunities or threats in the environment.

Decision rules and information, then, are linked to the strategic planning and programming process where agency or department objectives and policies are translated into plans and programs. The information system becomes the primary mechanism for supporting decisions related to the overall goals and objectives because it provides guidelines for operational programs and the basis for controlling progress by comparing projected and actual performance. In this way, information is used to implement plans and evaluate progress in achieving them. The strategic process in public organizations is bombarded with multiple and conflicting forces that make the information system and information processing skills even more critical in deriving strategies, plans, and programs. A well-designed information system can permit more than reactive "firehouse" managing.

Very few public organizations have complete information, resources, or ability to control or reduce environmental uncertainty.

Admittedly, such factors as geographic or functional dispersion may be influenced somewhat by organizational actions or structures. Yet, on the whole, forces such as a threat to the stability of the organization or future changes usually constitute major uncontrollables. Nonetheless, the organization can obtain information about these influences with an investment of resources and specifications of the linkages to the operations of the agency or department to determine their probable effect on programs and service.

Many times geographic dispersion is a direct function of the organization's responsibilities. Many federal agencies have highly dispersed regional and local offices; state agencies have responsibilities tailored to statewide activities that may involve regional or district variables. Local governments may have fewer problems resulting from dispersion but more problems resulting from the impact of state laws on taxing or demographic shifts. The primary question is how important the dispersed functions are in either absolute or financial terms. Authority, responsibility, and financial factors are all variables that should be considered in terms of their direct effect on objectives when information or reporting requirements are determined for dispersed organizational elements.

Complexity is an ongoing environmental concern. Decision making at all levels of the management structure and the task-technology dimension of how government organizations perform their functions are the primary activities affected by such complexity. A major consideration in gathering information on complexity is how the state of the art in management, economics, or technology of the organization's primary task is affected and how efficiency and effectiveness are affected. Quite often, it is difficult to control complexity in the environment; however, key information needs should be identified to reduce the impact of complexity. Out of a given array of complex relationships with forces in the environment, some will have higher priority than others because of their direct relevance to discernible effects on key operations. All complexity cannot be reduced, but decisions regarding the primary sources and reliance of the complex can be defined.

Threat to a public organization has a variety of dimensions, ranging from the routine to critical. Additional attention will be given to this topic in the discussion of the general and operational environments; yet one criterion for evaluating an element in the external sphere of the public organization that has or is exerting influence over the organization's mission and related basic resources needed by the organization could be considered a potential threat. This discussion is not to imply that the threat is an illegitimate influence but, rather, that the environment, through an action by a client, controller, or interest group, is calling attention to certain of the organization's assumptions or operations.

An effective information system that supports public managers and their decisions should, to the extent feasible, be capable of predicting the future. Oettinger (1980) identifies information resources as the most likely basis of knowledge and power in twenty-first-century societies and organizations and argues that information is a basic resource like energy and materials. He maintains that traditional processes and answers are inadequate and that we must gain mastery over such information processes as "compunication" (computers and communications) and related technology. Combined with these technological tools, Oettinger also sees this evolution resulting in more domestic and international struggles over freedom of information versus control over it. Of course, every manager and organization want to predict the future, but the growing importance and impact of information technology, information industries, and hardware capabilities (satellites, telecommunications, and the like) should make the more susceptible public organizations aware of the potential changes in the future.

GENERAL ENVIRONMENT OF A PUBLIC ORGANIZATION

Political Variables

Every public organization requires resources to achieve its objectives and survive in an environment composed of benign, hostile, co-operative, or competitive forces. Figure 2.1 categorizes certain elements of the general environment, but this grouping is not designed to be all-inclusive. It is only representative of the major influences that affect public organizations. They are not equally influential for all public managers because all organizations vary in their impact on the environment according to the nature of the organization's objectives, the competition for and use of resources, and, many times, the competence of their management. The word "political" usually refers to matters of legitimacy and distribution of power as they offset the propriety of an agency's existence, its functional niche (in society, political system or policy subsystem), its collective institutional goals, the goals of the dominant elite faction (if they vary from goals), major parameters of economy, and in some instances the means of task accomplishment (if the task is vague enough to raise value questions) or if values change sufficiently to bring established means into question. (Wamsley and Zald 1976, p. 64)

Though other valid concepts of the political variable exist, this definition introduces the reality and complexity of the public organization's political environment because it forces recognition of what public managers must consistently evaluate and understand as antecedent conditions.

The legitimacy of the agency's function is therefore legitimately influenced as much by external as internal prerogatives. The relevance of this concept for information systems is that the public manager has the responsibility to observe and integrate the political variables that influence the organization's functions so that the objectives are best achieved in the context of competing influences.

Market or Economic Influences

Every public manger is aware that economic factors influence his or her organization, but this awareness does not always translate into appropriate action, such as the collection of information. Economic essentially refers to the allocation of resources either externally to the organization or for task accomplishment inside the organization. The term "economic" as used here means the resource allocation process used by the environmental (national, executive, legislative) controllers that provide resources for public managers in government organizations. In the context used here, organizations do not necessarily control their economic inputs in the strict sense of the word. Rather, they influence the allocation process by providing either legitimation or justification to relevant controllers by how they achieve their assigned responsibilities. The responsible manager needs to understand the distribution and importance of the market or different economic environments. To perform managerial functions properly requires valid economic information in the information system.

Legal

The legal influences on public organizations may be very specific or general. All public organizations are charged with implementing a variety of statutes; however, there may also be conflicts in the way authority is delegated to achieve sometimes competing objectives. Often many conflicts are decided upon by judicial processes that supersede or exert control over routine personnel actions that may have major operational effects. Some public organizations, such as environmental, public safety, or welfare agencies, may be more influenced by periodic judicial or legal rulings regarding imprisonment or eligibility than by internal policies, which may exert little control. Overall, public managers and organizations are governed and sanctioned more by legal-statutory variables than other elements. Information systems and their management are a centralized managerial function that can be used to process and comply with legal-statutory reporting requirements as well as to feed information back into the system about compliance, equity, validity, or other legal mandates.

Technological Influences

Every public organization uses information to make decisions, achieve its objectives, and/or control its operations—but not with the same degree of efficiency or effectiveness. The basic technological process is most neutral but less subject to traditional administrative controls and more dependent on research and development and advanced uses, especially in state-of-the-art processes where such things as real time or costly decisions are important. Large-scale integration, photon telecommunications, optical memories, microcomputers, supercomputers, and software advances have increased the storage, retrieval, and processing capabilities of computers to the point where the major limitation is "wetware," or the human element (David 1980).

At this point, technology is available to provide cost-efficient and effective resources to public managers who are able to define and structure their informational needs. Rather than being a constraint, information technology is an asset that can be used to meet other organizational demands and objectives. For example, if the technology to communicate the equivalent of 70 pages of data in one-second spurts through congressional communication lines exists, and it currently does, can or should public managers master the same potential?

Demographic, Cultural, and Ecological Issues

Social and cultural values are difficult to measure, but their effects are usually undeniable. For example, the massive amounts of government support for social and human service programs far exceeds what self-sufficiency as a national value would dictate, as well as that spent on other services, including national defense, energy, development, and transportation. Yet the products of these social services and other programs are often difficult to measure. Both the demand for services and economic constraints are increasing. The rising demands for government services and concomitant competition for scarce resources, along with demands for dated accountability, require some cost-efficient mechanisms, such as information systems that are adequate for controlling and monitoring program delivery.

Media, Turbulence, and Contingencies

As government and public organizations and functions have proliferated, so have elements and interest groups in their environments that scrutinize and evaluate their behavior. The influence of the media has been in evidence in federal, state, and local affairs, ranging from gubernatorial, agency head, or a presidential resignation, as well as in reports on state and local governments where such issues as Proposition 13, chemical dumps, and budget deficits have been covered intensively. The media are not being characterized here as antagonistic but, rather, as a check on actions, power, and authority granted to public organizations. The media are probably one of the most visible tests of the "information is power" premise. It is reasonable to assume that public management would want to balance the effect of the media by having on hand information acquisition and dissemination capabilities to be able to respond to valid inquiries for information.

Figure 2.1 characterizes the elements of the general environment as moderating the effects of the contextual environment on the components of the operational environment. This illustration is representative of the complexity and interdependence involved, but it does not capture all of the reciprocal interaction and interdependence needed for designing information systems. However, the purpose here is to emphasize the role of the public managers in their organizations and to focus on the principal elements of the management and information processes as parts of the general managerial functions.

OPERATIONAL ENVIRONMENT OF THE PUBLIC ORGANIZATION

Warwick, Meade, and Reed (1975) characterize the environment of a public bureaucracy as remote or proximate, with the power-setting and operating environment as subsets of the proximate environment. The systems-contingency approach presented here is that not all elements of the environments are equally significant to public managers and that only specific parts constitute the most task-relevant influences. The general implication for managers of public organizations is that they should understand these actors and obtain information to determine the likely extent and direction of their influence. Figure 2.1 presents the main components of the operational environment in public organizations.

Statutory Authority and Legislative, Executive, Judicial, and Financial/Budgetary Controllers

The operating environment for public managers includes actors with recognizable authority linkages to the organization; that is, they have the staturily based formal authority and responsibility to regulate the organization, its resources, and/or activities. For most public organizations, these authorities are usually executive or judicial officials, appropriations and legislative committees and subcommittees, and the legislature overall. These bodies and their monitors (Office of Management and Budget, General Accounting Office) and their state counterparts perform inspecting, auditing, and evaluating functions that directly affect the operation of the organization.

The authority and financial/budgetary controllers and their monitors are particularly important because they have direct impact on the organization's functions and its long-term survival. These controllers may change the scope of responsibilities of the agency through direct statutory modifications or by adjustments in budgets. In turn, legislation, executive orders, or judicial rulings may have immediate and direct fiscal effects on how a public organization is managed. For example, annual appropriations may specify changes in functions or spending levels for different activities.

To deal with controllers in the operational environment, the objective of the public organization is to codify existing statutory requirements in terms of their importance. All requirements for reporting operational and financial information to higher-level authorities or controllers should be categorized to meet temporal and functional needs. If certain reports on efficiency or level of organizational output are defined by statute or regulation, the information management system in the organization should be designed to meet these requirements by producing the information in a cost- and time-efficient manner. For example, at the state and local levels, financial and accounting reports for expenditures and revenues are required periodically by the federal government. Welfare, personnel actions, or certain activities related to court-ordered actions may also require special reporting activities. At the federal level, operational and budget information may be required to justify budget requests.

Because the controllers mandate compliance with certain authority and financial standards, the public organization information structure should be able to generate the relevant information for both external reporting and internal control. In sum, the information system for public managers should be responsive to the number, importance, and type of controllers and their monitors, with some determination being made regarding priorities.

Service Recipients/Clients

The client or service recipient is that individual or group that receives or benefits directly from the service or product produced by the public organization. Though a separate factor, suppliers may also be placed partly in this category because they may stand to gain by furnishing raw materials and other resources. However, the focus here is on those clients who receive a service or product directly specified by the organizational mission and related objectives. For example, a human service organization has to establish eligibility for the client before the service or product (food stamps, welfare payments) is provided. This pool of recipients constitutes the client base about whom information should be collected in order to be able to forecast demand, provide targeted services, and still meet the formal obligation specified in the law.

Organizational Allies and Adversaries

Organizational allies and adversaries are entities that either support or compete with the organization. Allies usually aid the organization in obtaining resources or making its operations more effective. Adversaries may be competing with the organization for resources, clients, or even similar functions. The environment of allies and adversaries is not necessarily stable or routine, and allies and adversaries may change according to pressures for change or availability of resources in the environment. These elements in the power setting of the public organization are complex due to multiple interdependencies and shifting coalitions between organizations.

Constituencies

Constituencies are usually defined as groups or individuals external to the organization that are interested in but have no formal authority over its actions. An example of a constituency is an interest group that is indirectly or economically affected by a public organization's policies or services. These interest groups may be either powerful commercial lobbies or ad hoc groups with vested political interests oriented toward changing the operations of the organization to benefit them. Similar to adversaries and allies, they may also have positive or negative influences with long-standing relationships with the organization that may enhance or detract from the mission accomplishment.

Individual Allies and Adversaries

There are times when the public organization may have influential individual allies and adversaries. These individuals may or may not be part of other organizations or elements of the power setting; however, they may warrant special attention. This statement is not intended to be manipulative or co-optative but realistic in that managers of public organizations should be cognizant of the significant, or potentially significant, pressures that affect specific internal or overall functions. A relevant example is given by Warwick, Meade, and Reed (1975), who examined certain individual influences on a federal department:

> The most powerful controller of the internal operations of the State Department is the House appropriations subcommittee chaired by Congressman Rooney. During his tenure Rooney has become the scourge and scrooge of the State Department. (p. 73)

A similar phenomenon may also be present at the state and local levels of government where individuals exercise their power to affect public organizations.

Interorganizational Relations

The relevant environment of public organizations is composed of other government, nonprofit, and private sector organizations. Many interactions between the organization and others in its "set" or ecological niche (Hall 1977; Aldrich 1979) may be specified by statute, whereas others may have evolved in response to the mission of the organization. These relationships may not necessarily be supportive or competitive, but the issue is whether they affect a focal organization, providing inputs to or receiving outputs from the organization. It has been argued that interorganizational relationships are the most important aspect of society (Hall 1977).

The basis of interorganizational interactions is usually some form of interdependence. In the public sector this may mean that such resources as political support, financial assets, clients, or human resources are in contention or provide important bargaining tools or means of exchange. The exchange relationship may be mutually cooperative, competitive, or conflictual. The frequency, formalization, and intensity or nature of the contacts are appropriate variables to understand. This category of information may be extensive in organizations with complex functions, but the resulting information can be managed to support the decision-making framework of the different levels of management so that the substance of the interorganizational relations can be made more effective or productive.

Public

Use of the word "public" or "public interest" sometimes evokes debate that produces more heat than enlightenment. The public here is defined as that segment of the environment that does not neatly fit into the authority setting, client, constituency, or other categories but, rather, has a general interest in how effective government is. The public may overlap with the external categories or be the dominant factor on any given issue or it may be acquiescent and not visible. The media may represent or invite the public to action, but the public policy process does have mechanisms for translating public needs and opinions into relevant statute and policy. The public is not strictly a residual category but does exert, through its presence and constitutional role, a general influence on the general and operating environments of public managers. The information structure should deal with public interest as an overarching objective and criterion for determining how the information serves this interest.

OVERALL ENVIRONMENTAL ISSUES
AND INFORMATION SYSTEMS

Management at all levels in public organizations needs mechanisms for reducing ambiguity and uncertainty, both externally and internally. The external environment includes elements that have general effects, but it also includes authority or financial controllers, clients, allies, adversaries, constituencies, and public interests that exert powerful influences over functions, budgets, and even survival. It is in the best interest of management to deal explicitly with the variety of forces by identifying the key elements—those factors that have significant influence on organizational operations—and collecting information to deal with the particular issue. This information systems and management process should, in turn, support the decision-making structure of the organization.

The subsequent material in this chapter focuses on the internal operational and organizational structure and related information issues.

INTERNAL ORGANIZATIONAL STRUCTURE AND PROCESS

Internal System

As noted earlier, managers in public organizations have the responsibilities characterized in the POSDCORB acronym derived from classical management and organization theories. However, they also are required to integrate neomodern behavioral knowledge, technical issues, and, more recently, systems perspectives with their existing knowledge. This means that public managers should be conversant and skilled in applying knowledge and experience within a complex web of competing authority, multiple-objective, and resource constraints. The systems perspective provides an overall view of an organization and its interdependent subsystems. In it, each subsystem has a specialized function, such as managing human resources or dealing with the primary tasks or operations that constitute the core technology of the organization.

The model in Figure 2.1 represents the internal organizational structure that complements the external setting previously discussed. The basic assumptions are that the external environment includes both general and operational influences that affect organizational processes and that part of this exchange is affected by the interdependence between the specific parts of the organization and relevant subenvironments. For example, some organizations or large government agencies may command enormous amounts of political, financial, or human resources and can exert great degrees of influence over a specific task or general environment, possibly even some of the controllers. A less powerful organization or small local government, on the other hand, is more susceptible to demands for change from these same sources in the environment. This same parallel can be drawn for the internal elements of the organization; that is, the more resources, such as critical information, that are made available, the more control that can be acquired.

Internal/Functional Information Requirements

Accurate, timely, and complete information is absolutely essential for managing operations. Information on input, operations, and output, and the collection and processing of that information, are needed to do anything, from identifying stolen vehicles to estimating revenues for state taxing purposes. Rosenthal (1982) presents qualities that operational managers need in decision making: Information must be reported rapidly and accurately; the information must be presented concisely in an easily understood format; the data/information should be updated regularly; and specific information is of more value than aggregate data. Illustrative decisions for using the information are capacity utilization; effectiveness assessment; demand management (fire damage); cost performance (adherence to budgets); personnel or facilities planning; and trend analysis.

Operations/Tasks Subsystem

The operations or tasks technology of a public organization constitutes the central concern, as it encompasses the resource conversion process where raw inputs are transformed to outputs that may influence, for example, fire safety or air traffic control where many lives may be at stake. This conversion process, where humans and financial resource are converted to services, may interface with the environment if the technology involved is highly complex and subject to varying levels of control or uncertainty. The functions of the U.S. State Department are based on the responsibilities for promoting the long-range security of the United States and carrying out established U.S. foreign policy in a turbulent, uncertain, and many times high-risk environment. This type of technology and function inside the organization has to deal with multiple uncertain influences because political, social, national, international, and economic factors may directly affect how routine or nonroutine tasks are handled. The threat and risk associated with even minor actions in hostile countries may directly influence how U.S. foreign policy is implemented.

Management has the responsibility to coordinate and control the interdependence of the operational core of the organization, other internal functions, and the environment. In addition, it is the task of management to coordinate and integrate the relations between core technology and the other support or staff functions, such as personnel or budgetary processes, in the organization. If the core technology is ambiguous or complex, such as used to deliver welfare or public safety, then the relationships and required information to support the decision-making process will be correspondingly complex to meet the demands of the operations management process. The point is that management must understand the critical components of the core organizational processes to design an effective information system to support and control them. Information systems are means to operational ends that can only be properly designed by public managers who understand their role.

Project/Matrix Organizational Structure

If the public organization faces a turbulent, heterogeneous environment with multiple pressures and demands, the organizational structure is likely to be highly differentiated and difficult to integrate. This type of structure will require more in-depth analysis of what information is needed to structure and control the separate functions toward the organizational objectives. For example, if there are many levels of vertical and horizontal departmentalization, information flows that correspond to each of the functions will have to be developed. The organizational structure is, therefore, the explicit representation of how operations are integrated to achieve the objectives of the overall organization; and information flows must naturally support this integration. Many times functional organizational structures that have evolved from the traditional forms of management are not easily adopted to achieving new approaches or organizational forms. Newer forms of organizational structure called project, or matrix, management, which superimposes project over functional forms, are used to accomplish unique, one-of-a-kind purposes. These structures require information and control subsystems to achieve projects on schedule, within budget, and in accordance with technical criteria. The supporting project management information system should provide decision-relevant models, a database, interactive computer hardware and software, relevant and sophisticated reports (displays), and a language that is user friendly (Cleland and King 1983).

Human Resources Subsystems

Human resources are a vital part of the public organization; they must be effectively integrated with the primary functions, structures, and operational tasks of the organization. Because most public organizations tend to be labor-intensive, accounting usually for more than half of the costs, human resources have to be systematically managed and controlled. Legal requirements, such as validity determinations, preference, equal employment, and merit-based performance evaluations, are placing an added administrative requirement on existing personnel systems and their information bases.

The concept of human resource information systems has been treated in the literature; however, in addition to the data requirements and personnel management uses, the information system should address overall resource policy and planning issues. The human resources, or personnel subsystem and management function, support and maintain the organization's central tasks and operations. This human resource information function will have internal personnel management needs to consider, as well as supportive relationships with other parts of the organization.

Recruitment, placement, selection, classification, training, work measurement, compensation, performance evaluation, promotion, benefits, transfer, and retirement information are associated with all individuals in public organizations. These facets of human resource management should be linked to their organizational function and integrated with the needs of the most proximate level of management. These elements of information can also be used to develop personnel planning models to match projected organizational requirements and personnel-related decision making.

Financial/Budgeting and Accounting Functions

Resource proceurement and management functions of public organizations are central to the goal of servicing and producing programs or products. Though these functions have often been translated into more specific budgeting and financial management items, which many times serve as ends rather than means, they form a key focus for information systems. As discussed earlier, though other indicators of effectiveness should exist, the financial/budgetary status of public organizations has become a crucial indicator of how well the organization appears to be performing. It is a highly visible internal and external measure that has become in many respects a surrogate for effectiveness or agency success. Though budgeting is a traditional part of the management process, it appears to have become the single issue that the executive and legislative controllers understand and use to exert pressure on public organizations. This emphasis may not be the most productive because certain organizations can frequently mobilize allies, clients, and/or constituencies to apply pressure on the executive and legislative controllers using the budget as a cause célèbre rather than improving the effectiveness of the organization.

Regardless of the distortions to which the budget and related financial management processes are subject, the allocation of resources to public organizations should be controlled and monitored to promote at least some accountability for the use of public funds. At the local and state levels, one of the primary means of financial control is the use of fund accounting procedures. Recently, exhortations to adopt accrual- or modified accrual-based reporting procedures have surfaced and are being used to improve financial rating for borrowing purposes.

Planning and Research and Development

Managers of public organizations need adaptive devices and mechanisms for monitoring and responding to changing external factors or anticipating future conditions. This planning or strategic function is usually performed by top-level management, as it involves issues of broad organizational objectives, policies, and allocation of resources. It calls for a practical and valid understanding of the major environmental elements that exert influence over the organization. It also enhances the ability of the organization to forecast the most probable future conditions that the organization may confront.

Research and development and supporting studies will not eradicate all uncertainty but will provide management with an analytical approach to evaluating alternative courses of action, making choices and decisions, and designing action plans to achieve results. The planning, research and development, and forecasting functions, then, give managers the edge in reducing, if not eliminating, the uncertainty associated with directing and controlling complex public functions. Much of current public management has been characterized as reactive, but cutbacks in public, political, and financial support portend a future where public managers will have to develop all of their resources, including information and related systems, to meet the other internal needs of the organization and the external mandates from society and the controllers. Information systems may not displace many costs in the short run, but given the required data and input from the managers who use them as tools, they can become useful apprentices in the planning, research, and forecasting function.

INFORMATION SYSTEMS AND
INTERGOVERNMENTAL COORDINATION

Federal, state, and local governments consume approximately 33 percent of the gross national product of the United States, and much of this sum is directly related to intergovernmental transfers of one form or another, such as general revenue sharing, subsidies, block grants, entitlements, grants-in-aid, and matching monies. The federal share of some state and local government expenditures may range from 15 to 40 percent, yet only recently have these influences been made explicit under the premises of the new federalism, which is still undergoing a shakedown. Many current state and local financial management information systems are not capable of meeting federal reporting requirements or determining exactly what the level of dependence on the federal government is. These and similar problems also extend to the area of local government unfunded pension liabilities, where the states are being asked to bail out municipalities that have extreme deficits.

The shifting of financial support and responsibilities across the different levels of government has created a highly turbulent set of interdependent relationships where the effects are not totally understood at any level of government. Information systems should be designed to support decisions related to the increasingly diverse needs of intergovernment relations.

INFORMATION NEEDS FOR STAFF
AND SUPPORT FUNCTIONS

Public organizations perform line functions, such as providing transportation services, building highways, providing aid to families with dependent children, preventing crime, extinguishing fires, providing vaccines or controlling diseases, educating children and adults, and even providing recreation. These line functions usually require some sort of support, ranging from evaluation studies to janatorial services. In some public sector functions or organizations, the evaluation function may be a central operation; however, it still supports some other line or management function of government. The degree of importance of the staff (support) functions varies by organization type, as does their consumption of resources. At one time the management information systems function was primarily attached or subordinate to financial or accounting departments, but recent technological and software advances have made both computers and related information systems more ubiquitous in public organizations, from dispensing billions of dollars in social security checks monthly to checking fingerprints or National Crime Information Center data on individuals. So the importance of the staff and support function varies, but information may be the key ingredient in determining the validity of an evaluation or the identity of a criminal.

INTERNAL INTERDEPENDENCE

The internal functions, structures, processes, and elements of the public organization are not as discrete as characterized in Figure 2.1 because varying degrees of interdependence are required and found among the subsystems. There should also be explicit guidance and provisions for resource allocation, leadership, communication (formal and informal), competition, conflict, decision making, and the supporting information system that structure the interaction and interdependence between the components. The subsystems have separate functions, but they must also be coordinated to perform their individual tasks that contribute to broader organizational goals. Overall, the managerial information system should document the type and degrees of interdependence required and should also have a capability to aid in evaluating the effectiveness of the ongoing interaction. Substantive internal interdependence can only be achieved by defining the most important dimensions of the required interactions in terms of their directions and degree. The required levels of interdependence can then be maintained using structural (authority, rules, regulations) or processual (ad hoc groups, coordinating committees, steering/project groups) integrating devices to achieve and maintain the desired relationships.

TABLE 2.1. General Information Structure for Public Organization Managerial Levels

External Elements	Strategic	Mid	Operational
Authority and financial/budgetary controllers	Identify key executive and legislative elements that control authority and budgetary matters	Translate organization objectives to internal rules and procedures and set up information for control systems	Specify basis of authority for information needs for operations and relate costs to services or products and meet authority-budgetary controllers information requirements
Service recipients/clients	Specify recipient population and derive eligibility standards based on law. Evaluate service or product	Articulate organization methods for providing service or product and develop measure for evaluation	Develop information related to tasks and technologies that provide the service efficiently and provide information for review and feedback for evaluation
Individual allies/adversaries	Identify key individuals in the organization environment	Provide organization information mechanisms for controlling organization interactions with recent individuals	Set up operational information procedures to deal with individuals with whom organization members come in contact
Organizational allies/adversaries	Identify key organizations in the organization environment and monitor contacts with them	Provide organization information mechanisms for controlling organization interactions with relevant organizations	Set up operations based information and feedback procedures to mid- and top-level management on organization contacts with significant other organizations
Interorganization relations	Develop schematic of statutory- and nonstatutory-based interorganizational relations	Design organization information and control mechanisms for dealing with most significant interorganizational relationship	Develop information and feedback procedures on extent and relevance of interorganizational relationships
Constituencies/unions	Understand who constitutes the major constituencies and unions	Maintain managerial prerogatives and decision-supporting information and control systems	Design operational information procedures to use in dealing with constituencies and recording outcomes
Public interest groups	Identify central "publics" and interest groups	Design organization information and control methods to ensure effective interactions with the public	Provide operational and specific information relative to organization contacts with "publics" and interest groups
Internal Elements			
Operations-technology/tasks	Understand key operational issues and develop key indicators for operational performance and include in periodic information reports	Develop operationally based information and control procedures to manage control elements of the operations technology using measurement and evaluation	Design efficiency, scheduling, and complementary information-reporting systems for the important decisions associated with the operations technology
Organizational structure (number and type of programs, vertical and horizontal differentiation)	Monitor key programs and structural elements using information and control procedures	Develop information and control procedures to measure and evaluate significant elements of the organization structure	Design and follow up on specific information and control procedures for key parts of the organization
Human resources	Understand key human resource issues using key and critical information	Provide mechanisms for integrating human resources information with other elements of organization	Develop specific personnel management information system to support organization objectives
Resource procurement and management (finance, budgeting)	Monitor and control resource issues using key and timely information	Design and implement information and control systems for resource procurement and allocation	Provide operations-based resource, budgeting, and financial management information
Planning, research and development	System planning, R & D, and forecasting information to ascertain most efficient future strategies	Provide mid- and long-range research and planning information to top-level management using mid-level organizational information	Provide information based on operations—technology research and planning needs—to mid- and top-level management
Internal interdependence	Primarily mid- and operational-level specification of direction and degree of cooperation, interdependence, and mutual problem solving or decision making		

Source: Compiled by the author.

MANAGERIAL INFORMATION SYSTEMS STRUCTURE

Table 2.1 reduces the general interactions discussed here to more specific indicators of what kind of information may be used by different levels of management across the various functions or subsystems. This overview is not all-inclusive; however, it provides an approach to structuring the information collecting, gathering, analyzing, and using process that has to be designed by management at all levels. Operations, organizational objectives, managerial competence and incentives, external demands, and intergovernment variables will vary for different types of government organizations at the federal, state, and local levels. The contingencies and most relevant influences on these information systems will have to be resolved by the informed manager who can specify what information is needed to make what decision to achieve what objective.

SUMMARY

Chapter 2 provides a practical and conceptual framework for managers to use in thinking about information systems that are anchored in reality. Many piecemeal and computer-based information systems have failed because they relied on the technological promise of specific hardware or software approaches to the detriment of antecedent managerial and/or user requirements. The major information-based contingencies facing public managers are technological, operational, organizational, political, and economic. Rarely will it be true that the hardware or software technology is not available to meet a public manager's information systems requirements. Rather, the deficiency may be in management's ability to specify the appropriate decision framework in the context of the organization's objectives, structure, technology-task, political, or resource-economic picture.

The underlying premise is that the public sector organization and manager are interdependent internally and with the environment; they exchange a service or product for resources (financial, political, human). In exchange for the resources and authority, the legislative, judicial, and executive controllers often exert direct or indirect influence over the organization and its management. However, the organization also influences and sometimes controls the many actors in the environment by its actions and effectiveness. The different levels of management (strategic, mid, and operational) have varying degrees of responsibilities that have to be fulfilled if the organization is to achieve its objectives, satisfy contextual controllers or service recipients, and understand the key contingencies in the environment in which it operates. The overall environment and its constituent categories or subenvironments with more or less specific influences will interact in different ways, depending on the mission of the organization, but the management of the organization will have to adapt their decision making approach to design an effective information and control system to meet the specific contingencies that it must manage.

3

Computerized Information Systems Components: Hardware, Software, Files, and Database Management

In the era of supercomputer technology, where computer capabilities exceed even human imagination and calculations take one-billionth (nanosecond) or one-trillionth (picosecond) of a second, some organizing device is needed for managers to understand the role of technology in computerized information systems. Figure 3.1 provides a structure that can be used to link the technological aspects of computers to managerial tasks. The public manager's constant companion is the need to make decisions, and related to the decisions is the use of information. Whether a personnel action such as a reduction in force, a change in a position classification system, or a productivity improvement effort is being made, the manager requires timely, accurate, valid, and relevant information.

Information to support decision making, operations, strategic planning, or inventory control has the common process characteristics of collection, storing, processing, analyzing, and outputs or reports. Through generic processes in information systems, managers must define what and how information is collected, how it is stored for use (temporary, long term), how it is analyzed (statistical, operations), what kinds of reports are produced (length, frequency), and how the information will be used in the decision-making process. Each of these parts of the managerial and information system process illustrated in Figure 3.1 has implications for electronic, mechanical, and technical components of a computerized information system. A small local government human service department may only require a microcomputer with limited storage or word processing capability to

FIGURE 3.1. General Structure of Information Systems Processes for Public Managers

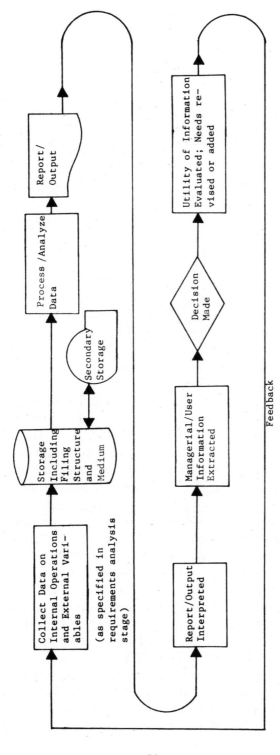

Source: Compiled by the author.

FIGURE 3.2. Basic Components in Computerized Information Systems

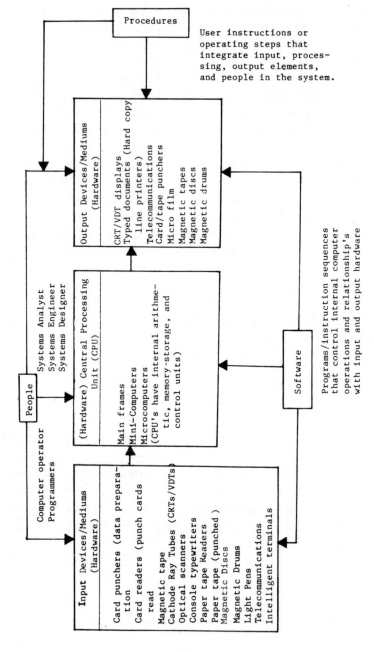

Procedures

User instructions or operating steps that integrate input, processing, output elements, and people in the system.

Output Devices/Mediums (Hardware)

CRT/VDT displays
Typed documents (Hard copy line printers)
Telecommunications
Card/tape punchers
Micro film
Magnetic tapes
Magnetic discs
Magnetic drums

People

Systems Analyst
Systems Engineer
Systems Designer

Computer operator
Programmers

(Hardware) Central Processing Unit (CPU)

Main frames
Mini-Computers
Microcomputers
(CPU's have internal arithmetic, memory-storage, and control units)

Software

Programs/instruction sequences that control internal computer operations and relationship's with input and output hardware

Input Devices/Mediums (Hardware)

Card punchers (data preparation)
Card readers (punch cards read
Magnetic tape
Cathode Ray Tubes (CRTs/VDTs)
Optical scanners
Console typewriters
Paper tape Readers
Paper tape (punched)
Magnetic Discs
Magnetic Drums
Light Pens
Telecommunications
Intelligent terminals

Source: Compiled by the author.

deal with 20 clients, but the collection, storage, processing, and reporting functions are still necessary and must be structured to make decisions about numbers and types of operations in terms of how data are collected (for example, standardized forms), entered into storage (terminals, tapes, cards), analyzed (billing), and reported (bills or letters to clients, periodic summary statistics).

Figure 3.2 presents the basic systems model and associated roles of computer hardware, software, procedures, and people that act together to produce a basic computerized information system. According to Senn (1982), hardware, software, procedures, and people are elements that work together to produce the information required for the manager or user. Different configurations of hardware, software, procedures, and people should be designed to meet the company requirements of public managers. For another view of the basic information system, Davis (1974) also adds files (database of tapes, disks, cards, documents) as another physical component of the overall system. Batch processing using card punchers and readers may be adequate to do monthly water or periodic tax billing; but such a method is hardly adequate for processing patrol car or police inquiries on license plates or evaluating food stamp applications at the county level when a central state database is maintained with terminal connections for timely inquiries and replies. The function and managerial needs dictate the most effective combination of hardware, software, people, and procedures to meet the requirements for the different phases of the information systems process.

INPUT, PROCESSING, AND OUTPUT HARDWARE

Hardware usually consists of the central processing unit (CPU), input and output devices, and file storage devices, including data preparation units, such as keypunch or paper tape punches. Because of the incredibly quick processing times of the CPU (which has mathematic, memory storage, and control units), the major bottlenecks in information processing usually occur in preparation, input or output devices, or all three.

Input Devices

Input devices such as card or paper tape readers or magnetic tape readers are considerably slower than CPUs because of human or mechanical interaction with the system. The most common input devices are (or were) card readers, which read 80-column cards that have been keypunched; magnetic tape readers, which read magnetic characters from oxide-coated tapes by using heads similar to those on audio equipment; and terminals (CRT, VDT), which are electronically connected to the central processor. Also, some CRTs are called intelligent terminals because they have built-in memory capacity that can be used to check data before they are entered for processing.

Other input devices are magnetic ink character readers (MICR), such as those that read magnetic ink account characters on bank checks; optical scanners; and optical character readers (OCR), used to read data from specially marked documents or forms. Paper tape readers, key to disk, key to tape, and light pens are primarily special-purpose application input devices where data are temporarily sorted on tape or disk. A light pen can be used in conjunction with a CRT in architectural or engineering design or other uses. Other special devices such as voice-provided data or information and electronic or photo cell sources may also be used as input devices in certain specialized applications.

The current trend is for punched cards to be replaced by faster, quieter, direct entry devices where information can be input and corrected as quickly as possible. Console processors and various terminals are also being used to input data, usually in time-sharing situations, where several different users may be sharing the computer at one time. Certain input devices, such as the CRT, tape reader/puncher, console typewriter, or teletype, may also be used as output devices.

Output Devices

Devices to punch cards or paper can be connected to central processors as output devices, as are line printers that produce hard copy or terminals that present visual displays. An impact line printer, which may also use a chain or a drum, has a hammer and device drive that comes in contact with paper (for a chain printer). It is commonly used for output and can produce multiple copies with varying speeds.

Drum printers have characters arranged in engraved rows on a rotating drum, and hammers strike the ribbon and paper against the type, which produces the printed character. There are also nonimpact printers, which use laser, thermal, electrostatic, or ink jet technology. A nonimpact printer may produce 20,000 lines per minute, whereas an impact printer will probably not exceed 5,000 lines per minute. Ink jet nonimpact printers using electronically controlled jets of ink may reach 45,000 lines per minute. Dot matrix printers push wire rods against the ribbon and paper to produce dot-composed rather than solid characters (Senn 1982). Console typewriters (used by the computer operator), teletype terminals, CRTs, and graph plotters are linked directly to the CPU and produce different forms of output. Also, interactive terminals are usually for online uses where the output is displayed on a CRT or output on a hard copy terminal that gives either impact or nonimpact copies.

Output devices for micro- and minicomputers and word processors are usually much slower than the printers mentioned earlier. These systems print one character at a time and have speeds ranging from 10 to 65 characters per second. Other output devices are audio response units (audio output), microfilm (COM-computer output to microfilm), and microfiche; these are gaining in popularity because of their unique applications and space-saving qualities.

Another form of commonly used output is telecommunications. Communication lines can be used to send signals from a computer to remote receivers. A simplex line transmits in one direction only, and a duplex line can transmit in both directions simultaneously. Transmission speeds can vary from 110 bauds (110 characters per second) to approximately 50,000 characters per second. Communication signals are commonly connected between digital computers by modulators for sending and demodulators for receiving (modems). Computer communications, especially with satellites and multiple-channel networks, is becoming a highly technical branch of computer systems and is sometimes called "compunications."

Central Processing Unit

The engine of the computerized information system is the central processing unit (CPU). All other devices are connected with the CPU and are under its control. Figure 3.2 illustrates the elements generally contained in the CPU.

If equipment is directly connected to the CPU, it is described as "online"; if not connected, "offline." For example, interactive terminals and primary storage devices are online, and secondary storage devices or card punches are considered offline. The CPU contains registers that hold instructions that are decoded or hold data during the arithmetic execution operations. The arithmetic registers are used to speed up computations, and the address and buffer registers are used during the instruction/fetch (bring instructions from memory) and execution cycles (instruction interpreted and operation performed) (Lucas 1978).

Computers store and process data in what is called binary form. Groups of binary digits or bits (0 to 1, which basically means an off or on electrical signal) can be used to form characters called bytes (commonly composed of 8 bits). Bytes form words when grouped. These computer-created words are units that have storage locations in the memory units of the CPU. Words can mean different things in the control and arithmetic units of the CPU, depending on how they are used.

Alphanumeric data are converted to bits, bytes, and/or words. Words can be 12, 16, 24, 32, 48, or 60 bits for word-oriented machines, although other lengths can be designed by manufacturers (Senn 1982). Machines can be designed on the basis of fixed- or variable-word lengths where specific meanings are attached to symbols. The computer memory is similar to a group of mailboxes where each piece of data or the instruction has a specific address where it can be obtained for CPU operations. The CPU then controls the operation of the arithmetic unit with its logic circuits by using the program instructions from the memory according to address or location.

Primary Memory/Storage

Data and instructions for computer/CPU operations must be stored in the memory of the computer to control the operations to be performed. The address of the data or instruction is maintained by the control unit, which also has the function of inserting or removing these pieces of information from their locations (Senn 1982). Instructions contain operator codes (add, subtract), which are combined with other addresses of data to be operated upon. If the operator is a subtraction, the address is the memory location of the data that are to be subtracted from data in the CPU.

Though only one data element or instruction can be stored in one location at a given time, storage locations can range from approximately 4,000 in microcomputers to several million in large mainframe computer memories. Computer memory technology has made great advances in moving from magnetic core storage to the use of semiconductor or silicon chip technology. Instead of a magnetic core with wires and an iron ferrite "doughnut" the size of a pinhead with either an on (1) or off (0) current of charge, integrated circuits or semiconductor memories are composed of transistors arranged on a thin silicon wafer that is chemically etched to control the flow of electrical current. The silicon chip has extremely small storage circuits in which the switch is set to a 1 or 0. One chip can store several thousand bits of data. The silicon chips are then integrated to form groups of chips, circuits, or a memory module.

Arithmetic/Logic—Control Units and Registers

Computers perform such operations as addition, subtraction, division (special case of subtraction), multiplication (special case of addition), and exponentiation. The computer uses a different number base than our base 10 system. Our base 10 numbers are converted to binary numbers (0, 1) for use in the computer. For output, the binary numbers are then converted back to base 10 numbers. Instructions composed of operation codes and data addresses (operands) are transformed to the instruction and address registers; then the specified operations are performed under the direction of the CPU control unit. The control unit is directed by a program of instructions, usually established by the computer manufacturer. In addition, the control unit directs the operations of peripheral and secondary storage devices (Senn 1982).

Computer registers are assemblies of electronic circuits that have specific functions, such as receiving, holding, or transferring data or instructions used by other CPU elements. They are usually temporary in nature and have changing functions during the instruction and execution cycles. They can hold the instructions, addresses, data going to or from storage, and accumulate the results of arithmetic operations. The registers perform functions that are critical to computer operations and also increase the speed at which they can be performed.

Secondary Storage

Secondary storage is used to hold data in files and programs that are not being executed and normally have to be accessed during data channels. Because primary memory online storage capability is very expensive, and some computations demand large amounts of data, secondary storage of data provides a flexible device. Some common secondary storage devices are disk, magnetic drum, magnetic tape, and mass storage (magnetic tape strips). The access speeds are much slower than with primary storage, but secondary storage provides a feasible and economic approach for supplementing primary storage.

MINI- AND MICROCOMPUTERS

Minicomputers

In the mid-1960s computers that were smaller and less expensive than the large mainframes were introduced. These minicomputers were limited in capacity and were used mainly for engineering and scientific applications because of their decreased need for software or programming. A minicomputer is difficult to define properly because of the great range of computer sizes and functions that overlap with those of the large mainframe computers. They may stand alone, and some are the size of an office desk and are used primarily for process control, such as those used in oil refining or educational applications. Although it has not yet happened, possibly because of microcomputers, some predicted that they would replace mainframes. Minicomputers range in price ($10,000 to $50,000) and storage capacity (approximately 32K to 250K) in primary memory (Senn 1982).

Microcomputers

A microcomputer, a relatively recent phenomenon, is small enough to place on a desk. It usually has a keyboard, a CRT (display tube), a microprocessor (which controls the activities and arithmetic and logic functions), and read-only memory, with the capability to add storage, printers, and other devices such as modems that can link the computer to other computers through communication channels. They can use flexible (floppy) disks, hard disks, or cassette tape for memory or storage. Microcomputers have the storage and speed that were possessed only by large and minicomputers a few years ago. Depending on the capabilities required and additional equipment, they may range in price from less than $200 to well over $10,000. The microcomputer is slower than larger machines. However, the growing software support for micros (or personal computers), which ranges from various forms of word processing to complex financial analysis with graphics, offsets the minor disadvantages of the slower processing speeds for small users.

As the use of microcomputers increases, the functions they perform will also expand. At one time, microcomputers had less speed and storage capabilities than the larger machines, but with the growth of integrated programs, they can perform most of the functions formerly reserved for larger, more expensive, sophisticated hardware and software. They usually possess read-only memory (ROM), such as the set of instructions used for starting the computer, and are pre-programmed by the manufacturer. Random-access memory (RAM) contains software that is related to a particular job the operator enters from the keyboard or disk. Larger additional memory capability can also be acquired. Further, as the trend toward distributed processing systems (a hierarchy of large and small processors) grows, undoubtedly more use will be made of microcomputers at the local level of organizations to interface with centralized, large processors. Information flow will then be structured to correspond to the needs for information used in decision making at the different levels of government organizations. An emerging issue is whether the proliferation of microcomputers has contributed to managerial and organizational effectiveness.

INFORMATION SYSTEMS SOFTWARE/PROGRAMMING

Managers need to understand the role and components of software/programming of both large computers and microcomputers if they are to be capable designers of information systems that meet their decision-making requirements. Software/programming is essentially the instructions or computer programs that direct or tell a computer what to do. Without relevant software, the computer hardware system cannot fulfill the tasks for which it is designed. Management has to understand the uses and limitations of programming to supervise formally and make informal decisions about its role in supporting decisions, computer applications, and information systems design. Software/programming is the critical link between managerial responsibilities and computer capabilities.

Because of advances in technology, hardware costs have dropped significantly. However, software performance rather than hardware potential has become a problem. Some major problems have been the failure to meet manager/user requirements, increased costs, untimely performance, difficulty of maintenance, and errors. Many of these problems still exist, but the current direction in information systems design is oriented toward meeting user needs and increasing productivity with new applications.

Software has generally been classified as either systems or applications programming. Systems programming is usually that group of programs associated with particular hardware supplied by a manufacturer or software house to make applications writing and execution simpler. Systems software has traditionally been categorized as master programs, programming languages, and general-purpose programs. Operating systems (OS) are the overall controllers or executives in the system and provide the master programs for use of the hardware, language processors, and database system. The operating system controls job scheduling, job accounting, facility allocation, and communication functions if they are part of the system. Language processors provide the ability to compile applications programs prepared in particular languages. A high-level language (usually user-friendly languages, such as BASIC, *B*eginner's *A*ll-purpose *S*ymbolic *I*nstruction *C*ode; COBOL, *C*ommon *B*usiness *O*riented *L*anguage; or FORTRAN, *For*mula *Tran*slation, program must be translated into machine language, and the software that performs this is called a compiler.

Programming Languages

Programming languages help more individuals to use and program computers and facilitate the effectiveness and general utility of hardware/computers and information systems. These high-level languages have been in use since the late 1950s. FORTRAN was originally designed for IBM systems to help scientists and engineers solve mathematical problems using a computer. COBOL was designed primarily to support business and commercial functions where large numbers of records are maintained and many transactions are performed. Thus FORTRAN is geared more toward mathematical functions, whereas COBOL primarily deals with sequencing or sorting of records.

The BASIC programming language is similar to FORTRAN, but was developed primarily for time sharing or interactive environments and rapid program writing, though it can also be used for batch (noninteractive) processing. BASIC is easy to learn and may only be written for a one-time run or purpose. Another online language is ALGOL (*ALGO*rithmic *L*anguage), which was used frequently in Europe but formed the basis for certain computer developments in the United States. One multipurpose language PL/1 (*P*rogramming *L*anguage *1*) combines the features of FORTRAN and COBOL. APL (*A P*rogramming *L*anguage) is an extremely powerful language with complex but compact notation.

Some special-purpose and problem-oriented languages are SPSS, RPG(II), GPSS, and SIMSCRIPT. SPSS (*S*tatistical *P*ackage for the *S*ocial *S*ciences) is a special-purpose, high-level language written in FORTRAN that has widespread applications in the social and administrative sciences. It performs multiple data management, file creation, and statistical functions. RPG is used to generate programs for report formatting or presentation of data already in the computer. RPG(II) is an update of RPG that is designed for the nonprogrammer to specify programs for routine administrative applications that are output format oriented.

GPSS (*G*eneral *P*urpose *S*ystems *S*imulator), designed in the early 1960s, is a language for discrete simulation problems using a block diagram approach. Its primary application has been in such areas as simulated queueing systems, work in process, or facilities usage such as fire station location or police dispatching models where there are interdependent components to model. SIMSCRIPT also performs discrete simulation problems using FORTRAN.

Characteristics of and Considerations in
Selecting Software/Programming

Because software/programming are necessary to translate managerial needs into computer instructions to perform required operations, managers have certain issues to consider when selecting them. Davis (1978) proposed that several variables be considered when selecting a programming language: type of problem, skill level of programmer, terminal or offline program entry, complexity of problems, portability, availability, availability of consulting, general-purpose versus specialized, and language versus package. Some languages are designed for specific problems (COBOL, RPG, GPSS); therefore the type of problem or need should be considered in selecting a programming language. Some languages require high skill levels, whereas others are designed for occasional users, and some languages are more relevant to interactive/terminal entry (BASIC) rather than batch/card processing. Some problems are complex and may require complex programs (scientific applications using FORTRAN). If a standard program is to be used at several organizations/installations a "portable" standard language is desirable. Adequate program support should also be available, and specialized functions (simulations) require specialized (GPSS) as opposed to general languages (COBOL). Also, a package that performs multiple file management and statistical procedures such as SPSS may be preferable to specific languages that have limited uses.

Senn (1982) provides other characteristics that are important in programs: correctness, accuracy, completeness, generality, efficiency, and documentation. "Correctness and accuracy means that the program should accept data, process them and generate results without error either in syntax or logic" (p. 159). Syntax errors are improper symbols used in instructions, and logic errors are improper instructions. A complete program performs all necessary computations and data manipulation. A generalizable program can be used in different numbers of transactions and on different data and have several options available. Efficiency means that instructions are written to process data as quickly and easily as possible. Documentation means that adequate explanation, flowcharts, and descriptions of the system process, procedures, and data are included, along with documentation on process sequencing and purpose of statements.

Software packages can greatly reduce the cost of information systems and personnel, but one disadvantage is that a program may be inefficient because its generality exceeds the client's needs. Packages can perform data management, retrieval, and computation and generate reports or update files according to user needs and data. Many packages have been developed to meet the increasing requirements of public organizations and have many advantages that indicate their use will increase in the future because the labor-intensive task of developing special-purpose programs is so expensive.

Flowcharting and the Programming Process

Most programming progresses through a logical sequence of steps that parallels the managerial definition of a task in operations other than information systems. One standardized approach to representing systems (procedure chart), program (logic diagram), or computer program (detailed) logic is called flowcharting. Flowcharts are diagrams that represent a sequence of operations using commonly accepted symbols. Figure 3.3 presents the symbols of the International Standards Organization (ISO). The American National Standards Institute (ANSI) also uses these symbols with minor variations. These symbols and flowcharts are used to illustrate all phases of information systems development.

Different levels of flowcharts present a simple visual diagram of complex relationships in the overall system, the structure of information flows within the system (by diagramming the sequence of transactions), and the detailed computer logic that represents the transactions and sequence of information flows to computer programmers. The flowcharts provide a common frame of reference for the dialogue between the manager and information systems specialists (programmers, systems analysts).

Flowcharting conventions are to establish the level (system, program function, computer program); chart from top to bottom, left to right using standardized symbols (templates with standard symbols are easily acquired); start from known to unknown; chart main data/information flow first; label each page clearly, identifying the project, chart, date, author, and page number; use connectors to reduce complex flowlines and crossovers; and be consistent.

Flowcharting is a useful tool for presenting and validating managerial or systems designer logic to others involved in the systems design process. Flowcharting also illustrates complex relationships

FIGURE 3.3. International Standards Organization Flowcharting Symbols

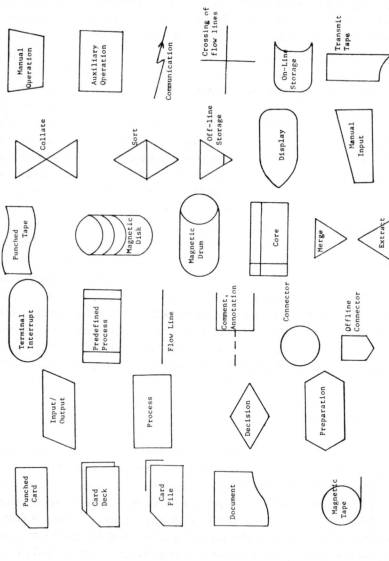

Source: American National Standard Institute (ANSI) 1971. *Standard Flowchart Symbols and Their Use in Information Processing.* New York.

between information systems processes and the information itself. The flowchart should present the flow documents, data files used, decision points, processes, and overall accuracy of transactions or flows.

Figure 3.4 illustrates three different flowcharts that address different levels of specification. The systems diagram or flowchart is a general approach to defining a systems view of operational decision making and control. The program flowchart identifies steps in a general process of designing and evaluating programs, and the computer program flowchart illustrates how a budgetary assessment of welfare costs can be converted to a computer program that translates the logic of the cost program to specific programming language. The manager can use flowcharting to great advantage in presenting program logic and producing a common framework for managers and systems analysts to use in designing information systems. Chapter 4 examines how some of these concepts can be applied to designing parts of accounting and financial control systems using additional data and information flow diagrams.

The proper use of flowcharting standardizes the process of information systems development through all of its phases because it can be used to link logically the operations, decisions, and information needs. Flowcharting can identify procedures, related decision-making points, and supporting information requirements integratively. This approach, then, provides a conceptual tool that the manager can use in thinking about how procedures, people, hardware, and software interact to produce information required in the tasks of management.

Programming Process

The manager or user must be able to specify exactly what needs and decisions are being supported and be capable of communicating them to the systems analyst or programmer. If the processing of welfare clients involves specific information, such as detailed application and screening or review procedures, and a computer program is being revised to achieve error detection to make a determination of payment, then specific processes, such as error-level detection and calculation of payments, have to be described in detail. This purpose, then, defines the common foundation for both managers and programmers.

FIGURE 3.4. Different Types of Flowcharts Using Common Symbols

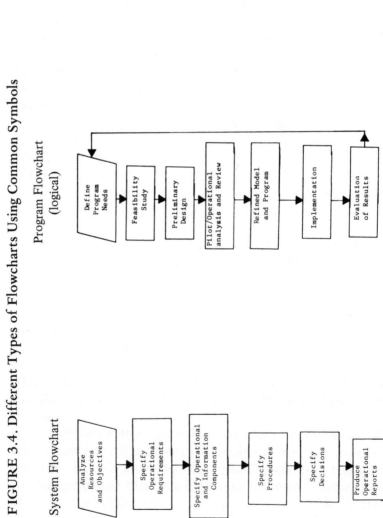

Computer Program
Flowchart (detailed)

Program Flowchart
(logical)

System Flowchart

Source: Compiled by the author.

Another important part of the programming cycle that has to be understood by the public manager is the structure of the data. The manager must have previously defined what data will be processed and how the data are arranged (input and output), input, and output medium. For example, in a welfare application, a welfare payment will probably require the recipient's social security number, number of dependents, eligibility, qualification for one or more payments (AFDC, food stamps), rate of payment, total payment, method of payment, and time of payment. These conditions and processes determine what information is required either from the application, centralized database, or outside sources (financial checks). All programming requires some managerial assessment of the source, validity, arrangement, input, and output of the data to be used in the program.

Processing logic determines the operations that will be performed on the data, and this logic is usually diagrammed using the flowcharting symbols and processes described earlier. The data and processing steps in the cycle provide the basis for selecting a programming language that will be efficient in meeting the purpose of the program. When the preceding phases of the programming cycle have been completed, the program is coded (translated into computer readable instructions), input into the computer system, diagnosed for errors, and debugged if any errors are found.

INFORMATION FILE STRUCTURE, STORAGE, AND DESIGN

A public sector manager must understand the relationships and interdependence among files and their structure and storage media, and the other components of an information system, such as hardware, procedures and software. Files with data and information are the basic foundation blocks in a computerized information system that have direct impacts on the effectiveness of the overall systems, and managers should have the knowledge to structure and influence the design of files.

A file is a coherent, systematic collection of data and/or information that relates to the functions of the manager and organization. Files are arranged logically and physically to correspond with their use in the system. Files are organized into items, and records are composed of items, which are the most elementary units in a file.

Files are composed of records that have the same items. The record is usually the key concept because of its relationship to the organizational function. For example, a single welfare client will have a record with numerous items of data, such as name, social security number, age, income, and dependents, as well as other required data. A police file may contain incidents or reports with time, location, type of crime, witness, and loss data items. The records composed of the same data items constitute a file or data set that is stored and processed. Files or data sets can be accessed, modified, copied, erased, used, sorted, or stored in different logical or physical arrangements or different media.

File Storage and Organization

Files are usually permanent or semipermanent collections of records, some of which in government attempt to deal with more than 230 million Americans. It has been posited that there are, on the average, 15 files on the average American in federal government agencies for a total of 3,529,743,665. They range in substance from social security and payroll data to criminal charges and loans or grants. Large files such as these are likely to be stored on secondary storage devices.

Secondary storage (not in primary memory or online) devices usually consist of magnetic tape or disk, which are offline, that is, not directly accessible. Data on secondary storage devices can be retrieved or accessed using data channels to transfer the data to the primary storage work space where they can be processed in accordance with instructions. The magnetic tapes can be placed on tape drives and the removable or fixed disk pack (several disks) placed on a disk drive to be "read." The characters (letters of the alphabet, numbers, and so on) in the items in the record will be transformed to electronic symbols and stored on the magnetic tape or disk. The tape can hold 800, 1,600, or 6,250 characters per inch, depending on how they are arranged, or "packed," and the data are normally filed sequentially on tracks (seven or nine horizontal tracks along the length of the tape), that is, recorded in the same order they are received or processed. The data are electronically recorded on the tape by a write head, which arranges the data on a magnetized coating, just as in home recording devices.

Data can now be stored on disks (similar to phonograph records) more economically than in the past, and the current trend is toward use of secondary storage units composed mostly of disks because of the number of units that can be attached to processors. As an example, a disk pack can be sealed, fixed, or removed. The data are placed on the disk with a write head where the disk drive rotates rapidly and the read/write heads (usually on same arm) perform their read or write functions without touching the disk itself.

Primary memory storage is usually described in thousands of bytes. For example, 16K primary memory storage is 16,384 bytes where the K means "thousand" (actually 1,024). A large computer may have a primary storage of from 512K bytes to 16 million (mega) bytes. The primary storage part of an information or computer system is directly related to the number of cases or records and complexity of applications related to the organization functions.

The most current advances in microelectronic semiconductor research allow for low-cost, low-heat, fast, low-power, reliable, and compact storage of data using transistors on semiconductor chips. Semiconductor storage devices are used in most computer systems because of their incredible speed, low cost, and heat efficiency. In this technology, complex circuits designed by engineers are etched or placed on silicon wafers. There are predictions that by the year 2000 technology will allow for each semiconductor chip to contain more than 1 billion circuit elements.

Storage Methods

The most common method of storage is random-access memory (RAM), which requires direct access storage devices (DASD), such as the disks and disk packs previously described. RAM provides for very rapid access and retrieval of stored data. The read/write heads can be moved in or out between the disks to access data on the tracks, which form what is called the cylinder (the same track on each of the disks in the disk pack). Records do not have to be stored sequentially as with tape, but rather placed on the disk in various locations as they are processed. Records can be fixed or variable length, with each form having advantages and disadvantages. Variable-length records add to the complexity of determining overall file requirements but may be required for organizational purposes, whereas fixed-record lengths provide for economy and efficiency when working with known fields and field sizes. However, the nature of the records (decision-making requirements/evaluation, eligibility determinations) and the specific task or operation being performed should form the basis for determining the length of the record.

Master, Transaction, and Sort Files and Record Key

Because files and the records in them are the basic information-building blocks for an organization's information system, they have to be systematically designed, maintained, and updated to meet their potential in the managerial decision-making process. In the overall category of files there are three distinct types that the manager should understand and keep in mind. A master file, such as budgets, accounts, inventory, clients, or personnel files, contains the more or less permanent records that form the core operations of the organization. A welfare or AFDC department or office should have a master file of clients, and a finance or budgeting department should have the budget, program categories, and/or funds/accounts on file to control the major functions of the organization. Police and fire departments will have incident reporting and filing systems, and water and utility companies will have files of customers. These files are known as master files because they constitute the major operational focus of the organization. They must be carefully maintained to provide the most timely, complete, and accurate information available because they constitute the core of the information system.

Master files are updated by other files called transaction files, which collect, edit, process, and report data for the master file. Transaction or "detail files" collect records that reflect relevant organizational transactions, such as changes in client status or budgeting allocations/expenditures, edits them for accuracy, processes the changes to the master file, and reports the change. In this way the temporary transaction file keeps the master file up to date and relevant for decision making.

Another temporary file is a sort file, which is used to sequence other files using a record key. A record key may be something such as the social security number, client number, account/budgetary number, name, or date that is used to order or sequence a file. Depending on the need of the manager or user, the sort files can rearrange the master file according to need.

DATABASE INFORMATION SYSTEMS

Martin (1976), an influential architect and chronicler of information systems technology and developments, defines a database in the following way:

A collection of interrelated data stored together with controlled redundancy to serve one or more applications in an optimal fashion; the data are stored so that they are independent of programs which use the data; a common and controlled approach is used in adding new data and modifying and retrieving existing data within the data base. (p. 4)

The person who presides over and controls the overall structure and the task of developing the database is called a database administrator. Large organizations may have many databases and database administrators where a top-level management official is needed to manage the overall information resources of the organization (Martin 1976). In databases, physical data are independent and separate from logical structures, data are nonredundant, accessibility is real time, data are secure, and application programs give the manager or user flexibility in using the data.

A database schema is a "chart of the types of data that are used" (Martin 1976, p. 74) and a subschema is an applications programmer's view of the data item types and record types (p. 76). Though the major trend in information systems has been the growth of online database systems, because of their timeliness and flexibility, the administration of the database structure is complex and requires other functions, such as data definition (data dictionary or items and meanings), database design (to physical structuring, security), data operations (day-to-day operations), and security (investigates security breaches) (Martin 1976).

A database is usually centralized because it contains important operational data and because control over access is needed. The advantages of real-time access is achieved by using direct access storage devices (disk, drum). The database administrator usually uses a database management system, a supporting software system that provides for creating, updating, retrieving, and reporting accurately and consistently. Many users can access the base, as controlled by the database administrator, by using applications programs/programmers to meet specific manager/user needs. Single files replace the separate file systems and thus reduce redundancy and efficiency of retrieval using a special database command language. Database systems can be self-contained with their own language or use other languages. The major hardware and software vendors have database management and file management systems.

To be effective, databases should also have the characteristics of integrity (secure and accurate), sharability (access to all users), availability (accommodate diverse users), and evolvability (responsive to changes and user demands) (Senn 1982). Because database information systems possess these advantages, in addition to the others cited earlier, they provide an effective means of collecting information and managing large- and medium-scale government operations (welfare, AFDC, transportation systems or departments). They are becoming increasingly relevant to government managers at top, middle, and operational levels of organizations where demands are increasing and added flexibility is needed in managing the information resource.

DISTRIBUTED DATA PROCESSING SYSTEMS

Distributed data processing is usually described as a hierarchy of processors that allows for "much of the processing logic and storage to be placed at or near the transaction while maintaining some of the advantages of large, centralized computers" (Davis and Everest 1976, pp. 248–49). The lowest level in the hierarchy is a small computer with local storage and processing capability. Large tasks not possible at the local level are performed at a higher level in the system, which has larger computers. An example of a state welfare-AFDC system using this concept will be discussed in Chapter 4.

Distributed processing is gaining in use because it can be adopted to the geographic dispersion and local autonomy issues facing many government operations where networks of information are required to perform both local and centralized functions. It also has the advantage of economic flexibility because local users have to provide information for higher level as well as local processing, and mainframe computer systems at the local level may not be feasible. These systems can also use the processing and storage capabilities of the growing number of microcomputers in public organizations.

COMMUNICATIONS AND INFORMATION SYSTEMS

The distributed processing system is possible because of communications technologies that allow for linkages between processors geographically removed from each other. Communications over short distances (500 to 2,000 feet) may employ a direct connection (hard wire) to carry the flow of signals between processors. Phone lines (with proper speed capability), dedicated leased lines, or microwave transmission can be used. For example, local terminal/processors in one organization can be directly connected to each other while one of these local terminals or processors may be connected to a centralized mainframe hundreds of miles away by microwave transmitters and receivers.

Communication facilities used in computer networks may be simplex (communication in one direction only), duplex (communication in both directions, one at a time), or full duplex (same time communication in both directions). Multiplexors transmit data from several slow-speed terminals to a centralized computer or transmit data from the central processor to the terminals. A "front end" processor or computer is a piece of hardware that may be used to manage transmission or reception functions without loading up the central processor with communications. The front end processor can store, receive, edit, and assemble blocks of data for the central processor or transmit back to the terminals. Software for managing and connecting remote terminals and the main computer is called teleprocessing or telecommunications software. There are many other technical details associated with computer telecommunications, including satellite communications, that can expand upon the basic framework provided here and provide a state-of-the-art assessment of trends and prospects (see, for example, the special edition of *Science*, February 12, 1982, especially the articles by J. S. Mayo, B. I. Edelson and R. S. Cooper, A. Newell and R. F. Sproull, and R. M. Davis).

COMPONENTS OF COMPUTERIZED
INFORMATION SYSTEMS

The capacity of computerized information systems (CIS) to support organizational and managerial objectives in this complex milieu of the public sector will be directly related to the capacity of managers to define their roles. To define and analyze the managerial role in the context of multiple, competing influences in public sector organizations can be aided by CISs, which, in turn, can be used to achieve the objectives resolved from the analysis. The CIS, as a subset of the manager's set of functions, will be as effective a tool as the manager is effective in designing its use. The CIS, as most tools, will reflect the competence of the user and manager of users. Therefore, it goes without saying that computer is not an information system or substitute for the manager, but rather, it is one of the components that must be made interdependent with the other managerial functions and processes.

Figure 3.5 illustrates the level of interdependence needed to link the constituents discussed here with the model of an organization and managerial elements provided in Figure 2.1. Figure 3.5 puts the relationships in their interdependence perspective for the purpose of clarifying the linkages between a CIS and an organizational/managerial system. The center of Figure 3.5 characterizes the key role of information and control systems to achieve both coordination of internal operation and external environmental structures or processes. As discussed in Chapter 2, most public sector and/or government organizations cannot afford the luxury of defining the context of competition for resources as benign, so an open systems or contingency approach provides the most viable model of organizational and managerial requirements. The CIS is subject to and part of the response to complexity. The CIS not only has a great potential for improving management capability but also has the capacity to introduce problems if not designed and structured in correspondence with the critical needs of the organization.

As illustrated in Figure 3.5, the CIS supports the operations, human resource, finance-budgeting, and other functions by providing information and control for each of them. If timely, accurate, and complete information on appropriations or fund balances is needed to support the finance-budgeting functions, then the hardware, database, operating system (executive controller of the hardware), applications software (special-purpose programs), storage devices (primary and secondary), and the requisite telecommunications should be designed to provide it to the manager. Required linkages (for example, hardwired internal linkages and/or microwave of phone lines to external terminals in agencies) have to be determined. For example,

FIGURE 3.5. Integration of Systems Contingency Model with Computerized Information Systems Elements

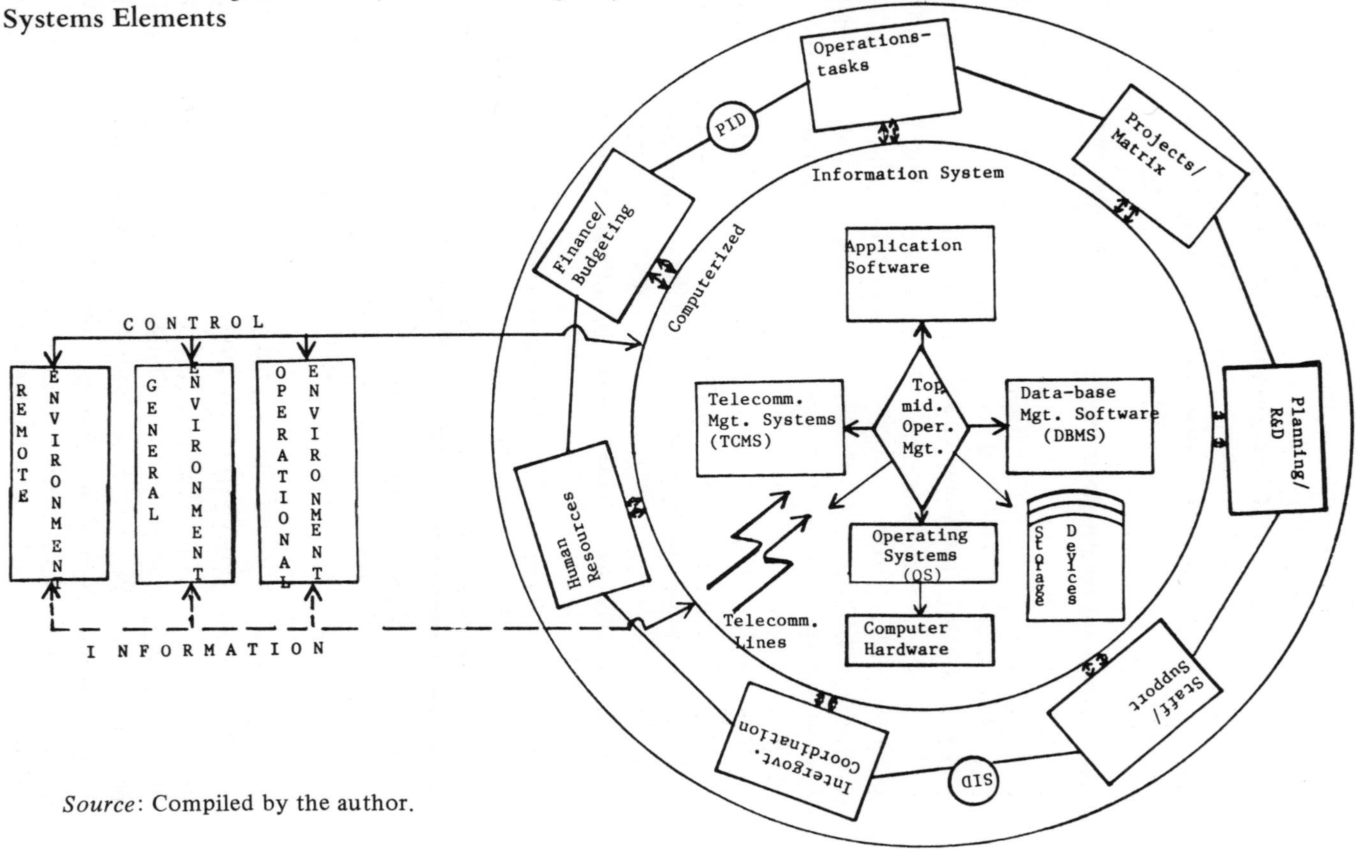

Source: Compiled by the author.

75

if a state government requires an integrated financial management information system within a generally accepted accounting principle framework to meet top-level executive (centralized budgeting and management) and agency level management needs, a real-time online capability, a centralized database with regional offices, retrieval, and update capability, an intensive and sophisticated database and operating system with appropriate applications software (forecasting models, revenue projections), telecommunications (for the regional offices), and adequate primary memory or online storage may be needed.

If the state is large, has complex intergovernment relationships with federal, other state, and its own or other local governments, a statewide personnel system, and special projects such as economic development, or support studies/research, the computerized financial management information will have to be designed to support these functions. Without a CIS, they may still be achieved, but in an age of growing unemployment compensation, unfunded pension liabilities, welfare-medicare transfers, and educational programs, management needs an information resource capability to make valid decisions. This is true at the operational level in government functions as well as the top levels of the state, urban, and federal agencies.

External statutory requirements such as federal reporting or eligibility determinations, clients, media, technological, or energy variables may have direct or indirect relevance to any given program, procedure, personnel action, or budgetary decision. External structures, such as legislative or judicial bodies, exert direct control over a managers's actions and provide sources of information for internal operational requirements, if there are great demands on an agency with complex functions and many employees or clients. The computerized information systems database, hardware, communications, storage, and software subsystems will have to correspond to those needs.

Local governments or their agencies have similar open and internal systems requirements to meet. Local governments have multiple relationships with external funding and statutory bodies that dictate reporting or operational requirements, as well as such personnel matters as equal opportunity, compensation, and selection.

The diagram in Figure 3.5 could also be used to design a computerized information system for a local agency such as a police department. An urban area of 100,000 people may require computers with linkages to state or federal data banks to process license numbers or fingerprints and, depending on operational needs, hardware, software, and storage capability to do online analyses of crime patterns with regard to time, location, or type of crime. Other factors or projects, such as team policing, automated dispatching systems, or computer terminals in patrol vehicles, may determine what applications software or operating systems are needed.

Another purpose of Figure 3.5 is to show that computerized information systems are not discrete, disembodied electronic boxes that have a separate life from the strategies of management. They are tools or subsystems of the overall top, mid, and operational functions that should be designed to do what they do best: support the knowledgeable and informed manager. The office of the president of the United States is undergoing a computer revolution that ranges from use of word processors and electronic mail to increased use of communication links between computers. The proliferation of personal and microcomputers, the reductions in the cost of computer technology, robotics, use of home and desk terminals, supercomputers, optic transmission lines, electronic mail, telecommunications linkages between large databases, and teleconferencing have made it mandatory for government managers to understand and use computerized information systems to make themselves more effective.

DEVELOPMENTS IN AND SUMMARY POINTS ON COMPUTERS, HARDWARE, SOFTWARE, AND ELECTRONICS

The revolution in computers and associated technical processes has not ended. Enormous changes in large-scale integration using semiconductors have changed the size, reliability, efficiency, and cost of computer and storage devices, and major strides are still being made in areas such as integrated software, networking, and superconductors for supercomputers. SQUIDs (*S*uperconducting *Q*uantum *I*nterference *D*evices), which consist of circuits made of Josephson junctions or other superconducting switches, may further improve the electronic technology of computers. However, the manager will still be the primary linkage between this evolving supertechnology and public/organizational needs.

Chapter 4 addresses issues relevant to computerized information systems at the federal, state, and local levels of government. It builds on the model in Chapter 2 and the knowledge of hardware, software, and computerized information systems presented here. Chapter 5 discusses how these issues can be integrated using a systems analysis/ design process approach to information systems in public/government organizations.

PART II:

INFORMATION SYSTEMS ANALYSIS, DESIGN, AND IMPLEMENTATION

4

Information Systems Issues at Federal, State, and Local Levels of Government

In a recent book of readings by Horton and Marchand (1982), several problems and issues concerning the management of information resources in the federal government were identified. These issues were derived from several sources, including the Commission on Federal Paperwork (see Horton and Marchand 1982, p. vii), which resulted in 770 recommendations for reducing paperwork and red tape. The book provides an invaluable service to public managers by defining the meaning, process, and challenge of information management in public organizations.

Horton and Marchand present the arguments against information management in public organizations: Current information policies and practices in the public sector are adequate; information cannot be managed; it is too late to change government policies and practices in this area; and information manipulation will result in stifling creativity and open inquiry and threaten individual privacy. The authors concluded and answered these arguments by stating that extensive evidence shows government information policies are inadequate (these are documented in their book); methods are needed to define the value of information to government; the "crutch" of paperwork is used too many times to mask government ineffectiveness and the lack of answers to critical questions; the use of information for manipulation and control depends on how viable the policies are that prevent abuses; information can enhance individual growth; our citizenry must be informed to participate intelligently in the democratic process; and a careful approach to information policy and management is needed.

These objectives are also part of the purpose of this book, and the exploration of information systems issues at different levels of government provides such a mechanism.

The purpose of this chapter is to present and discuss the major information systems and related management issues at the federal, state, and local levels of government, along with intergovernment relations, and to outline how these issues may be understood using the previously discussed framework and principles. Each of the government levels and their interactions have unique information problems related to roles and functions, but there are also common dimensions to their problems that contribute to an integrated perspective on using information systems and the related technology as a management resource and tool. For example, in 1977 there were 79,913 federal, state, local, school district, and special district governments in the United States whose spending in 1980 exceeded $869 billion, that is, approximately one-third of the gross national product (Savas 1982). Services and products ranging from trash collection to satellite telecommunications are provided worldwide by government organizations that require more economical and efficient approaches to management and operations.

The approach taken in this chapter does not presume total system integration or managerial rationality, but is, rather, designed to emphasize what can be understood, structured, designed, and implemented. Comprehensive rationality methods such as Planning, Programming, and Budgeting Systems (PPBS), Zero Based Budgeting (ZBB), and Management by Objectives (MBO), do not always address the behavioral, organizational, and political context in which they are designed to operate; for one variable missing in these budgetary and managerial models is the failure to utilize effectively information systems. Information systems do not replace judgment or negate the contextual and internal variables as outlined in Chapter 2, but they do provide a means for further identifying the commensurables and incommensurables in any given decision situation so that managerial judgment can be more effective. Uncertainty will never be totally reduced, but a rational approach to defining what is known and unknown to make decisions is better than uninformed guesses or emotionally based criteria, especially if the public interest and demands for accountability are present. The federal perspective will be addressed first because of its enormity, economic impact, continuous development, and effect on the other levels of government; discussions of state, local, and intergovernment issues follow.

INFORMATION SYSTEMS AND MANAGEMENT ISSUES IN THE FEDERAL GOVERNMENT

It has been stated that "the Federal Government is the world's largest user of information technology" (OMB Memorandum on Improving Government Services through Information Technology, 1979). The impact from this scope of operations on society has been recognized at least since 1963, when a study of federal data processing was initiated by the Kennedy administration. The results of this study were submitted to the Senate in March 1965, and on October 30, 1965 the Brooks Act (P.L. 89–306) was passed to rectify problems found after House committee investigations of information resources management were completed (Report of the General Government Team, 1978).

The specific purpose of the Brooks Act was "to provide for the economic and efficient purchase, lease, maintenance, operation, and utilization of automatic data processing equipment by federal departments and agencies." This same law also provided that three government agencies—Office of Management and Budget, General Services Administration, and the National Bureau of Standards—assume the responsibilities for improving the management of information resources in the executive branch. An assessment of this trilateral approach to managing information systems in the federal government after 13 years of operation was that it

> has been confusing, contradictory, and in many instances detrimental to the effective application of information technology to support mission functions. Further the concern of the troika appears to be excessively hardware oriented. (Report of the General Government Team, 1978, p. 10)

Many of the findings of the Report of the General Government Team emphasized the weakness in the overall policy, definition of objectives, and management processes rather than the capability of the technical resources. Further, the report found that so-called "computer problems" really reflected poor policy management or program jurisdiction problems (p. 5). Federal government organizations typically have several functions to perform, so part of this chapter will be devoted to examining the general operations in specific service functions to emphasize the question of management responsibility.

Human Resources and Human Services

Human services and resource programs and agencies administered or funded by the federal government constitute a significant part of the total services provided by the federal government and reflect many information systems needs. A federal study reviewed four human services agencies as part of a presidential project on federal data processing. The four agencies under review accounted for a budget authority of more than $267 billion in 1979. The Department of Health, Education, and Welfare (now Health and Human Services) administered more than 375 individual programs during 1979. These four agencies are estimated to have spent more than $600 million for fiscal year '79 on information systems and related technology (Report of the Human Resources Team, 1978). This same report estimated that these programs, which now account for approximately 50 percent of the federal budget, touch the lives of more than 100 million Americans. In addition to multiple agencies on the federal level, the programs are partially administered by "grants to states and local government by 140,000 local nonprofit, nongovernmental community human service agencies, more than 28,000 local governments and at least 200 different State human service agencies" (p. 6).

Many of the findings associated with the administration of information systems in the human services programs indicated that, overall, organizational and management issues precluded effective information systems management. That is, a key finding and conclusion of the information systems study of human services was that "no set of definitions or standards have been adopted for Federal human service programs" (p. 9). Given the competing political, economic, and statutory environments associated with administering human services programs, the condition of inadequate or insufficient standards from either external or internal sources is a major problem for the managerial use of information. If standards exist or are developed, management can design information systems that acquire, process, and use the pertinent information. Whereas if management does not use an information system for deriving the organizational standards or objectives, information does not support the achievement of objectives or individual decisions. This state of affairs leads to confusion, inadequate management and control, lack of performance criteria, and uncoordinated delivery of services. These conditions are evident in the area of human services management. The basic information technology exists to support human services programs; however, the management problems are the result of inadequate public policy and management rather than deficient information systems. The information system is a tool that is as effective as the human services program manager.

An examination of the human services management issue illustrates the massive financial and substantive implications of external demands and poor internal management rather than the failure of technology as a causal factor. Some of the other management-related issues identified in the report on human services that affect the utilization of information systems and related technology in the federal government are unclear assignments of responsibility for service delivery; weak federal enforcement, monitoring, and evaluation of policies and programs; poor coordination among federal agencies; inadequate classification schemes for human services programs; fragmented eligibility determination; failure to use off-the-shelf technology to improve service delivery; and failure to work effectively with state and local governments. This list of federal problems with human services management is not intended to be exhaustive or critical but, rather, indicative of the causes and effects of deficient utilization of information systems within a government management context.

One implication for managers who use or need information resources to acquire or maintain control over government functions is that decisions relating to general policy, internal management, and organizational objectives influence information systems operations, and the capability of the information system also has a reciprocal effect on how capable managers can be. Another implication is that organizational and managerial objectives have to be understood in the context in which they exist for information systems to provide the proper support.

Information Systems Issues for Top Program Management in Federal Government Agencies

The information systems and managerial implications of the top-level program management part of the presidential management study in federal organizations were that information resources should be managed and allocated to achieve objectives just as financial and human resources are. That is, the information resource can be no better than the use to which it is applied in supporting the internal functional operations used to achieve organizational objectives, many of which have been determined by external controllers, statutes, and general environmental influences, such as technology and economic policy.

The presidential study on top management in government agencies stated that they (top managers) "do not effectively translate political goals and priorities into mission responsibilities," which results in "inadequate specification of information system and technology requirements" (Report of the General Government Team, 1978, p. iv).

Another major finding was that "the management style of high level career managers is reactive in dealing with information resource decisionmaking" (p. 10). These findings emphasize the premise that top-level management has to translate political influences and goals but does not exhibit the capability to plan and control important organizational processes such as information management. These findings do not imply that all top-level managers possess this reactivity characteristic, but, rather, that to manage dictates an ability, probably a proactive posture, to move an organization, agency, or group toward an objective, usually using a plan and other mechanisms such as an information system to attain control.

Other findings from the study were that there is inadequate linkage between information processing and telecommunications, a lack of achievement of the Brooks Act's goal of improved executive leadership, and inadequate management and technical assistance for the use of information technology in the federal government. All of these findings support the premise that inadequate information systems management is a direct result of management. The study further recommends that the president emphasize management objectives and criteria in using information technology, that the Office of Management and Budget be designated to improve the management of information technology, and that central agency assistance for program management be expanded among the executive agencies. The specific assignment of responsibility is not so easy; but the important point is that in the effectiveness of information systems, the critical variable is the competence of management at all levels in the federal government.

Federal Information Standards Study

Another report of the presidential reorganization study produced several findings that are of direct relevance to the argument that management plays the central role in determining how effectively information resources are used and managed. One corollary relevant to the management of information and documented in the federal study is the implementation and use of operating standards: "The purpose of the federal information processing standards has been to further economic and operational advantages through the standardization of automatic data processing hardware, software, and systems" (President's Reorganization Project, Standards Team Report, 1978, p. 1). The other findings of the study classified the related problems into such categories as lack of goals and objectives, insufficient management direction, inadequate taxonomy for standards, and potential conflict between data processing and telecommunications standards.

One of these findings is based on the perception of users that the federal standards program lacked discernible goals and objectives and that this led to lack of prioritization among the standards. Another finding of interest was that "management direction by the Department of Commerce, the General Services Administration, and the Office of Management and Budget has frequently been lacking in purpose and commitment" (p. 6). This finding supplements further the significance of the management function in affecting the outcomes of the information systems process in organizations. The influence of management could also be extended to deal with coordinating and resolving conflict between related subsystem functions (for example, telecommunications and data processing), especially in emergency or defense functions, and classifying priorities among development, implementation, and measurement. The report on standards also concluded that, if not corrected, the managerial, conflict, and operational problems will get much worse with time.

Information Technology and National Security

The substantive and financial impacts of national security are significant and pervasive in the United States. The use of computers and information systems in the Department of Defense (DOD) is widespread because they influence weapons systems use and development, intelligence, navigation and guidance, and scientific as well as administrative functions (President's Reorganization Project, October 1978, p. 4). Though DOD is usually acknowledged as a leader in the management and use of computers, the report identifies areas where improvements are needed.

Some of the major findings of the study were that the computer resource is not managed as an entity (that is, separate policy and information structures exist); Defense spends $10 billion in total annual informations system costs; career specialists are dissatisfied with training and career opportunities; relations with Congress pertaining to information technology are strained if slippages or failures occur; and each military service has experienced some difficulty in organizing and managing optimal use of computer resources (p. 5).

Federal Personnel Issues and Information Systems

The purpose of the Personnel Team Report (1978) of the President's Reorganization Project was to assess the significant problems and issues associated with the management and utilization of federal data processing personnel. The findings of the personnel study reflected the approach taken in this book, namely, management's understanding of and responsibility for use of information systems and related technology. For example, one finding demonstrates the centrality of management:

> The ability of data processing personnel to contribute effectively to the goals and objectives of Federal agencies is a direct reflection of top management's perception of information technology's function and significance to the agency's mission. (Personnel Team Report, 1978, p. 1)

The noteworthy point here is that the management function appears to affect personnel and information systems issues not only separately but together as they contribute to organizational effectiveness. In terms of the model presented in Figure 2.1, each level of management has the authority and responsibility to integrate the information system and personnel functions to obtain control for purposes of coordinating all subsystems to achieve common objectives. That is, if management understands the external and internal systems requirements, especially the key influences or contingencies, the internal information system can be designed to support the decision-making framework by formulating related information personnel policies, particularly in such areas as assessing performance and overall productivity.

The second major finding reinforces the need for defining job requirements. For example, it was found that job standards frequently did not reflect the nature of data processing and resulted in ineffective position management. If managerial objectives are not adequately rationalized in terms of division of labor or control procedures, the corresponding position classifications will not support the organizational functions. This is becoming more critical in areas that require information-intensive operations and advanced training or skills (such as information systems analysis and processing). Management must be instrumental in designing standards for data processing/information systems personnel that support the work required and reflect the specific nature and demands of the information systems job.

Operational Management and Information Systems

An examination of the requirement for valid information systems management for operational functions provides the opportunity to make the information and control process explicit. The critical link is the relationship between who uses information and for what purposes. For example, one of the key points made by the presidential study of operational management concerned a balance between agency autonomy and control needs. That is, line management could be strengthened by "earned autonomy" from central control with the objective of vesting authority and responsibility with the agency itself. Central controllers are agencies such as Office of Management and Budget, General Services, headquarters, regional, or departmental top-level control. However, the underlying concept is how managers can earn their own operational autonomy from central control by competently using information systems.

The operational study report presented several broad conclusions that it considered common to all aspects of operational management. Its first conclusion appears to demonstrate that even a basic principle of traditional management is violated: "Users of data processing services are not assigned appropriate responsibilities. Users are not held accountable for their use of data processing" (Operational Management Team Report, 1978, p. i). This problem exemplifies the worst possible situation in terms of managerial accountability in the use of information systems. That is, if management does not design the information system to meet coordinating, control, and operational requirements or support decisions, then neither management nor subordinates can be held responsible. This is a common pathology associated with the misuse of information systems.

Acquisition Issues and Information Systems Management

With the financial and substantive impact of information systems on public organizations, the acquisition of multimillion dollar, critical information systems becomes a significant action. The Acquisition Team Report (1978) estimated the annual computing expenditures of the federal government to be between $5 and $15 billion, depending on the measures used. Though the Brooks Act was supposed to provide the basis for dealing with many information management and related acquisition problems, many of the old complaints predominate: excessive operating costs, unnecessary acquisition costs, and degraded services to the public.

The study's findings covered the acquisition process, policy guidance concerning "people adequacy," and financial planning deficiencies. The most telling observation was that the acquisition problems were "symptomatic" of more basic problems and "at the heart of the data processing acquisition difficulties is a failure by OMB and GSA to staff themselves properly and to carry out their responsibilities prescribed by law" (p. 3). The core recommendations to alleviate such difficulties centered on policy aspects of acquisition and the role of the Office of Management and Budget in unifying and formalizing the process. The major prescription for accomplishing the recommendations emphasized the role of the president.

Senior Executives and Information Systems Management

Because many dysfunctions associated with the use and management of information resources can be traced to top-level or senior management in public organizations and agencies, it is therefore appropriate to examine the emerging role of top managers as described in the reports. The Small Users Team Report (1978) noted the following:

> Overall information processing performance in the small agency leaves much to be desired—with the agency's top management primarily responsible for the condition. In most instances, agency top management has not given its information processing effort the consistent necessary support, attention, direction and interest it needs to provide the sophisticated support to the agency's missions that current technology is capable of . . . more often than not, information processing is *not* effectively integrated with either the immediate and/or longer range mission and program goals and objectives of the agency. (pp. 2–3)

This report further stated that part of the problem is due to frequent changes in top management. It also noted that the potential of information technology is not being used to support program needs. Among other things, the recommendations recognize that the information systems management function should be integrated with both the short- and long-range objectives of the agency.

A Representative Legislative Perspective on Information Systems Management in the Federal Government: The Case of Software Technology

Information systems management functions are becoming increasingly important in public organizations, and their financial implications ($25 billion accumulated costs in 1977) are more important and pervasive than ever. This visibility and the applications of all facets of information systems are coming under more intense scrutiny by many controllers of public agencies or their staffs. For instance, in a cover letter to a report on computer software to Congress, the comptroller general of the United States, Elmer Staats, stated that "computer software is the most important part of automatic data processing systems today" (U.S. GAO 1980, p. 337).

The GAO report concluded that the cost of computer usage by government can be reduced by millions each year if software technology is coordinated and shared across government agencies. The report identified the ongoing problems of "reinvention of the wheel," excessive software conversion costs, lack of deliberate management emphasis or direction, and lack of governmentwide coordination and adherence to standards as management information systems issues to be addressed. The major recommendations, using additional input from OMB, GSA, and the Department of Commerce, focused on the role of centralized and top-level management in increasing the effectiveness of software use. Specific recommendations concentrated on defining agency head information system responsibilities, establishing governmentwide research and development, and promoting standards and inspections for the management of information technology and systems.

Summary of Federal Government Information Management Issues

The major theme to emerge from the federal government is consistent with the emphasis in the book: Information is a function of management that should be utilized to achieve agency or program objectives. However, it is also found that, in general, "agency or program managers do not exercise the required responsibility, and the users of data processing services in the Federal Government are seldom held accountable. . . ." (p. 4). It was also found that this dysfunction could be identified in such central agencies as the Office of Management and Budget, the General Services Administration, and the Department of Commerce.

The President's Reorganization Project and multiple GAO reports represent the most current, comprehensive analysis of federal information systems management. Though completed in the late 1970s through 1980, the presidential studies paralleled and succeeded the Commission on Federal Paperwork and ongoing GAO analyses of related information systems issues. One of the results of these studies was a Senate amendment requiring a "paperwork assessment" for proposed legislation (Horton and Marchand 1982). Congressman Frank Horton clearly captured the emerging concept that must be mastered by managers of public organizations and functions in the following statement: "It is critical that public administrators at all levels of government regard data as a valuable resource, not simply as some ill-defined obstruction or mundane commodity like paper clips" (1982, p. viii).

Another key statutory impact of the preceding federal commission and studies is the Paperwork Reduction Act of 1980 (Public Law 96-511, December 11, 1980). This act, more than any of the preceding statutes, recognizes the role of information in government activities and provides for a federal information policy, an implementing Office of Information and Regulatory Affairs in OMB, and federal agency responsibilities. Other elements of the Paperwork Reduction Act of 1980 establish an information locator system responsive to Congress, and provide for specific powers of the director of the Office of Information and Regulatory Affairs.

Federal Information Systems Management and the System and Contingency Perspective on Public Organizations

The interdependence of the top and operational levels of management and information systems functions was well described in the various reports and studies that examined the central themes of information systems management in the federal government. The explicit determinations were that overall managerial effectiveness has to be improved (program/manager relationships) and interactions between managers and technologists have to be improved. Also, the theme of interdependence between external and internal systems and the corresponding role of the managerial element were illustrated.

In the function of information systems management, integrating devices are critical because they support the decision and objectives framework by providing the means for control of different functional resources within an overall organizational context. A dynamic model that provides a structured approach to integrating managerial functions with the turbulence of the political, economic, technological, statutory, and uncertainty of the public organization environment allows managers to integrate their experience and practical needs. With 18,474 central processors, not counting the Federal Aviation's air traffic control system, Central Intelligence Agency, National Security Agency, or other classified systems, and hundreds of thousands of word processors, massive tele- and satellite communication systems, and congressional information systems, the potential and vulnerability of the federal government are difficult to comprehend, but public managers have the responsibility to do just that.

Information Systems Issues at the State Level of Government

Though computer technology has been available since the 1950s, the rate of adoption has not been consistent across levels of government or even across the same level of government such as the states. States are sovereign entities subject to varying regional, natural resource, cultural, and economic conditions. This diversity is also reflected in management and organization structures, as well as use of information systems. For example, one of the primary uses of state information systems is for budgetary purposes, which is a laborious process involving refinement, justification, and relegation at several decision levels (Kelly 1978). Kelly argues that the application of computers to the budgetary process is limited by the user's imagination and understanding, but that common uses such as the following can be found: (1) preparation of the text of the budget document, because virtually all large computers and most minis have powerful text-editing features, (2) balancing and keeping financial data and tables consistent, (3) structure agency budget request electronically where aging computers can "talk to" control computers, and (4) in other areas such as budget execution, expenditure controls, revenue forecasting, purchasing, and planning (1978, p. 382).

In a survey of the states it was found that of more than 40 states that had begun computerization, 34 used the computer for budgetary calculations, 27 received agency input via computer, 24 used computers for printing the budget, 15 used it for text preparation, 18 implemented online processing, and 8 used packaged programs (Kelly 1978). Only four states had not initiated some form of computerized budgetary or other uses. Some of the unanswered questions in state usage are related to computerization and the roles of the branches of government, user acceptance, implementation strategies, and methods of developing systems.

In another state-related study of information systems, McGowan and Loveless (1981) found public managers to be critical buffers between external developments and internal impacts. Their study of 19 state executive agencies showed that sources of information were federal agencies, other state agencies, the private sector, professional associations, and universities. The results of the study also identified such problems as need for expertise, low managerial mobility, lack of consistent policy direction or communication flow, competition with other state agencies, changing federal influence, and insufficient information. They concluded that there are still critical issues, such as defining the nature of public functions and their influence on external-internal relationships and reliance of managers on past practices that may be inadequate. One recommendation was that "key information managers" should be selected and nurtured so that the exponential increase of information can be managed.

Petersen, Spain, and Stallings (1983) have examined state roles in local government finance. Their review of nine states showed varied regulatory and/or assistance positions with regard to financial management and information reporting. The states were differentially involved in accounting, auditing, budgeting, debt management, pensions, cash management, property tax assessment, and revenue administration activities of their local governments, but with no common information reporting requirements. For example, California requires annual financial reports, exerts no control over quality of preparation, permits local government to issue debt but does not reinforce the limit, and exercises extensive controls over the property tax assessment process. Minnesota prescribes reporting requirement methods to obtain reports if they are not submitted, sets limits on debt, requires independent audits, regulates permissible investments, and has strict limits on revenue sources. Pennsylvania has no common accounting standards or auditing controls for local government, approves nonreferendum long-term debt, mandates annual revaluation of property, which is almost universally ignored, and sets limits on percentage of market value property taxes collected.

Another issue at the state level is patterns of the use of information systems. They may have some desirable or undesirable effects, depending on the perspective taken. For example, Meyer (1979), in a study of finance agencies at both the state and local levels, has attributed the growth of centralized departments of administration to, in part, "the incorporation of computer technology and modern budgeting concepts." In addition, he found that, of the automated administration departments he examined, all operated their own computers—a phenomenon he later attributed to expansion of organizational domains achieved by using information systems.

The states have various roles and requirements ranging from partnership to regulation, but they also have the authority and responsibility for the local governments that carry out state functions. The states have different constitutions and different political, economic, and cultural environments. Common information regarding local government effectiveness, taxation, finances, and operations is required at the state level to implement the assistance and their regulatory functions. Integrated accounting and information systems produce reliable information for decision making at the state level. Petersen, Spain, and Stallings (1983) concluded that assistance without regulation is an ineffective state financial management strategy.

Welfare Information Systems

Another widespread and important financial issue facing state governments, and having information system implications, is the administration of welfare programs, such as AFDC (Aid to Families with Dependent Children) and food stamp and medicaid programs. The federal government has encouraged the use of computer-based information systems for the states' welfare functions (Chi 1982). Many states have sophisticated welfare information systems, including Wisconsin, where a Computer Reporting Network (CRN) has been developed and used as a prototype in other states. Wisconsin had error rates as high as 50 percent in 1975 in the food stamp program and 33 percent in AFDC. With an administrative reorganization and the CRN system, the Wisconsin Division of Economic Assistance administered the AFDC, food stamp, and medicaid programs in 72 counties and 9 Indian tribal agencies. As of May 1982 the state had 217,374 AFDC, 293,402 food stamp, and 290,782 medicaid recipients with a total unduplicated count of 352,079 across the three programs (Chi 1982).

In the CRN system the central component was a set of standardized policies used to standardize and collect client data and design a distributed data system with the main database in Madison and smaller processors in the counties. This allowed for some local data storage to be used in local processing and higher level managerial decisions to be made using a centralized database similar to that illustrated in Figure 4.1. Some local resistance problems were encountered from county officials; however, the CRN has the capability to initiate, maintain, and terminate cases for one or all of the welfare programs (Chi 1982).

Information is collected, partially edited, and transmitted from the county local processor to the data center where computer checks are performed to ensure eligibility, benefit levels, and information

FIGURE 4.1. Representation of Wisconsin's Distributed Information System in the Computer Reporting Network (CRN) for AFDC, Food Stamp, and Medicaid Programs with 81 Local County and Tribal Indian Agencies

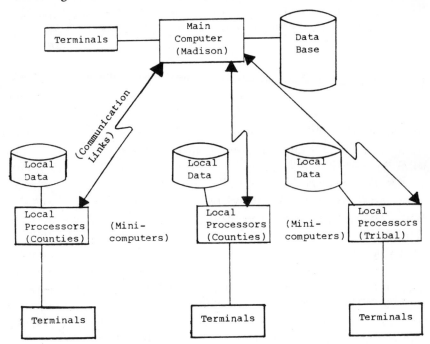

Source: Distributed information system diagram derived from text description of Wisconsin's CRN system by Keon S. Chi (1982).

integrity. The CRN produces automatic reports on client eligibility, entitlements, benefits, and notifications for the local agency, in addition to caseload management, tracking, and statistics for agency management, plus special reports for the Division of Policy and Budget, the Departments of Industry, Labor, and Human Relations, the U.S. Department of Labor (for the food stamp program), and the U.S. Department of Health and Human Services (for the AFDC and medicaid programs). With the CRN and the resulting uniformity of management in all 81 local agencies, the estimated dollar savings for one year was $21 million (Chi 1982). Evaluations of the CRN by the U.S. Department of Health and Human Services identified some weaknesses, such as lack of automated interface between work incentive programs, verification and automated eligibility determination procedures, quality control, cost control documents, and application forms. However, several federal government programs (Project Match, National Recipient System, Medicaid Management Information System, and Family Assistance Management Information System) are being used to promote computerized state information systems (Chi 1982).

Though many other states, such as Georgia, Illinois, Michigan, and New Jersey, have computerized welfare systems, the Wisconsin CRN illustrates the systems influences at work in the design and use of state information systems. The federal government is a highly visible partner in most major programs, other state agencies and local governments have vested interests and needs, and the legislative branch must have a central role in both the appropriations and substantive operations of the information system. Also, internal policies and rules addressing standardization are required, geographic dispersion and recipient needs have to be analyzed, local official autonomy and timely and accurate reports are needed, and organization structures have to complement the information system or vice versa. Also, most ongoing information systems have problems or weaknesses that require continual attention and update by the public managers involved. Information systems are an integral part of management and organizational operations and processes that have to be used to perform state functions. With increasing direct and indirect long-term costs of personnel, the need to control costs in competing public programs, and increasing requirements for fiscal and program accountability, the role of information systems needs increasing examination by state-level public managers in all functions.

State Accounting and Budgeting Information Systems

State governments require accurate and timely information to forecast revenues, control expenditures across functions, pay vendors, resolve payroll and personnel problems, including retirement system weaknesses, meet federal reporting requirements, prepare and review budgets, improve productivity, make policy and operational decisions, and meet the diverse needs of state-level public managers and users statewide. A project team consisting of budget, administration, personnel information center, public welfare, financial management, health, transportation, liquor control board, environmental resources, retirement system management services, affirmative action, and employee relations officials in the state of Pennsylvania has analyzed requirements in these operations and has designed an information systems project called the Integrated Central System (ICS) that will eventually affect most departments within the state. The system was designed to support and facilitate shared information across functional lines, decentralize operations and accountability, and centralize policymaking and control—to be implemented over a five-year period.

The objectives of the ICS project are to develop an online database that integrates accounting, budgeting, personnel, payroll, and purchasing functions. Related to these objectives are such others as the development of agency accounts to reflect and identify organizations and their relationships, provide online inquiry capability for the accounting system, provide state managers with timely and accurate information, and allow access to the five modules with a single computer-generated entry.

Some of the explicit features of the ICS information system are integrated, shared database, remote terminal input, inquiry, and update, report generating for all users, communication networks to all permanent work sites, security controls, reduction of redundant manual inputs and data, proper controls, and audit traces for all accepted transactions. Figure 4.2 is an overview of the components and relationships of the proposed ICS system. The discussion here will focus on the accounting system because it is tied into the other ICS components and illustrates many of the financial control issues facing state managers with a feasible approach to dealing with them.

Accounting Systems Design Subsystem and Information Flows

The accounting system of the ICS is an important part of the overall state management concept because it includes the financial data that represent authorizations, expenditures, and controls and interfaces on a daily basis with every other system to provide validation and control in the agency and state-level decision-making processes. The relevant functions tied into the accounting system are state receipts, appropriations/allotments, encumbrance processing, disbursements, accounts receivable, inventory system, fixed asset

FIGURE 4.2. Proposed ICS Integrated Control System Overview for the Commonwealth of Pennsylvania

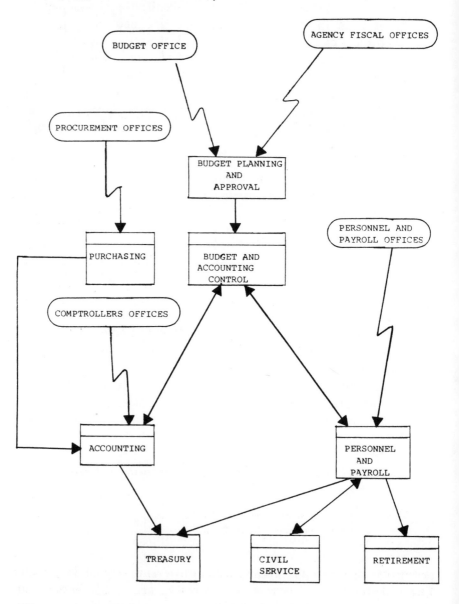

Source: Commonwealth of Pennsylvania Report on Feasibility for an Integrated Central System, November 1983.

FIGURE 4.3. ICS Accounting Subsystem Functions

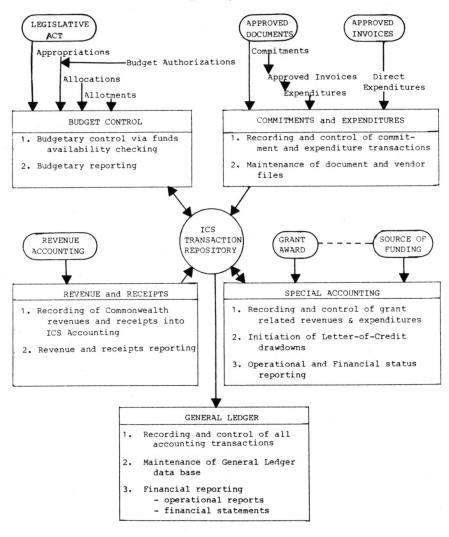

Source: *ICS Accounting System Design Summary*, Commonwealth of Pennsylvania, Office of Budget and Administration, December 15, 1982.

inventory, special and federal accounting, and general ledger and financial statements. These functions will be changed from predominantly manual preparation to online or automatic initiation, inquiry, verification, billing, payroll processing, and update system.

The primary objective of the ICS accounting system is to enhance financial control of state resources using budget-administration, controller, agency, and field officers who operate under the authority of the governor. When the legislature appropriates money for state operations, this level becomes the legal spending limit. Figure 4.3 illustrates the uses of and interdependencies in the various subsystems of the accounting system, which exhibits integrated database (to minimize data redundancy), online processing (immediate response), modularity (set of modules directed to functional tasks), flexibility (to meet varied user needs), and table-driven (with numerous sets of reference data, for example, valid users, object number, organizational units) design principles. An account code structure is used with fund, department number, appropriation, ledger, organization, object, subobject, fiscal year, and cost function and category attributes for transactions.

The accounting system subsystems are independent yet interdependent because spending and budget control and the grant subsystems may be involved in given spending transactions where the relevant databases must be continuously updated. All subsystem transactions will be posted in the ICS transaction repository, which will provide the basis for audit trails and updates in the general ledger, which is the focal point of the accounting system. The system will also produce reports on the status of appropriations, allocations, suballocations, allotments, funding status, and transaction updates on either terminal, hard copy, or both with optional formats. In this way, the accounting system can be used to give budget control to the state managers.

The accounting system is planned to be the first of the five models to be implemented and put online so that the existing centralized accounting system can be terminated. As usual in information systems, elements of the entire system are first tested and then cutover where the new replaces the old system or subsystem. The new accounting system, specifically the general ledger subsystem, will change the accounting basis for the state to modified accrual standards for standardized financial reporting purposes and also maintain cash accounting. These changes conform to the generally accepted accounting principles recommended by the Municipal Finance Officers Association and the National Council on Governmental Accounting (Municipal Finance Officers Association of the United States and Canada 1980).

State-Level Automated Offices

There is an increasing trend for state agencies to automate or integrate their office data processing and/or information systems. With comprehensive office automation systems composed of micro-computers, ink jet printers, electronic mail, information sharing, intelligent terminals, diskette storage, and high-speed printers (900 words per minute) with ink cartridges that will produce 4 million characters (2,000 pages of text), standard office equipment appears to be on its way out. State agency managers try to maintain as much autonomy as possible in automating their offices; however, some state studies have examined automated offices and made certain conclusions.

One study has found that the typical investment in a multiuser integrated data/word processing system is approximately $200,000, but can be more than $600,000 for an integrated text/data/voice system (Kettinger 1983). Kettinger, in a State Office Automation Pilot Study (SOAPS), found that state general service departmental managers expanded their standalone equipment because centralized leadership and direction were lacking. He also found that, when compared to data processing, office automation is less structured, intensely behavioral, unpredictable, sensitive to external factors, difficult to measure, more visible, and more people-oriented. The lessons from his study were that office automation requires a strategic plan, clear understanding of the benefits it desires, a high level of commitment from top management, a creative and determined project director, a preimplementation study, and active involvement of end users. Further, equipment should satisfy all functional requirements—be tested and well supported—a comprehensive installation and technical support plan is needed, a comprehensive human factors approach is crucial, and training is vital.

State-Level Information/EDP Planning/Strategy

In addition to detailed operating and accounting information systems, states need to consider the requirements they are likely to face in the future. Implementation of information systems usually takes place over a long period, especially if the systems or agencies perform complex functions. As needs change or external demands from legislatures, technology, or clients increase, information systems may require modification. Because public sector environments are rarely stable for long, it is reasonable that state managers plan for the future. As states usually have unique needs and pressures, plans and strategic objectives should be as specific as possible.

Some states have embarked on a planning venture to assume that information systems needs will be met using strategic objectives that will be implemented by a central staff agency or bureau (for example, see Commonwealth of Pennsylvania, 1983). Such plans may consist of objectives based on contract studies or government studies, technological trends in hardware and software, agency multiyear plans, and experience of other states. The plans, which are derived by steering groups or special committees composed of agency and user representatives, may include milestones, objectives, and associated costs or benefits with the various strategies or objectives outlined in the plan. In addition, this committee or group could set up various groups or agency/user structures to implement the objectives and schedule their achievement.

Strategies used in existing plans include establishment of statewide EDP/information systems standards programs or committees, distribution policies for processing of data for specialized functions, training and career development program, procurement and contracting of hardware/software and related services, integrated fiscal and executive management information program, contingency plan for disaster recovery, and efficient use of EDP resources. Each of these strategies addresses different internal and external variables, but the plan should also focus on the interdependence between the strategies and the projected requirements and available resources. Each strategy then can be broken down into specific tasks and time frames associated with each. The master plan approach to information systems provides for all participants, including agency and central managers, to identify their needs in the context of overall state needs and projected trends in costs, benefits, uses, and technology. A plan is also one method for managers to ensure support for achievement of their own objectives.

Some information systems plans have problems of being too specific, vague, or representing multiagency compromises; however, there are few alternatives to meeting overall state objectives and supporting managerial objectives and decision making. Plans also anticipate the growing piecemeal demands from the operating levels where office automation, microcomputers, and word processing are increasing without proper integration at the managerial levels. Telecommunications, sophisticated software, database management, and the trend toward automation are all factors that have to be taken into consideration when plans or information systems strategies are developed for or by public managers.

General State Information Systems Needs

States may have as many as 20 to 30 different functions or agencies, such as welfare, education, health, and protection, consuming as much as 80 percent of a state's budget with little or no state control. Billions of dollars can be appropriated and spent with little evaluation or systematic approach to information systems to support either executive or legislature analysis or decision making. State governments have to be able to define their data processing, reporting requirements, information systems hardware/software, telecommunications, and applications in various functions by identifying general state needs and focusing on functions such as welfare where the benefits of efficient systems are likely to be great. Purchasing, payroll, inventory, budgeting, and accounting functions can also be greatly improved if managers understand the functional requirements, related decisions, and supporting information. States also have responsibility for the fiscal condition and operational effectiveness of their local governments. Without supporting standards, common reporting/information requirements and state-level analyses or audits using well-designed information systems, legitimate, management-based state oversight over local governments operations, effectiveness, or revenue functions is doubtful.

LOCAL GOVERNMENT INFORMATION SYSTEMS ISSUES

Present Applications

Since the introduction of computer technology in the 1950s, the rate of adoption by local governments has increased at an exponential rate; virtually every city and county with populations of more than 50,000 and nearly all of the governments with populations between

10,000 and 50,000 use computers in one form or another. Investment costs in computing operations may average approximately 1 to 3 percent of the annual budgets of local governments with about 1 percent of the total personnel devoted to data processing activities.

Concerning the applications of computer and information management technology, a survey of city and county governments revealed that there are nearly 300 distinct applications in 27 different government functions. The overall distribution can be readily grouped into the following activity areas (Perry and Kraemer 1979): record keeping (42 percent of applications), calculating/printing (35 percent), record searching (8 percent), sophisticated analytics (5 percent), and process control (3 percent).

Examination of the organizational areas that have been involved in the adoption and use of information technology reveals that most applications are in the areas of accounting and finance, including such functions as taxation, accounting, assessment, utility billing, and payroll preparation. This is consistent with the historic trend of government to automate formerly routine processing functions. A close association among the record maintenance, record searching, process control, and computational activities of local government fiscal organizations is found as the government shifts to data processing. Routine information in the local government functions is readily stored and retrieved, permitting high payoff for local managers with a relatively low level of financial or human resources investment.

Coupled with an increase in the use of government accounting standards and the need to maintain current audit trails, applications of information technology at the local government level have been quite successful in filing, processing, and analyzing revenue and expenditure data. Other areas that have been exposed to new developments include public safety (police command and control and fire protection), courts and judicial systems, and control. The tendency for future growth in local units of government appears to be in those areas requiring innovative and sophisticated forms of analysis, such as financial management—including cost control—police command and control, record keeping, human services delivery, and planning.

Colton (1980) studied police command, control, and communication systems where certain successes were found but that outcomes and process measures did not meet expectations. He concluded that the emphasis should be on performance standards and development of a common framework for assessing computer-based information systems. Other specific local government information systems studies have examined other facets of municipal management, such as cost control using a database concept (Buffa and Fowler 1981). Their schematics for batch, disk, and online inquiry database systems are based on a cost model for municipal departments. Further, their system provides cost summaries for each facility, maintenance task, resource, and labor and detailed analysis for task costs. They recommend a database management system to deal adequately with file maintenance, access, update, and file interdependence issues so that user needs can be met.

In examining databases for local government, there are additional managerial considerations, such as existing skill levels and existing hardware/software in the local government. Also, as Buffa and Fowler (1981) conclude for public managers, there are multiple advantages to database information systems; however, their cost can be in excess of $100,000, thereby making them economically feasible only for larger cities with greater demands for information processing and cost control.

Computers and Local Government

Planning and Management Policy

An organizational perspective views the planning and management function as the predominant framework within which decisions are made in the organization. Particular steps must be taken at this stage to ensure that information policy is consistent, supports the management, and is responsive to change. Specifically, Kraemer and King (1977) recommend that the following actions should be considered:

1. The chief administrator or executive should insist on a thorough, accurate analysis of any ongoing government activity before it is considered for automation or computer assistance.
2. It is important that all relevant parties, including top management, participate in the planning, development, and operation of computerized information systems.
3. Frequent and thorough evaluations of computerized information systems should be conducted to ensure a high level of efficiency and procedure. (pp. 29-39)

Financial Considerations

While comprehensive planning and evaluation are critical ingredients for deciding whether new forms of information technology should be adopted or whether current activities are effective, the ability to maintain financial control is fundamental. In the current environment of constrained resources, this element becomes acute, requiring a careful assessment of their utilization.

Personnel Policies

A corollary to the control of financial resources in assessing the effectiveness of information management in local government is the planned nurturing and development of personnel resources—those individuals currently within the organization as well as those who have to be attracted to it.

Concerning other aspects of human resources management that warrant consideration, Kraemer and King (1977) indicate that

1. It is advisable to have well-formulated personnel policies to facilitate introduction and use of computing technology.
2. Training in relevant aspects of the information system should be provided to any employees who are affected by the system. (pp. 79-80)

Local government administrators—managers, mayors, department heads, and personnel officers in particular—should pay close attention to the needs for information and the impacts of related operational changes on their policies.

Utilization Policies

Control of both financial and human resources is, in fact, focusing on two of the primary inputs to the information system. As stressed in the previous chapter, a critical part of an information system is the utilization process.

Disclosure and Privacy Concerns

As the final policy area to be considered, the issue of disclosure and access to personal information is certainly not of secondary concern. With the passage of the Freedom of Information Act and the Privacy Act, government organizations at all levels must ensure that information systems are responsive to the protection of individual rights. Kraemer and King (1977) correctly point to the paradoxical situation in which governments find themselves:

> In recent years, a concern for the privacy of individuals has arisen in the face of the collection and use of personal information by governments. Fueled by both fact and fiction, predictions of suppressive control of the individual by the government have emerged. More often than not, these predictions refer to the existence of computerized files of personal data as threats to individual freedom. Computerization of personal data did not create this "privacy problem"; it merely called attention to a new aspect of an old problem: *the tradeoffs between government's need to know certain information about individuals, and the individual's desire to maintain personal privacy by withholding information.* (p. 71)

They recommend that state and local officials remain sensitive to individual concerns, at the same time cognizant of federal and state legislation that will affect developments in this area.

In all of the five policy and management areas outlined, it is apparent that the chief local government executive/administrator is in a crucial position to determine organizational policy with regard to information systems applications. In determining and implementing this policy, executives at the local levels have enjoyed a moderate degree of success; applications in automating former routine and clerical tasks have proceeded relatively smoothly, while adaptations to management reporting and analysis functions remain tentative at best.

Local Government Financial Management Information Systems

A series of recent initiatives documents the concern with a central function of local government—financial management. Hayes et al. (1982) and Harrell (1980, 1981) have identified common issues and approaches. For example, Hayes et al. argue that over the next five years one of the critical decisions to face local government managers will be the role of financial management information systems in integrating the accounting, budgeting, performance management, and auditing functions. Their key argument is that an integrated financial management information system (IFMIS) has the capacity to provide not only financial but also performance data to meet operational functions. They list the cities that installed integrated IFMISs and cite the components as being a unified database, computerized internal audits and controls, modification for flexibility and analysis. Each of these IFMIS elements is discussed in detail by Hayes, et al., as are levels of integration, system benefits, and costs. In addition, the benefits and costs can be sizable, with "bureaucratic and political turbulence" the major problems; however, the economic case for IFMISs is getting progressively stronger. The pros and cons of independent and integrated financial management information systems are discussed in detail. The author describes both the opportunity costs of inaction and shortsighted action that fails to consider long-term needs. Strategic steps and environmental steps are recommended to achieve more useful and integrated systems.

Harrell states that many of the fiscal problems in local government today can be attributed to inadequate financial management information systems. Because many times scarce resources are given to more visible services, such as police or fire, this allocation process may intensify impending crises such as the cases of New York City, Washington, D.C., and Cleveland have demonstrated. According to Harrell, the financial management information systems (FMIS) development process can be broken down into three phases: the acquisition (needs capacity, selection), implementation (organizational, documentation, testing), and operational (training, operational, enhancements) processes.

The report by Harrell also provides multiple views on the systems development process, all of which are relevant to local government managers; however, five principles that transcend the particular phases were summarized. They are the following: Involve the local government data processing staff in planning, implementation, and training; comprehensively review, define, and meet user needs; have a committed management; use consultants only as advisers; and provide adequate resources for training. In addition, the final lesson presented by Harrell is that local government managers must learn to control the computer or be controlled by it.

Framework for Local Government Information Systems

As evident in the preceding discussion, local government managers have many internal and external variables to consider in their use and development of information systems. The lessons appear to be that no simple procedures or approaches address the complexity faced by local government managers who have to or want to develop computerized decision support/information systems. Internal organizational, operational, staff, training, and performance requirements are influenced by and influence external variables such as level of economic resources and political and public pressures. The examples of New York City and Cleveland are only exaggerated cases of what can go wrong in all local governments. The current state of affairs indicates that information systems can be valuable if management understands and controls them in terms of their internal and external potential and accrues support from internal users and external forces, such as executive and legislative controllers.

Figure 4.4 links the points presented in the discussion with the framework provided in Figure 2.1. Different functions within local government require specific types of financial, operational, organizational (to include special projects), intergovernmental, human resources, planning, and staff information to meet their objectives. Each of these functions can be supported with specific parts of the overall information system or separate information systems that are tied together or integrated by management. Top-level managers, such as the mayor or city manager, will need information that supports policy decisions across functions that address uncertainty, external political or economic factors, and overall budget or planning issues. Departmental managers will need information relating more to departmental budget, performance, personnel, operations, and possibly the impact of federal or state mandates on their particular functions. Though each top or departmental manager may require accounting or auditing information for his or her respective control systems, the manager would not be the major focus of the information.

Operational level or first-line supervision in police, fire, public works, and utilities (enterprise fund type operations) or even recreation functions require information on specific personnel, facilities, equipment, material, and financial resource allocations to their tasks. Patrol cars, number of officers, beats, demands for service by type of crime/call, time, and location are more relevant to first-line police supervisors than overall departmental budgets or interrelationships with other departments. Personnel managers are more interested in recruitment, wage, position classification, merit systems, preference categories, benefits, and performance evaluation at the individual

FIGURE 4.4. Information Systems Framework for Local Governments

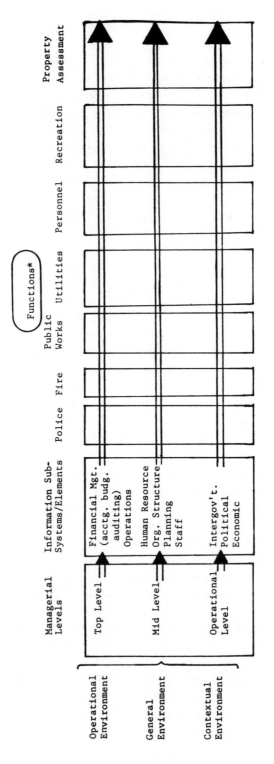

*For purposes of clarity and brevity, other local government functions, such as licensing, libraries, purchasing, inventory control, information and referral, data processing, transportation, and court applications, were not included.
Source: Compiled by the author.

rather than general level of the organization. Though many areas of financial and personnel management overlap, their essential focus and effect on the organization differ in their respective contribution to achieving local government functions. Also, political, economic, or intergovernmental factors may influence even line supervisors, but top-level managers have the primary decision-making responsibility to deal with problems related to these areas.

INTERGOVERNMENTAL ISSUES AND INFORMATION SYSTEMS

Whether one subscribes to the view that local governments are battlegrounds for federal agencies, or that the federal government actually helps local managers do their jobs, there are many intergovernmental links between the federal, state, and local governments. Many local governments may rely on the federal and state government for as much as 40 percent of their revenue. "Since 1970 more than one-fourth of the states' general revenue has been obtained from the national government" (Wright 1978, p. 37). States are in the middle of a seesaw with local and federal governments at either end with constantly shifting policy and resource constraints (Wright 1978). States play a critical role in determining local priorities and the federal government has multiple linkages with state and local government because of education, welfare, transportation, unemployment compensation, and other general programs such as pollution.

States and the federal government attach reporting requirements to their grants to local governments, and most states require annual financial reports or audits of local government. Local government information systems should meet the external reporting requirements for funds received, but attempts should be made to standardize so that multiple forms are not required to report the same information.

The intergovernmental revenue arena is fraught with political, economic, and authority issues, but each level of government depends on the other for information regarding how programs are complemented and resources to carry out the programs. Information systems at each level of government should address the appropriate reporting requirements and revenue transfers while the primary recipient of funds and implementors of programs, the local government, should be given financial and managerial support for standardized reporting systems by the state and federal governments. Not only is a unified federal-local policy on information systems needed, but an emergent information/reporting systems policy linking the federal, state, and local levels is required if one level of government expects and funds another level to perform many of its functions. Recognition of the need for an integrated approach to information systems may profitably start with the education and welfare programs that consume the largest amounts of funds. Because the federal government has much more at stake, it should develop an approach to designing intergovernmental information systems using the principles codified in the 1980 Paperwork Reduction Act.

Each level of government has specific objectives and influences, but the overarching design presented in Chapter 2, which encompasses a general model of the public organization information and control system, can be used to outline the major external and internal variables facing public managers. External controllers in the legislative, executive, and judicial sectors impose requirements, statutes, and objectives that must be understood and implemented using every effective means, including information systems. General classes of clients, constituents, and technological factors influence public managers differently in the levels of government but must be considered when information systems needs and development are defined. Local government managers have fewer absolute demands, but many constraints and resources emanate from the state and federal governments. States have sovereign roles and authorities, but they also implement federal programs that address a similar but much greater complexity in their environment. Chapter 5 attempts to reduce the uncertainty associated with information systems issues by providing a structured perspective on the analysis, design, and implementation of information systems.

5

Information Systems
Design and Development:
An Approach for Integrating
Management Needs and
Information Systems Capabilities

The preceding chapters have examined many major issues and outlined important points that are emerging as critical demands on public managers at all levels of government. The existing literature, ongoing research, and managerial practice are replete with too many examples of how information systems have failed or could not meet their initial promise. The examples of and reasons for failure range from the technical to economic, behavioral, and/or operational problems. However, a careful examination of the patterns in cases where information systems fail or work effectively can usually be traced to the level of managerial understanding of operational, behavioral, technical, and organizational requirements. It has also been observed that rarely are economic and technical factors the major problems associated with failed information systems.

Computers and information systems have capabilities and characteristics that make them extremely valuable to government managers. They can perform great numbers of routine or repetitive tasks and operations, such as standard analyses (application/eligibility forms, social security checks, tax returns, accounting transactions), or complex computations, such as missile guidance or satellite orbits. They can rapidly perform such arithmetic operations as addition or subtraction (determine payrolls, costs), accurately compare massive amounts of information (welfare rolls or delinquent educational loans against federal agency employment rosters), store enormous volumes of information (3.5 billion files on individuals kept by diverse federal agencies), retrieve information from files almost instantaneously (produce data or records on a terminal or search files for license numbers or fingerprints), and process complicated transactions with unerring accuracy (statistical analysis or update financial files).

The computer can also store millions of instructions and present reports or the results of any and all of its operations in multiple forms. The computer can extend the manager's potential because of its speed, accuracy, consistency, and ability to perform over extended periods of time. Batch jobs, which process operations singly or in groups, perform periodic tasks (water billing, taxing, inventory control), or online (immediate response or real time) can be used, depending on the organizational or operational requirements. Immediate processing of financial transactions or personnel actions can be designed into information systems so that at any given point in time an exact assessment of the financial/budgetary or personnel situation in any agency or department can be made. Entire agency or departmental functions can be simulated using key information and assumptions to examine such things as fire station locations or police dispatching systems or to produce cost models that predict the effects of certain changes in appropriations or revenues.

Computerized information systems can also be used to keep control over complex projects or programs with the use of CPM or PERT to analyze the scheduled activities. The enormous number of calculations in determining scheduling, start, completion, slack time, and cost information are performed routinely and accurately. These capabilities further extend the managers' potential to understand and systematize assigned managerial responsibilities. With the aid of an information system, client needs can be assessed and relevant decisions about client problems made in shorter time with less human intervention in such high-volume operations as welfare services, license processing, or computer-assisted education/instruction. Computerized information systems can assist clerical, operational, and managerial personnel with routine transactions, scheduling, analyses, reporting, projection, and decision-making functions that can increase a manager's effectiveness, control, and cost-efficiency objectives.

The technology of information processing—semiconductor technology, real-time computation, electronics, memory-storage, microprocessors and telecommunications—has in many situations exceeded the capability of the "wetware," or human, element in the human-machine information system because an integrative perspective is required to use them properly. Economic problems associated with information systems are usually identified early in the inception or feasibility stage of systems design, or enter the design picture when added capabilities are exceeded or existing systems need to be replaced. The technical and economic criteria are basically very important assessment factors to use in the preliminary design stages for information systems, but they are secondary in many situations when management has not adequately defined management and organizational requirements or properly codified the key elements of the decision cycle.

Ackoff (1967) examined the following basic assumptions about information systems: More is better, managers need the information they want, decision making will improve if managers get the information they need, more communication means better performance, and managers do not have to understand how an information system works in order to use it. For various reasons that he presents, Ackoff labeled these assumptions as mistaken and having enormous impact. He advanced what he considered to be a more appropriate design procedure, including decision systems analysis, information requirements analysis, decision aggregation, information processing design, and control of the control system. His concluding points, which are still relevant in information systems design, are that three groups should collaborate: information systems specialists, operations researchers, *and managers* (emphasis his) (p. 39).

Ackoff and others (for example, Lucas 1978; Murdick and Ross 1979; Davis 1974; Senn 1982) examined and described elements of the information systems design and life cycle, and all emphasized the role of user involvement, information requirements, decision systems, and control procedures. The most pervasive and currently accepted underlying premise is that management participation in the design process is necessary. Ackoff (1967) stated the case:

> The participation of managers in the design of a system that is to save them assures their ability to evaluate its performance by comparing its output with what was predicted. Managers who are not willing to invest some of their time in this process are not likely to use a management control system well, and their system in turn, is likely to abuse them. (p. 155)

Further, Mason and Mitroff (1973) concluded that managers need information that is geared to their own psychology and managerial problems, not only to those of technical systems designers. In addition, Nolan (1982) stated that one approach to effective implementation is to involve the user and the designer so that a total commitment to the information system will result. Various approaches have been suggested to deal with this participation issue; however, the major requirement is that the manager-user be the central coordinator rather than letting authority for the information system lapse by default to the systems analyst or information staff designer.

GENERAL MODEL OF INFORMATION SYSTEMS DESIGN AND LIFE CYCLE

An acceptable approach to information systems design is needed to address the issues of user involvement, needs definition, and development. This approach should address the information-decision and managerial control process in public organizations. Figure 5.1 outlines the general management information systems process that can be used to conceptualize the steps that should be considered in the information systems design cycle. The assumptions and systems design phases implicit in the diagram will be treated in more detail when the design and development process is described. However, the important point to make initially is that *all levels of management should understand, actively participate in, and control the systems design process.*

One point emphasized in Figure 5.1 is that management oversees the entire development process and makes the decisions that provide the structure and control for the needs definition, data/information collection, information management, and information processing and reporting steps. It has become conventional wisdom that the availability of hardware-computers or technical specialists should not drive the systems design, but rather that they should support the manager-user who participates fully. Then managers use the decision framework and organizational-operational needs to manage the information systems life cycle and information resource. This means that the decision flowcharting symbol (see Figure 5.1, step 6) is the critical step that serves as a reference for the whole process. For example, if management has prescribed strategies, budgets, or operational-level

FIGURE 5.1. General Model of Information Systems Needs, Management, Design, and Control Process in Public/Government

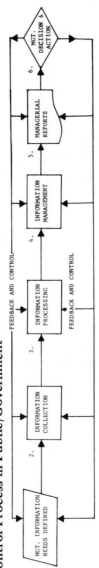

Activities Associated with Elements of the Information System Processes

1. FOR TOP, MID., & OPERATN'L LEVEL MANAGERS

   a. Operations/work Flow Needs
   b. Financial Measures
   c. Human Resource Issues
   d. Intergovernmental Req'ts.
   e. Project & Functional Needs
   f. Planning & R&D Req'ts.
   g. Critical Staff Elements
   h. Coordination needs to Address Substance
   i. Define Most Critical Operational, General & Remote Environmental Influences

2. COLLECTION ISSUES

   a. Frequency
   b. Substance
   c. Sources
   d. Instruments
   e. Cost
   f. Privacy
   g. Reliability/ Validity
   h. Documentation
   i. Quality Control
   j. Hardware & Software Req'd.

3. INFO. PROCESSING

   a. Preparation
   b. Cleaning/editing
   c. Entry
   d. Timeliness
   e. Completeness
   f. Accuracy
   g. Retention/storage
   h. Hardware/software
   i. Batched/on-line/ Interactive

4. INFO. MANAGEMENT

   a. Analytical Use
   b. Routinization
   c. Exceptional
   d. Decisions & Operations Supported
   e. Managers/users Involved
   f. Integrity of System
   g. Applicable Hardware & Software

5. REPORTING

   a. Format
   b. Number
   c. Distribution
   d. Frequency
   e. Availability
   f. Applicability to Operations or Decisions
   g. Destruction

6. DECISIONMAKING/ACTION

   a. Specific Decision or Need Supported
   b. Function or Object- ive Achieved
   c. Comparison with Standards or Rules
   d. Additional or Different Information Needed
   e. Definition, Collection Processing, or Mgt. Reporting Changes Required to Update Decisionmaking, Info or Action

Source: Compiled by the author.

objectives or standards based on valid information, then those standards become the basis for defining needs, designing information-collecting instruments (in addition to specifying frequency, substance, and sources), managing and processing information management, and generating relevant reports.

Another overarching premise evident in Figure 5.1 is that management must remain sensitive to the different phases of the information systems process by continuously monitoring the development of the system and its contribution to organizational performance. The feedback and control loops characterize the mechanism that can be used by management to make minor and major adjustments to the process. For instance, if discrepancies between standards and performance arise, or if the reports are not addressing the required uses, management focuses on the appropriate part of the design process and corrects the information flow that matches the need. In summary, then, Figure 5.1 represents a general view of the information systems process that can be used by management to control the degree of support required from the system. It also illustrates that *management has the central role in determining the structure and resulting effectiveness of the information system.*

INFORMATION SYSTEMS DESIGN AND DEVELOPMENT LIFE CYCLE

There is general consensus that management information systems design and development, sometimes called the development life cycle, should be systematic and follow certain key steps. There are variations in how specific parts of the design process are implemented, but there is also agreement that it constitutes a coherent, logical, information-based and operationally valid procedure to incorporate management-user and information-specialist knowledge. Some approaches to information systems design present details related to hardware, software, storage, records, and technological characteristics before addressing organizational or operational issues. However, the approach presented here presumes that the managerial and organizational context is the critical referent in the system, so that the systems design cycle is used as the linking mechanism to integrate management and organizational requirements to the information systems means.

General Process and Participants

Figure 5.2 presents the general steps in the systems design cycle. Note that several views of this cycle and functions exist; for example, the general phases in Figure 5.2 have been given different names by others. However, the content and substance are similar. And though consensus about the general approach is clear, the detailed steps may differ. For instance, Davis (1978) describes the information systems development life cycle with three general stages and internal elements for each of these stages. His first stage, called the definition stage, includes feasibility assessment and information analysis steps. The physical design stage has systems design, program development, and procedure development elements. The implementation stage includes conversion, operation and maintenance, and postaudit steps. Davis also presents an instructive view of the relative effort expended in each of these stages in rough percentages (p. 60); for example, the definition stage is 25 percent; the physical design, 55 percent; and the implementation, 20 percent. He also presents three important criteria to assess system feasibility: technical (Is the system feasible with existing technology?), economics (Are benefits greater than costs?), and operational (Will it work when installed?).

Senn (1982) also supplements his systems life cycle with what he calls the most likely data-gathering tools to be used in the life cycle: interview, questionnaire, observation, document examination, and measurement. For example, interviews and questionnaires can be used in most stages of the cycle, with observations most heavily used in the testing and implementation stages (p. 376). Senn also proposes that technical, economic, and operational criteria be used in the feasibility assessment phase. In each stage of the life cycle, a set of detailed steps should be systematically executed to provide the basis for the subsequent steps.

The structured approach to systems analysis and design provides a sound basis for managers to systematically approach a complex, usually time-consuming, expensive, and operationally important task. It also demands the active participation of managers in most of the stages because many of the general stages and inclusive detailed steps are embedded in operational needs and managerial requirements. The technical, operational, economic, and organizational feasibility criteria are best understood from a managerial rather than a purely technical or economic perspective.

FIGURE 5.2. General Model of the Information Systems Design and Development Life Cycle Process

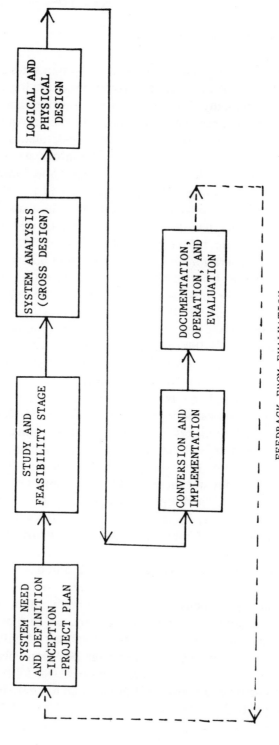

Source: Compiled by the author.

During the systems design life cycle usually other individuals and specialists are involved in the design and process stages. They can be external consultants or vendors or internal information services staff or combinations thereof combined into a study (or steering or project) group or committee under the leadership of management. Some of the involved information service specialists are systems analysts (individuals with systems and programming background who aid the decision maker or user in defining requirements and designing the system to meet those requirements); programmers (individuals who are proficient in hardware and software and types, tests, and programs that address the systems information needs; in large systems there may be specialized programming functions that deal with maintenance or applications functions); and others, such as departmental representatives (information systems task forces project group), who address specific functional requirements.

The information systems design steering committee is responsible for integrating user and management needs with hardware, software, and procedure issues in the appropriate stages of the design cycle. This is where top-level authority, financial, and overall management support and commitment should be visible and set the tone for the design process. Management is also responsible, in conjunction with the information systems staff, for outlining managerial/organizational objectives and providing sufficient resources. At this stage, it is also possible that management and the information specialists, depending on their level of knowledge, should be trained in the major requirements of each other's functions. Another general guideline for setting up project control that can be derived from past practice is that the role or use of existing information systems should be understood. Also, authorized user points of contact with substantive functions and operational knowledge of the significant parts of the organization should be developed and utilized throughout the design cycle.

Approaches to Systems Design

Several approaches or information systems objectives can be used to illustrate how to proceed with an information systems design; but some have advantages, disadvantages, and specific focal points that should be made explicit before beginning the discussion because they may provide an overall perspective for the design process. One perspective focuses on the structure of the database, retrieval of data, and manipulation of data; it is called the database or data bank approach. This method is quite useful if the management-users are very familiar with their decision-making requirements and have a relatively sophisticated information services staff that has extensive knowledge about how databases should be structured and accessed. Otherwise, the database approach places too much pressure on users, which may be a disadvantage if the user has not completely thought through the applicability of the data.

A data processing approach focuses on the processing part of the information systems cycle and emphasizes refinements in the manipulation of data, such as in repetitive operations (calculations, sorting) where routine actions are performed. Other approaches have been characterized as top-down (information requirements specified first) or bottom-up (hardware/software or lower level transactions shape the information systems capabilities). Integrated information systems involve an emphasis on the interdependence between subsystems and the development of collection, processing, database, and user parts of the information at one time. An organizational chart approach uses the structure of the organization as the referent for the design. One other design approach can be called functional development because specifications for information needs are based on functional requirements and the minimum information needed to support them. There are also permutations of these approaches ranging from a total systems plan to no plan or piecemeal development. Each of these general approaches has implications for how the design life cycle is structured.

The approach to systems design taken here attempts to integrate what have been identified as the top-down, organizational, and functional approaches, because single models of the design process restrict the use of many practical elements of other models. The functional approach emphasizes the functions that departments, groups, and subsystems perform so that the information flow supports and matches the functional requirements. This approach is especially useful in public organizations where specific responsibilities have been assigned in either statutes, administrative regulations, or formalized organizational duties. The organizational method focuses on the structures of an organization that are typically characterized on an organizational chart. This method tends to be somewhat artificial in the public sector because so many similar functions are performed in different organizations. However, many times the structures of public organizations reflect their functions, so the approach advanced here emphasizes the functional approach while taking into account the top-level or statutory requirements and organizational subsystems that perform these functions. In addition, this hybrid method does not rule out other approaches, such as incorporation of a database design or processing refinement, if the feasibility or requirements study or other design stages require them.

INFORMATION SYSTEMS ANALYSIS AND DESIGN CYCLE

Most information systems design processes begin with some pressure for change, such as identification of a need or a requirement for information either to support operational activities, management control, or implement a plan or other organizational strategy. In the public sector, an organizational problem may be identified or a reporting requirement instituted by an upper-level management authority. For example, the Comprehensive Employment and Training Act (CETA) and amendments of 1978 expanded reporting and record-keeping requirements for prime sponsors (U.S. Department of Labor 1980) and makes recommendations concerning information systems development. A related commission study, an executive order, or study recommendations are the norms in the public sector and may be direct results of requirements levied by legislative and executive controllers.

In conjunction with the overall information and control systems design presented in Chapter 2, most requirements for information systems illustrate that external controllers have interests in and control standard procedures that influence internal information systems while information processes have implications for operational, budgetary, financial, and/or human resource management. In the CETA example, the legislation also mandates that prime sponsors properly monitor, audit, and administer their program/recipients (U.S. Department of Labor 1980, p. 1).

Systems Need and Definition

Most well-designed and effective information systems begin with the need and definition stages. It is during this phase of the development cycle that a goal, objective, problem, issue, or mandate that makes the need for an improved or completely new system is identified. For example, the identification of a need may begin with an organizational plan or set of objectives that requires more accurate, comprehensive, and/or timely information than is currently available. The need may also arise because the existing system is not meeting reporting requirements or is falling behind in meeting demands from vocal controllers or clients. This need may be seen in a decreased ability to handle inquiries from service recipients, license applicants, or even suppliers of material. Or it may take the form of complaints or even financial or inventory deficits uncovered by inspectors general or auditing agencies, such as the GAO. One of the more common needs in public organizations is to meet the demand for information from higher echelons or as required by statutory mandates, such as the CETA amendments.

A standardized approach to the design cycle requires that systems goals, objectives, problems, or issues be explicitly identified. Just as in systems analysis, the information systems designers have to be prepared to match the systems capabilities with the proper need. The definition of the functional requirements becomes the critical driving force that structures the shape and capabilities of the information system that is to be designed. It is at this juncture that the external influences (authority, budgetary, client) are explicitly identified and linked with an information need. This same process is also needed for the internal organizational and management requirements. The internal operational, financial, technical, human resources, objectives, and requirements have to be established along with the interdependencies among the internal subsystems. When these overarching judgments have been made explicit, the feasibility stage of the design cycle can begin after a systematic project guideline is developed. A project needs or requirements plan can provide the foundation for a feasibility assessment study by clearly identifying the need/requirement or outline of the problem to be addressed. A project plan should define the purpose of the information system in terms of organizational goals and objectives, along with the evaluation of current methods and presumed disadvantages.

Study and Feasibility Stage

This stage of the information systems development usually examines technical, economic, and operational feasibility. However, because our focus is on government managers, another factor called political influence may be relevant in the feasibility study. Senn (1982) makes a strong case for behavioral factors associated with the introduction of organizational changes, such as automated/computerized systems. Another criterion related to the operational variable, but different in degree, is the organizational feasibility.

The purpose of the study and feasibility stage is to build on the previously defined needs and definitions to determine how the operational-organizational requirements can be met and what the feasibility of developing an information system is. There are several approaches to studying the feasibility of information systems. One of the more enlightened methods is to design an attitudinal survey of the organization before addressing the specific political, technical, operational, and economic aspects of the information needs. Depending on the needs and size of the organization and the financial or time constraints, the survey may be very extensive or concentrate on only a few issues or problems. If an agencywide or highly integrated system is being studied, the survey requirements will be more comprehensive than if an inventory or payroll system need has been identified. The project committee then prepares the survey to address the appropriate questions or needs defined in the project plan stage to prepare the way for the specific operational and informational flow analysis. The project committee also may use interviews, observation, measurements, or existing documents to supplement the feasibility assessment.

The project group should develop a study schedule and plan for its completion of the study, beginning with the preliminary survey and ending with a report giving recommendations and assessment of the feasibility. The information from the attitudinal survey and other methods should be targeted on the needs and objectives and *be as specific as possible*. Some of the questions may highlight such issues as perceptions and areas of information systems paper or work overload; specific needs for information (type, frequency); time required for filing or retrieving information; time required for reporting information; perceived benefits and costs of automated or computerized system; potential operational effectiveness of an information system; use of information system on both critical and routine tasks; and potential negative impacts. The survey questions should, to the extent feasible, address the technical, operational, economic, and organizational issues identified when the systems need was defined. The information obtained from this survey can be used to supplement the initial needs definition and for feedback purposes if certain points need to be pursued further.

Other elements of the feasibility study phase should emphasize more specific information needs. Reviews of relevant documents and interviews with key managers should be undertaken to link operational and information requirements. These reviews and interviews should identify and make explicit the basis of authority for the organizational objectives, managerial actions (identify pertinent laws, regulations), and related information needs. It may also be at this point that the significant executive, legislative, and judicial influences on the organization are defined. This definition should include basis, frequency, and financial or budgetary results of these interactions. This part of the feasibility study should also link information needs to the service, product, or process that is used to meet specific operational and organizational objectives.

The feasibility study should also make required interorganizational relationships explicit and identify the information needed to support these relations. For example, if a state department of education is mandated to, or does through other established practices, interact with health or safety functions in the state, these interactions, their frequency, related information needs, and outcomes should be documented and the supporting information needs defined.

It is also appropriate at this stage to identify other organizations, individuals, constituencies, or interest groups that influence the organization. This analysis should examine the extent of their influence and the related information needs. For example, some interest groups are more vocal than others in making demands on public organizations, and their political or budgetary influence may be felt through their legislative initiatives; thus it may be feasible to compile information to deal with these types of periodic demands. Further, this may be the time to document the financial impact of these demands on the organization's operations and budgetary picture.

The feasibility study is concerned with more general pressures, such as political, economic, and technological issues that are likely to affect operational and therefore informational needs. This may also be the most appropriate stage at which to chart the effect of more ambiguous factors, such as the major contingencies associated with the organizational functions, uncertainty, potential threats, and future influences on information needs. Overall, the study group should be able to analyze the most salient external and internal features of the organization that will influence the information systems needs.

Other specific results of the feasibility should be an assessment of the organizational sources required to support an information system to include financial and human capabilities. This means that the information needs should be defined in terms of support for the operational and organizational requirements that were specified in this phase of the design cycle. The recommendations from the feasibility study should provide analysis of technical, political, operational, organizational, and economic variables. There is also reason to believe that many obstacles to information systems are behavioral; therefore, these issues should be addressed in as much detail as possible in the attitudinal measurement-assessment phases so that they correspond to the organizational-operational assessments. The primary result of the feasibility study is an assessment of what is needed; what is technically, operationally, and organizationally feasible; how much the development and system will cost; and what the most likely alternatives are for meeting the information systems needs. If an information system is deemed feasible, the project group should establish a project control group and schedule to analyze and develop the required system further. This project plan should include cost, time, and operational objectives.

A network design such as that presented in Figure 5.3 could be worked out in detail to design and control the development project. Given the various configurations of public organizations and existing skill levels, the control and scheduling network could assume alternative forms to meet varying conditions but with the core process preserved. The variability is not likely to occur in the initial stages through the feasibility study, but regardless of initial conditions, the inception, analysis-design, implementation, testing, documentation, operation, and evaluation stages are standard steps that provide the structure for the design.

The feasibility study should conclude with observations, conclusions, and recommendations regarding the economic, technical, operational-organizational, political, and behavioral criteria mentioned earlier and an assessment of the alternatives. If the informational needs/problems have been found valid after reviewing the managerial goals, objectives, and operations, the feasibility study report should have assessed the economic and operational costs and benefits across the alternatives for meeting the requirements, as well

FIGURE 5.3. Approach to Control and Scheduling for Information Systems Development and Design Cycle

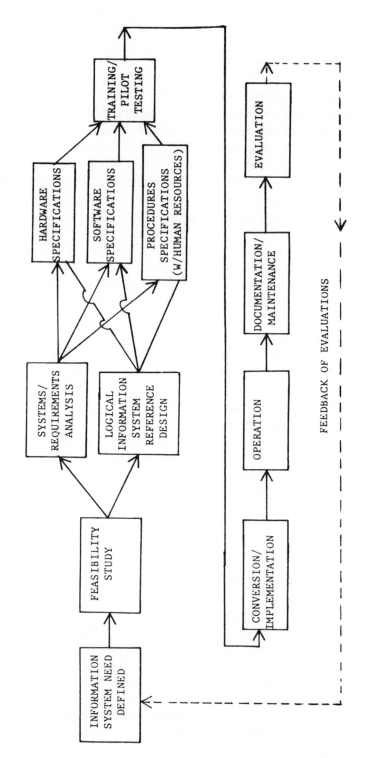

Source: Compiled by the author.

as concluding whether the project is technically feasible in terms of hardware, software, and personnel needs. However, many times the political, behavioral, and especially the operational factors will introduce additional dimensions to the study results. If the budgetary situation does provide for the financial resources, questions about the best use of money or even the long-term utility may arise. The conclusions of the study should assess the primary criteria and be prepared to answer the toughest possible "so-what" questions from any element of the internal and external environments, including the impact on overall organizational effectiveness, and draw on resources that may displace other opportunities. The weaknesses of unanswered questions in the feasibility stage will haunt the project development and implementation, so the critical points and issues should be addressed at this stage to provide a strong foundation for the subsequent stages.

ORGANIZATIONAL-OPERATIONAL
INFORMATION REQUIREMENTS ANALYSIS

One of the most important phases of the systems design cycle is the functional, operational, and organizational analysis that is used to identify the needs that shape the subsequent development cycle. This is the stage where management translates the organizational objectives, issues, problems, operational requirements, and information needs into the managerial and decision-making activities of the organization. The primary functions, related decisions, and information needs identified in the feasibility study provide the framework for further analysis of work flows and subsystems in the overall system.

The preparation phase of the requirements systems analysis should formulate an outline of the most important tasks to be achieved by focusing on the key subsystems/functions and the interdependence among them. Figure 2.1 presented a general outline that can be used to classify the information needs and the models in Figure 5.1. Figure 5.3 can be used to structure the process for each function. For example, once the key programs, operations, tasks, financial, human resources, intergovernmental, and planning functions have been defined, the required informational relationships inside and between them can be identified and the associated information needs codified.

At this stage, decisions and related valid information needs have to be determined if standards are to be derived and organizational control developed and maintained throughout the design cycle up to the evaluation stage.

Another important step in the system designs process is to identify, through observation, survey, measurement, or examination of documents, the strengths and weaknesses of the existing information system. The current information system may be a fully functioning data processing, computerized, or manual information system that has minor or major problems that were identified in the feasibility stage. The analysis step in the design cycle should analyze the existing hardware, software, economic, political, operational, and human factors that influence the operation of the information system. This step should also be used to identify adjuncts to the major functions, such as supporting or related systems (for example, inventory control or payroll administration). An assessment of the strengths and weaknesses of the existing information system is needed to provide a basis for the systems design.

A practical consideration in information system development is whether the existing system meets the needs of management. If there are too many ambiguities or if the system is grossly deficient, the problems have to be overcome because they may disguise more basic operational or organizational dysfunctions. Existing managerial problems have to be understood and rectified before the information systems design is completed.

Operational Focus

One important factor that has to be defined in the systems or requirements analysis stage is the organizational work flow and technology. The project team should be capable of developing a chart of the work flow in the different functions and designating the natural or organizational boundaries of the subsystems using skill groupings or levels of authority. These charts should properly trace the work flow from the input or intake stage through the organizational subsystems and pinpoint the key operational or decision points. The information required at each of these points has to be specified so that the information system supports the decisions made in the operational work flow. At this stage of the design, the specific subsystem work flowcharts should be checked for accuracy and completeness by upper-level and parallel managers. The subsystem work flowcharts should form the basis for the overall operational design.

Rosenthal (1982) characterized the production system for operational information as having input (data), process (collection, storage, manipulation, and retrieval), and output (information) elements. He argues, for example, that if the information system is used for emergency medical or for some policy purpose, information should be immediately available and online to facilitate rapid decision making. With public sector programs that require only periodic reports, and where speed of processing is not critical, batch processing may be sufficient.

Cleland and King (1983) focus primarily on information- or decision-support systems for strategic level decision making for the private sector; however, their analysis of the project management environment provides a view of what environmental information is necessary. In addition to relevant models, online capability, a database (and management system), graphical displays, and a user-friendly language (can be used by a nonspecialist), information from or on customers/potential customers, competitive, regulatory, and other "intelligence" sources are needed to deal with a changing environment.

Just as in the private sector, the environment or national/social conduct of government can be highly turbulent. Government "customers" may be clients, constituencies, interest groups, or controllers who have an interest in the organization's activities and operations. Government organizations and managers may or may not have well-defined joint relationships with other organizations/agencies/departments that may have authority or financial implications. They also operate with constraints imposed by internal regulations or external statutes that have long-term or short-range effects on client segments or needs. Key organizational or interest groups have backgrounds or characteristics that may have important direct or indirect effects on managers. The constituencies or voting blocs associated with welfare, social security, transportation, farming, health, education, defense, civil rights, and unions have direct and indirect short- and long-term impacts on many functions. The operational impact of their concerns or substantive interests should be understood.

These various demands have visible relationships with and impacts on internal budgetary, work load, human resources, planning, project, and intergovernmental operations. The information systems needs analyses should chart the requirements to develop a reference design to support the key decision aspects of the functions, as well as hardware, software, human, and procedures requirements. This reference or logical design then captures the key internal and external information systems requirements that form the basis for further defining the system in detail.

This systems analysis stage in the design process also presents logical flowcharts for operations and the supporting information that can be reviewed by the operational people and modified or corrected as required. The specific processes associated with who uses what information to make what decisions is also clearly specified so that the needs of the user form the basis for further systems development.

The information requirements analysis part of the systems analysis should produce schematics of data input forms (hard copy, coding forms, terminal formats) and copies or layouts of the reports or terminal formats used as output. At this stage a dictionary of definitions for data items and specifications for volume of information, processing times, and frequency of changes should also be produced. That is, each operational and decision-making aspect of the various functions should be circumscribed in terms of data/forms of input, reports/formats for output, a dictionary/documentation for the data items, and specifications concerning time, accuracy, updating frequency, and volume.

The operational work flow and decision-making analysis and charting of the supporting information flow can be used to prepare a logical or functional reference design that illustrates the important operational functions and processes and the interdependence between them. This operational and organizational information design then parallels the organizational/functional structure and defines the scope of the decision-making activities and the required information to match the decision making. It is here that the top, mid, and operational managerial control objectives and decisions have to be made explicit so that the required subsystems objectives can be integrated into the overall organizational objectives. This operational and decisional structure provides the managerial framework for designing what the general hardware, software, procedural, and human considerations are in the system. This overall logical-functional design then provides the link from the management structure to the information system and informs management what further management actions are required in developing the information system.

Logical, Physical, and Operational Design

One accepted approach to making detailed physical information systems design decisions is to feed the reference or logical design findings from the systems analysis back into the organization. This feedback process allows the key organization members in the different functions and managerial levels to become informed about the information systems analysis part of the project and derived needs. This feedback process also provides the opportunity for the design team to solicit input concerning the validity of the overall design and the operational and information needs that were identified. The logical or reference design also becomes a major mechanism for outlining the organization's managerial objectives. Information flows used in the decision processes can also be used for obtaining and structuring information resources from the various managerial levels of the organization, its environment, and functions or subsystems. The logical/reference design also informs the operational managers, staff, and other support elements that certain assumptions have been made about principal activities and implicitly if not explicitly related cost-benefit considerations and decisions were introduced.

Another important use of this design is to outline in detail what the major components of the information system are, their relationship, and the plans for scheduling and completing the project. This framework is then used to structure the detailed or physical design phase, which emphasizes further specification of operations and information needs in terms of hardware, software, or files/databases. For example, the major functions of the organization are segmented into specific operations that are flowcharted in terms of required functions and supporting information. Though many government functions may not be this detailed or extensive at present, the trend is toward the use of information systems to monitor decisions, operations, and compliance.

Physical and Detailed Design

The operational work flow and related information requirements developed in the systems analysis are used to specify inputs and outputs that can be used to control, process, support decisions, and measure program performance. When the logical design stage flowcharts are available, they should be used for disseminating the results of this stage of the project requirements and achieving intended information-related objectives for the overall organization. The operational and informational objectives can be used as a reference to elicit further information concerning equipment, to invite participation, and to resolve any misunderstandings concerning the design or objectives and reports to be produced by the project. In this way, the design stage can also be used to identify the major programming and procedure steps that have to be taken in meeting project objectives.

When the flowcharting of the major operations and routine and nonroutine decisions are completed, the information-support system should reflect the dominant information and cost trade-off criteria for the organization. For example, the costs associated with the intended objectives and trade-offs could be made between certain objectives, the related information, and other needs such as evaluation. In this stage of the systems design, managers should be able to specify what the most critical information needs are and what the relative priorities are in terms of paying for them.

Elements of the Database

The general and detailed systems analyses and logical/reference design stages provide the basis for further defining data collection, storage, and processing needs. If certain eligibility decisions, demographic tracking, or periodic or evaluation reports are required for a client population, they have a direct impact on how much and what kind of data storage and processing space are required. For example, as mentioned in the discussion on filing, it is necessary to compile a list of data elements that are needed to provide complete records and manage the program internally and provide reports to meet whatever external reporting requirements may exist. An information system requires a database or filing system that is a compilation of logically structured and related operational requirement files. There are a number of other databases, such as the software (systems or applications programs for using the data), database management system, and database procedures constituting the database subsystem. Data organization, such as data items (attributes of an object), records (combined data items), files (a collection of records), or databases with applications programs, have to be specified in the physical design phase, which translates needs and the logical design into the physical system.

The database subsystem should be integrated with managerial decisions by identifying all activity or transaction parts of the flow-charts that require data inputs. Also, a data worksheet should be prepared for each element or item, giving source of data, length and form, current and potential frequency of updating, retention schedule, and use of the data. All data worksheets should be grouped by activity and checked, with duplicate requirements eliminated. The master file or database should reflect the external and internal information needs that were derived from the systems analysis and information systems analysis. The master file or structure of the database should also support the functional subsystems of the organization and decisions that are made at the various points within the functions.

In addition to the logical design of the system database, the physical design of the filing or database system involves such elements as developing instruments for collecting the internal and external information, item elements and record formats, data structures, files (if database is not used), or overall databases. After designing the files, schemas, or subschemas, it is also appropriate and timely to define related hardware requirements to address storage, input, processing, output, and reporting needs. The hardware decisions must be made in the context of the economic, technical, managerial, decisional, software, procedural, and operational requirements specified in the previous design phases. For example, if large agencies or departments deal with thousands of clients for which large numbers of records are needed to keep track of applications, eligibility, payments/service, and outcomes frequently for long periods, then the storage, collection, input, and processing requirements will dictate a large filing or database structure. Further, if the data are centralized in another geographic location, such as a region or state capital, and there are real-time updating or online query or retrieval requirements to review, update, or display records or report on data analysis, there will be additional hardware, software, procedures, and telecommunications capabilities to acquire.

In addition to the hardware, software, and procedures requirements defined in the systems-logical design stages, the design should also specify personnel requirements. This set of specifications and recommendations should reflect the human resources that correspond to the other information systems requirements and address such issues as training and education of systems users and/or operators. For example, the project team should consciously emphasize the importance of well-trained systems personnel and define their duties as they relate to the degree of automation, the hardware capabilities, and the software use for automation and for the different parts of the information system to be used in the operations.

The use of terminals for online query or updating of records may also be supplemented with batch processing or periodic record changes or reports, but the hardware and software configuration or "architecture" should reflect the operational needs and decisions defined in the preceding analysis. This issue is very relevant to the acquisition stage when requests for proposals are written and systems are purchased from hardware or software vendors. Because qualified personnel—programmers, systems analysts, operators—are in demand in both the private and public sectors, plans concerning the training, compensation, and use of personnel in the overall system are needed.

Another specific task to be completed in the detailed or physical design stage is the development of the format, forms, and instruments used in the data/information-gathering process. The forms or other data collection instruments should reflect the quantitative and qualitative needs for information by specifying the sources of data, reliability, frequency, and linkage to different decisions or rules so that the information is useful to the manager who makes decisions. After the information is collected, processed, stored, and analyzed, it is then presented in suitable report formats (determined in the requirements analysis stage) for the users and managers. This reporting phase should undergo continuous scrutiny for report applicability and relevancy. Presentation of the required standard reports (usually using report-generating software) may be computer listings, hardcopy report summaries, or video displays where speed or flexibility is needed.

When the systems design has progressed to this point, the physical system should be tested and acquired (specific acquisition issues will be covered in the subsequent section of this chapter). The test of the system may range from complete conversion in smaller systems to piecemeal, functional, nonproduction tests of complex systems. The test is usually a simulation using real input, many times routine and extreme values, to measure the performance of the system against the operational criteria developed in the systems analysis design phase. This test is used to check accuracy, time lags, personnel errors, lack of understanding, relevance of managerial information, and cost variables. The test should also be used to determine that the inter-action between the various parts of the system are operating as designed and that unanticipated problems are identified. The testing stage should also produce information that will be useful in the con-version process as the system is implemented.

IMPLEMENTATION, DOCUMENTATION, AND EVALUATION

Conversion, Implementation, and Operation

One of the most critical, and many times most inadequately managed, phases of installing an information system is the implemen-tation. Depending on the absolute size of the project, the implemen-tation phase will consume more resources than the preliminary steps of the design cycle. It is at this point that the validity of the feasibil-ity study, systems analysis, logical, and physical design phases be-comes evident and execution plans receive their full test. According to Thierauf and Reynolds (1980) this implementation stage starting point involves the integration of operational requirements, personnel needs, programming, equipment selection, physical requirements, and conversion activities.

According to Thierauf and Reynolds, a comprehensive treatment of the systems analysis and design phases of information systems in a private organization presents several major steps in implementation, program development, equipment acquisition and installation, sys-tem level testing, installation, and conversion. They also advise against attempts to short-circuit the implementation process. When the hard-ware, software, procedures, and human resources elements have been properly tested and the problems resolved, the implementation stage should be started.

The conversion process includes creation of the master files/data-bases and conversion of programs to operations using four different approaches (Senn 1982): parallel systems, new system operated side by side with old; pilot system, one function connected at a time; phase in, new system gradually replaced by old; and direct cutover, conversion at one time. Each of the implementation approaches has some obvious advantages and limitations, but the direct cutover requires the most careful and detailed planning.

Senn (1982) also illustrated the types of behavioral problems that may influence implementation and made recommendations concerning reachable goals and informal managerial processes to deal with behavioral resistance to information systems. He correctly identifies the source of many problems as being the initial planning stages and lack of integration with users and managers. Information systems tend to be major interruptions that disturb organizational routines, scrutinize ongoing operations, reevaluate decision actions, and focus on resource allocation. Therefore, resistance is to be anticipated. The key lesson presented by Senn is that behavioral considerations are important, and user participation from the inception stage is crucial to implementation of an information system.

The implementation process should be scheduled using milestones and operational criteria. In addition, performance standards, cost, and time requirements should be used as elements in the implementation control process. Each stage of the implementation plan should have performance objectives to be met within time and cost constraints. The application of critical path and PERT techniques to this process is especially useful for controlling and scheduling the various implementation steps. The implementation data can also be used to maintain the participation of management and users by providing a common framework for interrelating the planned events.

Documentation and Maintenance Phases

The documentation phase of the information systems design and development cycle is a necessary step that fulfills several purposes, such as troubleshooting, replacing subsystems, interfacing with other subsystems, training operating personnel, and evaluating and upgrading systems (Murdick and Ross 1979). The most important use of the documentation phase for management is to complete the operation of the information system. Documentation is the physical record of the systems processes that describes the purposes, structure, operations, and basis for evaluation. It is highly unlikely that systems analysts or systems designers will retain all the important parts of the design in their memory, so some systematic approach to codifying the information systems processes and elements is needed as a reference. Though this phase of the design is tedious and time consuming, it should provide, among other things, a complete manual that addresses objectives, specifications, flowcharts, database organization, data dictionary, instruction programs, input-output definition, and a user's manual that specifies data preparation, specification of responsibility, and a glossary.

Because the information system is an ongoing reflection of and supporting tool for the organization's operations, it must be properly maintained. The technology associated with hardware and software in computerized information systems is constantly changing. Therefore, the system should be monitored to ascertain whether changes or improved methods will benefit the ongoing operations of the system. There are also periodic maintenance procedures that may be required by the manufacturers to maintain the hardware physically. The main questions to be answered by the manager are whether the operation is cost-efficient and sufficiently free of errors to continue the operation.

Evaluation of the Information System

Evaluation of information systems, once they are implemented and working, is a key function that should be performed by managers on a continuous basis. A primary criterion is whether the information system performs the objectives and meets the operational requirements specified in the feasibility and systems analysis phases of the development life cycle. Other important criteria are whether the benefits of the information system outweigh the costs, the impact of the system on organizational effectiveness and productivity of the operations, the effects of the changes, the accuracy and applicability of the information provided to the managers and users, whether the information is timely, user satisfaction, and attitudinal acceptance by the managers and users. The criteria of technical, economic, behavioral, and operational effectiveness should be used as ongoing bases for evaluating the information system. These factors apply to the internal, operational, and control objectives, as well as the analysis of the environmental influences that may directly affect internal organizational functions.

In addition to performance, time, and cost evaluations, the hardware and software operations of the information system can be evaluated by using electronic or software devices to record the frequency, time, and uses of the various systems components. Sensors may be used to determine how much time a CPU is actually working or waiting by measuring electrical impulses. This type of evaluation will indicate whether the hardware is sufficient for meeting the needs or requires such changes as dropping memory or storage units. Software monitors (usually programs/instructions) may be used to identify what programs are being used, when, and how much. The results and conclusions from the evaluation should be used to determine whether sufficient reason exists to undertake a review or analysis of the system.

SUMMARY OF INFORMATION SYSTEMS DESIGN CYCLE ISSUES

This chapter has examined a systematic, conventional, and generally accepted approach to addressing managerial and information systems issues—an approach that can be used in a public organization as well as private. It is called the information systems design and development life cycle. It emphasizes managerial involvement and operational requirements and uses the organizational and managerial context as the starting point. It provides a management-based, analytical perspective that defines a logical method for the manager to use in studying, designing, and evaluating the uses of information systems. This cycle also directly involves managers who ultimately have the responsibility for the effectiveness of the information system in the decision-making framework of the organization. The process begins (see Figure 5.3) with the inception stage, or identification of requirements-needs, progresses with a feasibility study to examine technical, operational-organizational, behavioral, political, and economic concerns, continues with systems analysis to logical and physical design phases of training, testing, conversion, and implementation, and reaches the end of the cycle with operations, maintenance, documentation, and evaluation.

The design cycle provides the manager with a coherent, management-based method for determining the primary needs, constraints, and operational objectives for the information system while still controlling the technical and economic facets of its operation. It integrates the manager with the information system and provides organizational control that may not be otherwise available, especially where resources are constrained, the environment turbulent, and demands for accountability increasing.

ISSUES AND CONSIDERATIONS IN
INFORMATION SYSTEMS ACQUISITION

The information systems acquisition process should occur after the feasibility study and systems analysis phases of the life cycle, thereby planning on and assuming the financial and authority support from top-level executives and legislative commitment. This is needed because computerized information systems potentially have great political, economic, and operational impacts on the public or government organization, and thus a systematic, careful approach to systems acquisition is needed. Generally, after the systems requirements have been defined, there are several alternatives for meeting them. Hardware, filing-database, and software systems or services can be purchased, rented, or leased; however, the important consideration is that the request for proposal (RFP) or specifications manual be based on the systems analysis and explicitly deal with the previously defined operational and information systems requirements. These RFPs or manuals should be used to inform vendors of the exact systems performance and components required.

The RFP should describe organizational needs and present systems and specify hardware requirements, such as cost, primary memory size, data channels, online, batch, time-sharing needs, peak loads, flexibility-expandability, special features, storage requirements, user interface, input/output speeds, processing time constraints, vendor support, security, and backups for emergencies. For example, if a large, centralized database system is needed to integrate project management and financial information with regional or district "smart" terminals capable of performing onsite analysis and storage, then certain types of hardware are required. A distributed database system with communications equipment (modulators-demodulators) and transmission lines or other forms of communication (telephone, satellite) with several geographically dispersed terminals or mini/ microcomputers may best meet the hardware needs. "Plug-in" or "turn-key" (readily available systems) may exist, or special configurations may have to be designed. In conjunction with the hardware specifications, the manager should also determine whether hardware-compatible software exists.

Software specifications derived in the systems analysis phase of the life cycle should address such issues as specific applications, modifications required to packages, the overall operating systems tasks, execution times, package availability, flexibility to meet changing needs, vendor support, user friendliness, maintainability (standard language well documented), report generation, and performance standards. Just as with the hardware specifications, conformance with the decision-making requirements and cost factors identified in the design cycle have to be explicit to control the acquisition process.

Issues related to hardware and software acquisition are personnel and maintenance costs. Personnel costs may consume more than half of the systems cost and maintenance costs as much as one-quarter because, although advances in technology have decreased the hardware costs considerably in the last 20 years, personnel and related costs have increased greatly.

Once the hardware, software, personnel, and related cost criteria have been examined, ownership, rental, leasing, or service bureau arrangements must be evaluated. Given the requirements of the system, is it more economical and/or efficient to buy, lease, rent, or hire a service bureau? Service bureaus provide a range of services that meet processing, time-sharing, report generation, keypunching, or specialized needs. Periodic reports, batch jobs, or even interactive processing may be available from service bureau remote terminals in agencies hooked up to the service bureau's central computer. Many times service bureaus are the first contacts with the capabilities of computerized information systems for local governments. They are usually low-cost alternatives for small government operations and provide a range of services that familiarize the public sector manager with information systems potential.

The acquisition alternatives can be evaluated using benefit-cost criteria, hardware and software systems performance measures, and vendor responses to the operational and service requirements. An independent assessment of the manufacturer and vendor capabilities may be needed where complex systems requirements exist, because systems and vendor capabilities have great variability.

Because there is very little clear-cut guidance provided by research in this area, the manager must rely on the performance, cost, time, benefit, and operational criteria developed in the feasibility and systems analyses to structure the acquisition process. Further, information from other government users, organizations of information systems specialists, academics, and nonprofit consultants will provide valuable information about acquisition—if the right questions are asked.

6

Approaches to Evaluation of Information Systems in Government

The previous chapters in Part II have dealt with a number of the technical concerns associated with the use of information systems in government organizations. As the reader can probably conclude, it is difficult for managers today—whether in public or private organizations—to function effectively without some rudimentary understanding of how computers and automatic systems operate. At the same time, the inability to design and implement properly such systems into the work setting can often spell the difference between success and failure for information systems and their users.

One necessary aspect of the role of information systems within government is the ability to evaluate formally and cost out their impact on the organization. Unfortunately, this is one area in need of the greatest improvement; and reasons for this vary. One factor is symptomatic of government itself, characterized by multiple levels of checks and procedures. Once a system is in place, it tends to become ingrained in the work process, and individuals develop work routines around it. Whether we prefer to think of it as status quo behavior or bureaucratic intransigence, it becomes far more difficult to make substantive changes to a system without alienating one individual or a group of individuals. In this instance, evaluation of the information system becomes futile at best. Whatever results that are derived are either overlooked or ignored.

Another factor is more personnel-related. To perform any type of formal evaluation requires knowledge of systems capabilities as well as organizational requirements. To put the two into a form that will be understood by administrators is no simple task. Fortunately, this is beginning to be less of an obstacle as government managers are becoming more sensitive to the impact that information systems can have on their organization. In addition, the level of professional training and background of individuals entering the public sector has increased. More and more such managers are beginning to ask questions about the expected return of investments in automation for their organizations.

Finally, the computer industry itself has added to the difficulties of evaluating the effects of information systems by often overselling the capabilities of such systems. Or the user is not sufficiently aware of the hardware and software needed to enable the information system to function optimally.

Although these factors may not be characteristic of all government agencies attempting to evaluate their information system, it indicates that a number of organizational, individual, and technical obstacles must be addressed. Before touching on ways to deal with them, we should begin with some discussion on how data and information can be evaluated.

DESIGNING INFORMATION SYSTEMS OF VALUE

A necessary first step in designing and evaluating information systems for public organizations is to consider the entire environment within which it is expected to operate. This would embody the key offices and units that make up the agency or organization itself, the skill level and expertise of managers who will be using the system itself, both directly and indirectly, agency allies and supporters, competitors, constituents, and, finally, the general public. For most organizations, the influence of each of these groups will vary—with agency personnel assuming far greater control than that of the general public—but each has a vested interest in both the amount and quality of information that is collected, processed, and disseminated.

Kettinger (1980), in a discussion of how to manage information resources at the local level, has suggested that government organizations should bring together these disparate groups through a *systematic* formalized evaluation technique, which he terms the information management study (IMS). The intent here is not to go over the five points of Kettinger's IMS; rather, any approach that begins with an overview and some understanding of the full environment of public agency information activities and routines would suffice. Unfortunately, most organizations, as previously noted, have been deficient in this regard, so the IMS will provide a necessary model.

Kettinger's (1980) approach to information systems evaluation suggests the following steps:

- Defining the scope of the study
- Defining top management support
- Identifying personnel for the study
- Communicating with participants
- Performing a prestudy survey
- Preparing a study plan

Defining the Scope

Perhaps the most critical portion of the evaluation is determining the boundaries that it will cover. For public agencies, it is incumbent that the value of the information system for assisting program performance in the public interest be considered at this stage; for too often the scope becomes limited, tending to focus on program continuation and maintenance with little or no thought given to constituent interest. In addition, studies that bring this into account have the benefit of having considered the broad ramifications of information systems on the community and can readily use the results for purposes of program justification.

Other points that should be considered in defining the scope of the information management study include legislative laws and mandates that may circumscribe an agency's activities and, consequently, its information practices. The Paperwork Reduction Act of 1980 was previously cited as one example here. In addition, laws that act to safeguard individual rights to privacy and access to personnel records also have considerable bearing on agency activities. While the technology exists to collect and process a great deal of data and information on private citizens, legal safeguards may act—and correctly so— as a deterrent to this. Beyond those laws, executive pronouncements, and the like that directly influence information collection and use, agency officials should consider the potential impact of any legislation—be it regulatory activities (for example, environmental and health safety), consumer protection, or direct service provision.

Also part of defining the scope of the information study would be changes/modifications in program direction. This takes on a variety of forms and shapes, from program termination in which funds have been withdrawn or the program's goal or intent has been satisfied, to program growth and expansion in which new emphasis is to be placed. In either case, information systems should be sensitive to such changes and be adaptive. A number of organizations have designed and implemented information systems around one particular program or practice, only to find that dramatic shifts in funds and resources have made these systems obsolete. Managers and those involved in information systems must be able, as best as possible, to consider the long-term nature of programs and their support activities. If they are unable to do so, or the future looks highly uncertain, the implementation of information systems may be a risky prospect. One alternative is to design the system in such a way that it can be readily adaptable to other uses or program activities. Ways to achieve this would include use of common language and database whereby diverse users can take advantage of the system and can access different types and sources of data.

Anticipated changes in information technology also have a direct bearing on determining the scope of the evaluation and the projected costs and benefits of the operating system itself. Unfortunately, this is one feature of the study that becomes highly speculative—relying on the ability of users, managers, and systems analysts to forecast organizational direction relative to directions in the field of automation.

To illustrate, in the mid- to late 1970s, government computing principally consisted of centralized operations, usually the control of an EDP staff, and dedicated to large-scale routine or batch operations. The technology during this time consisted of mainframes that could process large amounts of data in a systematic manner. The principal uses for the technology were centered in such areas as accounting and financial management, inventory control and procurement, and public safety (at the state and local levels).

As the technology underwent a period of change in the late 1970s and early 1980s, agencies that previously had large mainframe systems saw them as cumbersome and costly. Managers and departmental users alike came to view EDP offices as small fiefdoms, clamoring for additional resources but unable to design applications that could be flexible to change or modification. The advent of lower cost mini- and microcomputer systems alleviated a number of these problems and gave users the ability to design applications more in tune with their needs. The organization itself underwent a similar change as decentralization, user control, and distributed EDP resources became the watchword. Whether it is the case of the tail (technology) wagging the dog (agency) or the reverse, it is clear that managers and administrators must be aware of, and incorporate, technological developments in their information plans.

Finally, the shifting nature of budgetary resources should not be dismissed, for it is the very essence of public organizations themselves. The ability of agency officials to acquire and retain budgetary resources is viewed as a mark of success and power—not unlike a private firm's profit margin or return on investment. In today's climate of constrained resources and diminishing sources of revenue, EDP systems have often been implemented with the promise of higher productivity—more efficient service delivery with less cost. Unfortunately, studies have shown that this promise has, in many instances, become shallow, that computer applications have led to cost *avoidance* rather than *cost replacement*. Managers must therefore give increasing attention to the anticipated benefits relative to the total costs of information systems. At the same time, such benefit-cost evaluations should be calculated over the expected life of the system.

Defining Top Management Support

As the second component of the information study, defining top management support must also be addressed. To some extent, such support may be circumscribed by the external developments previously mentioned. That is, fixed budgetary resources may forestall the ability of agency officials to adopt new technology or make substantive changes. Or chief executives may wish to see new initiatives made in a particular program or policy area. To bring this into consideration, the evaluation of systems should clearly define how agency goals and objectives will be addressed relative to information collection and processing activities.

Top officials should be able to see and understand how the system relates to agency management activities and, more importantly, assists managers and users in reaching decisions. It is this last point that warrants further emphasis, as computer systems today are being judged on their ability to serve as true management information systems (MIS). While routine data collection and processing functions are fundamental to agency performance, the ability of managers to make nonroutine or unstructured decisions represents the future potential for improved agency performance. Top management should be counseled and surveyed on the extent to which such nonroutine applications will service its needs and be a viable portion of the agency decision-making process.

Finally, soliciting top management support can often provide valuable insight to users and system designers concerning the directions in which the agency is headed over the short-term as well as the knowledge of political constraints which must also be addressed.

Identifying Personnel for the Study

Kettinger here notes two approaches to performing the evaluation: the use of either internal or external personnel. As with any form of study or evaluation, there are obvious advantages and disadvantages, and a number of factors must be weighed.

The use of individuals from within the agency or organization allows for lower costs in terms of the direct outlay of funds. This does not, however, take into consideration the cost associated with staff time that must be redirected from other projects or program activities—in a sense, opportunity costs—but it does not entail the need to gain expenditure approval.

Another, perhaps primary advantage, is the knowledge of the organization's history and work processes. This will have a direct bearing on the ability of evaluators to ascertain the contribution of information systems toward improved agency decision making and program management. In many cases, such personnel can bring their personal assessments to bear on judgments of usefulness or value. In one midwestern state agency, for example, a sophisticated statewide computer system was installed that would, in terms of the vendor, allow geographically dispersed districts to communicate better and obtain instantaneous feedback. Upon investigation, it was found that the system was really a one-way communication device between central headquarters and the field. Field personnel saw this as another overture to control and monitor their activities and reverted back to a manual system that offered them some sense of control and autonomy. Clearly, the behavioral aspect of the automated system was not adequately addressed.

A third advantage of using internal personnel and staff can also be considered behavioral. Individuals who must live with the information system have a stake in seeing that it functions properly. Outside evaluators, naturally, do not share the same incentive and are charged with looking at the current or near-term configuration of the information system. In addition, they often fail to consider the behavioral impact of such systems on personnel, looking instead at objective standards for performance (such as the number of transactions performed, the turnaround time and the like.)

The use of external evaluators has its advantages and drawbacks, some of which have already been noted. Perhaps one of the primary strengths of this approach is that the necessary skill to perform an evaluation may be lacking within the organization. Particularly in medium and small jurisdictions or organizations, an analytic unit or staff either does not exist or such talent is not easily identified. One alternative is to inventory current personnel to determine whether individuals may have certain skills that could be tapped. But, at a minimum, the evaluation team should have people with knowledge of the technical aspects of information systems (hardware, software, database management), cost-benefit analysis, accounting and financial management processes, and systems design. In the case of using an outside evaluation team, the organization can ensure that these skills are at least provided in the request for proposal.

Another advantage in using outside personnel is that the information system may be politically sensitive or controversial in nature, and an independent assessment is warranted. Individuals who have been extensively involved with the system may be viewed by others as being too attached to it to remain impartial or objective. At the same time, there may be an internal battle for control of the information system. Either of these would be sufficient to question the objectivity of any internal evaluation. The use of an outside team here would be advisable—if only to head off such questions.

Whether the decision is made to use internal or external personnel, agencies should give serious thought to the costs involved and anticipated reaction. A compromise position, one which will hold down costs and forestall some dissent, is to staff the evaluation team with both: using outside personnel to guide the overall evaluation and internal support to provide background information and act as a sounding board.

Finally, the evaluation team, however it is constructed, should be apprised of the top officials' position and the overall objective of the information study. This last point is neglected and often leads to results or findings that fail to be accepted or ultimately implemented.

Communicating with Participants

This portion of the information study has been touched on in a few of the prior stages, but it bears repeating: Some formal mechanism should be established at the outset to ensure that questions or the need for clarification is directly channeled to appropriate personnel, whether they are top agency officials or line personnel.

One method for providing formal feedback is to prescribe in the study plan benchmarks or checkpoints at which an informal report on the team's progress is issued. The benefit of this approach is twofold. First, it will serve to keep the evaluation on course, preventing the foundering that often accompanies team or committee efforts. Second, it will serve as a channel for information on the study and inform managers of the expected results. In a sense, the final evaluation report should be pro forma if individuals who are responsible, or will be responsible, for the information system can gain some understanding of the content of the overall system study as it develops.

Another aspect of communication is providing agency personnel with some means of reacting to the study. This could range from a formal request for opinions or questions to informally soliciting feedback. Obviously, the individual traits of evaluators will be a key ingredient here. They must be able to communicate at the level of agency personnel and further serve to educate current and potential users. Too often, the personalities of evaluators serve to frustrate, and indeed alienate, staff and line managers alike.

Performing a Prestudy Survey

Here Kettinger notes the need for the organization to do some preliminary work *prior* to the actual assessment of information practices and procedures. This can take several forms, but an acceptable one should include some specification of organizational functions and responsibilities. In many cases, such information is readily available in agency manuals—listing enabling legislation, major program responsibilities, and structural arrangements. A necessary component of this material, as Kettinger stresses, is some indication of criteria for judging program effectiveness. Are there traditional measures of productivity that are used, for example, cases cleared or transactions performed? Does the agency have a program or performance monitoring system currently in place that could provide such data and information (MBO, PPB, or the like)? If not, it is incumbent that some initial effort be made to develop criteria, as the utility of information systems will be measured against these standards or criteria.

Middle- and upper-level management task criteria must be included as well, and are perhaps most critical for assessing the information system's capabilities in assisting managers in nonroutine decision situations. Such criteria should encompass the qualitative aspects of the managerial situation—the ability to make decisions given available information; meeting agency goals and program priorities; and the capability to respond to various constituent support groups and the like.

The final step in the prestudy phase is incorporating the information on prescribed duties, evaluation criteria, and information flow patterns into a working document for the formal study itself.

Preparing a Study Plan

As the fifth phase of the process, it is perhaps evident that the success or failure of the plan is really premised on the prior background work and analysis required. Nevertheless, this phase involves the development of a formal approach to evaluating the particular information system. This approach will be described in fuller detail in the next section, but here it is sufficient to note that Kettinger recommends that a formal statement of the agency's information policy be developed.

In many cases, this information policy will be contained in enabling legislation, that is, specific directives to the agency to collect and disseminate information. For example, the Bureau of Labor Statistics is directly responsible for collecting industrial statistics and making them available to the general public, other agencies, and industrial firms. In most instances, the information policy will be more subtle in form, viewed more as a necessary means for satisfying particular program objectives. For example, an environmental protection agency may have to establish rigorous, systematic procedures for collecting data from industrial firms on the level of effluents or emissions. Indeed, there are few exceptions to this because government activities are generally construed as information-intensive.

Finally, managerial and societal concerns should be imbedded in the organization's information policy. This does not mean that every facet of the management process be addressed. Rather, the concern here is to indicate that information is to be collected, processed, and disseminated in an efficient and effective manner with an eye toward cost and concern for individual rights to privacy and access to personal information.

CONDUCTING THE INFORMATION STUDY

Moving from the planning and prestudy phases to evaluating the actual information system itself will depend on several factors. One is the level of depth that is desired. A number of government organizations have conducted "formal" evaluations of their systems that are not much more than a cursory description of the hardware/software involved and their applications within the organization. The reader is assaulted with complex systems flow diagrams and examples of screen formats and comes away with a false sense of "Well, if it is this complex it must be good!" A few organizations have gone to the other extreme, conducting detailed unit-by-unit analysis with a long-term forecast of cost-benefits of the entire operating system. In this case, the second approach is better because critical or key information can be distilled from the more technical approach and channeled to managers and officials less versed in the technical aspects of information systems.

A second and obvious factor is cost—both monetary and time. Any extensive study of computer applications will require a sufficient amount of time to collect necessary information, analyze it, and present it in some meaningful form. Agencies that will be evaluating their system should allow sufficient lead time to perform the study and should build in some flexibility in expected target dates. It is not too uncommon to hear of agencies that have had to scale down the scope of the study when approaching critical deadlines. Whether this is due to unrealistic expectations or the inability to obtain necessary data or feedback, the final report will undoubtedly reflect this weakness.

Another factor, one that was previously discussed, is the availability of certain skills to perform the study. The more exhaustive the study, the higher the need for people who have knowledge of systems design, computer technology, organizational analysis, work flow logic, and the like.

In conducting the study, a number of components should be included. According to Horton (1979), the primary ones are the following:

- Analysis of organizational units and cost centers
- Information requirement analysis that details why information is needed, for what purpose, and to be used by whom, when, and where
- Total costs over the expected lifetime of use of the information, including both capital acquisition costs and annual operating costs
- Consideration of alternatives in satisfying the organization's information needs

Analysis of Organizational Units and Cost Centers

Beginning with the organizational structure information generated in the prestudy phases, it is necessary to examine specific activity areas by functional area. The benefit of the functional versus hierarchical perspective is that it permits better understanding of the information communication patterns within the organization—a perspective often lost when examining traditional organization charts or configurations. For example, a municipal government may want to look at the following functional areas:

- General administration
- Inspections
- Public safety
- Housing
- Public transit
- Libraries
- Parks/recreation
- Health/hospitals
- Social services

Second, and most difficult, is attaching costs to these functional areas, in this case, information-related costs. Horton (1979) refers to this as *information cost accounting* and recommends that both internal and external costs be developed. For internal costs, an objective class approach should be considered. This would involve adding up expenses for each functional area that falls into the following object classes:

- Personnel compensation and benefits
- Equipment acquisition and lease
- Materials and supplies
- Office space acquisition and rental
- Related contractual service
- Related guarantees, grants, loans, and investments

For external costs, Horton suggests two primary classes: those borne directly by the respondent from whom government collects information and those borne by some other element in the public sector (another agency or governmental body).

A firm or industry that must compile an environmental impact statement and supply this to a state department of environmental resources can be considered to have incurred costs in both the development and distribution of this document. Similarly, local agencies supplying computer tapes and information as a reporting requirement should also be considered to have borne costs in the process. Both must be accounted for as external costs by the recipient agency. One major flaw is that government organizations have traditionally focused on internal costs, ignoring external information-related activities or treating them as "free" (Morss and Rich 1980).

In computing internal and external costs, two approaches are possible. Horton (1979) terms these bottom-up and top-down approaches:

> Under the bottom-up approach, which is essentially an input-oriented approach, we are not at all concerned with the output side of the equation, that is the *uses* to which the information resource is to be put. . . . By contrast, under the top-down approach, we are concerned with the overall purposes of the organization. (pp. 174-175)

The bottom-up approach is traditionally based on the object classification scheme used to record financial transactions. It reflects the nature of the service or article for which an obligation is incurred and may be broken down into these components, according to Horton:

- Personal services and benefits
- Contractual services and supplies
- Acquisition of capital assets (buildings, equipment)
- Grants and fixed charges
- Miscellaneous (administrative expenses)

In addition, each major object of expenditure can be broken down into subcategories. Under this approach, internal costs for each area of the reorganization are aggregated by these objects of expenditures and can be appropriately displayed.

Under the top-down approach, the focus is on the overall direction and program of the agency and the following questions are addressed:

- What is the underlying, basic purpose of this program?
- What is it really intended to accomplish?
- What approach is to be taken in the program (capital-intensive, labor-intensive, information-intensive)?
- What role will each of the resources play in helping managers to achieve the program purposes?
- What role will the information resource play (primary, secondary)?
- In what form will the data and information be needed?
- How frequently will the information be needed?

Horton states that the object of expenditure classification scheme will also be used with this approach, but the focus is centered on the program rather than organizational unit.

Finally, a mixed approach is also possible—combining cost centers with a program orientation. The benefit of these approaches—bottom-up, top-down, or a mix of the two—is that it forces managers to assign costs rather than treat them in the aggregate form. At the same time, it fosters comparative analysis—examining trends over time and possibly highlighting initial areas for future action.

Information Requirement Analysis

The information requirement portion of the study should not be viewed as distinct from the organizational cost center section. Using the prior format, an effort is made here to document information flow and perceptions of information utility.

Information flow patterns can be broken down into the following phases (Kettinger 1980, p. 130).

- Transaction origination
- Transaction entry
- Information communication
- Information processing
- Information storage and retrieval
- Output processing

Transaction Origination

The particular set of tasks or activities here involves the control and monitoring of source documents and reports for eventual entry into an automated system. For example, a unit may be responsible for validating an insurance claim prior to its input into an information system for processing and payment. In this case, the source document will be the claim itself. The unit may also be responsible for a visual scan to ensure that it is properly completed and may batch or collect the forms for computer entry. In government organizations, source documentation and control is of critical importance and should be viewed not as adjunct to the system itself but rather as a key input. Finally, units responsible for transaction origination must also consider the steps necessary for the proper disposal/storage of the original source documents. In many organizations, a retention policy is in place that specifies the length of time that forms, reports, and documents must be held prior to disposing of them. In others, it is at the discretion of the individual managers or top administrators.

Further, public organizations are encountering numerous requests to examine documents and reports as part of the provisions of the Freedom of Information Act and related pieces of legislation. The impact, both present and future, on the disposal of documents can often place a great burden on the agency's information system—meaning in some cases that a dual system of manual and automated reports must be maintained. Public managers, in tracking this first information flow activity, must pay close attention to both facets— preparation for entry and disposal after entry; each will absorb costs in staff time and resources.

Transaction Entry

The manner of transaction entry will vary from system to system, but the two predominant types are batch and online. Batch entry systems, as the term implies, involves the collection of the necessary data and entering them into the automated system at one time. Often done in card format, but increasingly being done on terminals, batch entry is suited for large-volume, standard procedures. Posting property tax receipts in a municipality is one example of a process that is suited for this form of entry. In terms of information flow analysis, it is important to note here that the unit that performs batch entry, as well as any procedures that may be involved, must verify that the data are keypunched or recorded properly.

Online entry, on the other hand, involves updating or editing a current file in the system, most often performed through a data terminal. Online entry is largely tailored for low-volume entry or for tasks demanding a fast turnaround. One of the problems with this form of data entry is that validation of the entry is more difficult. However, certain procedures can be installed to ameliorate the situation. These range from using a job entry log, which records on hard copy each transaction that takes place, to exception reports, which are generated each time an entry is made, which violates prescribed conditions. For example, a report may be produced when a claim exceeds a certain dollar limit or the social security number on the form entered does not match that on a claimant file.

As with batch processing, the unit responsible for the online entry and procedures adopted for data validation/verification should be duly noted.

Information Communication

This area overlaps to some extent with transaction entry as information communication embodies the entry→transmission→receipt of data. Along with the precautions to ensure proper entry, the evaluation of information transmission would involve examining message-sending capabilities of the present system. Are the data transmitted on leased or dedicated lines? Are there periods of peak usage that may affect the ability to use the system or transmit data? Are the data being transmitted efficiently (a 300 baud line versus a 900 baud)?

Evaluating the receipt of data would involve noting the recipients. Is it point to point in which the data entered go to one user or location? Or is it a distributed or ring network in which multiple users can receive the transmitted data? A highway construction bid letting schedule is an example of this second type in which each highway district is immediately informed when changes are made to the schedule (see Appendix C, a case study on programmed project management in Pennsylvania). The evaluation should also consider the security of data reception so that access is not violated. Chapter 8 discusses a number of the specific steps that can be taken, but this information flow analysis should document the manner in which data transmitted are acknowledged.

Information Processing

Evaluating the processing capabilities of the information system entails a detailed examination of the hardware and software involved. Usually termed the "operating system," it is

> a group of programs that monitor and control all input/output and processing operations. As a software tool, it allocates and controls limited hardware resources. Programs that make up the operating system are usually developed by the computer manufacturer and applied to organizations purchasing their systems. They are designed to make the best use of the components for each *individual* computer system. Thus, an operating system that is effective for one type of system may be totally unusable on the equipment of another manufacturer. (Senn 1982, pp. 145-146)

This is an important point to bear in mind, particularly in evaluating the capabilities of a particular operating system. Each will be designed to address the needs of the organization, such as the number of users requiring online access, the priority of information processing requests, the ability to update and change files, and the like. Particular areas to look for here include the available software programs that tend to be accessed more often, and why. Are prepackaged (often termed "off-the-shelf") programs available that will suit users needs (BASIC, Visicalc, DBase II), rather than developing them in-house? Do these programs function smoothly, or are they prone to error?

In addition, it is necessary to look at the EDP support staff. Who controls the actual operation of the system itself? What resources does the staff have to handle and address user needs and inquiries? This may range from a full complement of systems analysts, programmers, and operators to a standalone system serviced by an outside vendor.

Does the organization time-share on its system, and to what extent? Time sharing is one avenue that organizations, particularly those in the private sector, have chosen in order to realize the benefits of optimal utilization of computing resources. Often, organizations find that their computing needs are not constant, and there are particular times during which they either peak or trail off. An alternative is to either purchase time with another organization's computer or to sell time with other organizations. This tends to be cost-effective, but it also presents the difficulty of determining access and priority. Even so, evaluations of operating systems should address the feasibility of this alternative.

Information Storage and Retrieval

Similar to the procedures involved in information processing, evaluation of information storage and retrieval will involve examining the hardware and software components of the computing system. In this area, however, attention is focused on ensuring the integrity of the data processed. For example, what procedures are installed for updating master files and handling transaction files? Are the master files periodically copied to tapes so that the system can be restored if there is an interruption? How are files maintained and archived? All of these questions should be sufficiently addressed in the evaluation, and the officials and units responsible for storage and retrieval noted accordingly.

Output Processing

As the last step in the requirement analysis, output processing refers to the dissemination of computer-generated reports and the disposal/archives of records and related data. We have previously mentioned that the organizational unit or division responsible for transaction origination should also be heavily involved in the archival function because computing personnel will frequently not be versed in the political or legal requirements for retaining or disposing of certain documents. Another activity in this area includes the distribution channels of various computer-generated reports and documents. It is necessary to evaluate the process by which users receive them and whether it is updated periodically to account for changes in personnel or changes in security access. Finally, output processing involves forms and form control. With the advent of such legislation as the Paperwork Control Act, control over the forms used for collecting and disseminating data is now an integral part of the information management function. Agencies should carefully document the manner in which forms are cleared for use and whether they are in conformance with such legislation.

The requirement analysis, as noted, involves a detailed look at the information management process from beginning to end. But it would be greatly deficient if it failed to incorporate some perception of the utility of the data and information produced. One way to address this question is to include a user survey at each stage (transaction origination, entry, processing, and so on). The particular unit and individuals involved would rate the information along the following dimensions:

- Accuracy
- Completeness
- Timeliness
- Understandability

For each of these dimensions, a scale from excellent to poor (or inadequate) may be used. Admittedly, this evaluation is often subjective and should not be treated separate from available indicators of information quantity or output; but it will provide a more complete picture of the agency's information environment. Based on the feedback received, the evaluation team may ask for specific examples of incomplete or inaccurate reports or information.

Total Costs over Expected Lifetime

Following closely on the requirement analysis portion of the evaluation, it is necessary to project the overall costs of the information system over its expected lifetime in the organization. This portion of the study should build on the previous cost center approach for first-year costs but is extended out over several years. Specific points to bear in mind here are the number of years to be included in the analysis and selection of the discount rate.

Table 6.1 shows an example of projecting the costs of computer installation and use over a five-year period. As this table illustrates, the first year will usually require the largest cost to the organization—nearly 49 percent of the costs over the five-year period selected. The reason behind this is the initial outlay required for hardware, software, and conversion; and once the system is in place certain assumptions are built into the analysis. For example, additional

TABLE 6.1. Example of Cost Forecast

Cost Element	Year 1	Year 2	Year 3	Year 4	Year 5
Software and conversion					
Database management system	$100,000	–	–	–	–
Communications software	15,000	–	–	–	–
Training programs	10,000	$ 5,000	$ 5,000	–	–
Other software	–	–	–	–	–
Conversion costs	20,000	20,000	25,000	$ 25,000	$ 25,000
Hardware					
Central memory	75,000	–	–	$ 50,000	–
Central processing unit	150,000	–	–	–	–
Storage devices	60,000	40,000	–	–	–
Terminals	15,000	15,000			
Other hardware	–	–		–	–
Personnel					
Database administration	75,000	80,000	80,000	85,000	100,000
Information analysis	–	–	–	–	–
Consultants	5,000	–	–	–	–
Other personnel	–	–	–	–	–
Total costs	$525,000	$160,000	$110,000	$160,000	$125,000

Source: Fred R. McFadden and James D. Surer, "Costs and Benefits of a Data Base System," in *Management Information Systems*, 2nd ed., ed. M. J. Riley (San Francisco: Holden Day, 1981), p. 343.

storage space and terminals will be required in subsequent years as new users and activities are added; personnel to oversee the operation of the system must be considered; and training of users is necessary. Naturally, the assumptions will vary from organization to organization, but they should be formally stated as part of the analysis.

In addition to stating critical assumptions, the analysis should be projected over a reasonable length of time. The example cited here is for five years, although the expected life of the hardware and software itself could be as much as ten to fifteen years. A five-year analysis is generally accepted as the norm. Technological, economic, political, and social developments will usually be of such an order that organizations must respond, and they will be different (whether structurally or in terms of procedures). In many cases, programs and priorities shift within and among agencies, so that analysis past the fifth year becomes risky at best. This does not, however, mean that managers should not consider long-term trends and directions. Rather, such long-term forecasts are better suited for narrative rather than analytic treatment and can still accompany the final report.

Another aspect to be addressed in calculating total costs of the information system over its expected lifetime is the selection of an appropriate discount rate and the use of present value techniques. The benefit of this approach is that it allows managers to evaluate the present worth of future costs. However, the critical issue concerns the discount rate used, as it must be sensitive to current and future economic conditions. Kraemer and King (1977), in evaluating the costs of municipal information systems, suggest that a discount rate of 8 percent is appropriate; but this may not truly reflect the opportunity costs of public investments. One alternative is to apply different discount rates in what is termed "sensitivity analysis." The benefit of sensitivity analysis is that managers can view the alternative scenarios at one time and assess the impact of changing discount rates.

The final step in cost analysis is measuring costs against some benefit standards. Unfortunately, articulating dollar benefits can be far more difficult, particularly in the area of information systems.

First, dollar estimates can be associated with cost reduction or avoidance. What this means is that the information system is expected to improve the efficiency of work activities or processes: The response time to clients or constituents is reduced, the number of errors in claims processing diminishes, projects are completed on time, and backlogs are reduced. This is one set of benefits.

Second, there are benefits associated with improvements. This may involve the ability to service more clients, to expand activities into areas that previously were not possible, or to provide managers with better data to make more informed decisions. The traditional contribution of information systems was to service the first type—converting manual operations and tasks to automated form—but we are witnessing increasing attention devoted to uses of information systems for program enhancement—the second type. Both types of benefits should be addressed in the analysis.

Finally, secondary or intangible benefits of information systems should also be noted. While dollar figures are often difficult to attach to them, they may range from improved office morale to increased level of worker skills and knowledge.

Consideration of Alternatives

As the fourth and final step in the evaluation study, consideration of alternatives to the present information system should be included as well. This will round out the study and provide managers and top officials with possible options to consider. Those performing the evaluation will undoubtedly have touched on certain weaknesses or limitations of the system, whether they are provided by managers or users surveyed or emerge from a close examination of hardware and software issues. It is important that they be included in this section because they are a germane part of any evaluation.

Alternatives that arise may include

- Restructuring the organization
- Better training of users
- Further decentralization or centralization of EDP systems
- Improved report dissemination
- Reduction of hard-copy reports
- Purchase of new hardware/software
- Time sharing with other organizations
- Improved access and security protection

This list is not intended to be all-inclusive, but it illustrates the mix of managerial and technical alternatives to be considered. One word of caution here: Individuals performing the evaluation itself should present such items for consideration by top officials and managers. Too often the impact of evaluations becomes lost or readily dismissed when officials sense a hidden agenda, and one alternative appears to be valued by evaluators over others. This doesn't mean that individuals involved in the analysis, when questioned, cannot offer a recommendation, but this remains outside the boundaries of the study itself.

IMPLEMENTATION OF THE STUDY

Upon completion of the information management study, the final report—consisting of the components previously discussed—should be compiled and presented to agency officials for consideration. Rather than take action on it immediately, the report should be circulated to agency managers for review and comment. Most of these managers will be current or future users of the information system, and such feedback is critical for determining future direction. But comments from managers not directly involved should be solicited because they are also part of the total information environment of the organization.

In addition, it may be in the best interest of the agency to obtain feedback from external bodies, whether they are funding agencies or oversight bodies. This has the added benefit of obtaining some assurance that data generated from the system are, or will be, in conformance with reporting requirements. At the same time, other agencies may rely on the organization for certain types and forms of information. Providing them with the information study is a further gesture of goodwill.

Not to be ignored are citizen organizations, advisory groups, and business associations that are the direct beneficiaries of the programs or services offered by the agency. Efforts to involve these external organizations and groups in the evaluation of the information system will often forestall future differences and can greatly facilitate changes that may be made.

SUMMARY

The value of information systems is an issue that must be directly addressed by managers, but it is also one that presents a number of challenges. The foremost problem is, of course, defining the value of data and information itself. For public organizations, information must be considered as having value when it contributes to the efficient and effective delivery of programs and services, *as well as* assists citizens in understanding and evaluating what government is doing. Unfortunately, this last goal remains the most elusive in designing and implementing information systems of value.

The evaluation of informations systems should also be approached in a systematic fashion, beginning with some understanding of what the study scope should include. Sufficient attention should be devoted to including the critical managers in the study and communicating the report findings to top management and appropriate external bodies. Whether or not the evaluation is rigorous, the organization should use this time to assess where it is with regard to its information environment and where it would like to go.

PART III:

POLICY, SECURITY, PRIVACY, AND FUTURE ISSUES

7

The Policy Implications
of Information Systems

The previous chapters introduced the reader to a number of the technical and managerial issues associated with computers and their role in public organizations. The focus of the discussion here will be at a different level—it will embrace both the internal and external settings of public agencies and the influence of information systems in the policy area.

One of the more interesting issues that concerns government officials today is the appropriate role of technology in shaping policies and subsequent program decisions. This same issue is further compounded when one considers the general impact of technology on organizations. Consider the following projections by Davidson (1984): "Worldwide sales in the computer and communications equipment market exceeded $100 billion in 1982. Growth rates for these markets as a whole are expected to continue at 15 to 20% per year for the foreseeable future. At that rate, total sales would exceed $1.5 trillion in 1999." (p. 97). In addition Hicks (1985) indicates that the sales of personal computers for business, home, science and education which were approximately $3 billion in 1982, and $6.5 billion in 1985, will grow at a similar rate.

Obviously, a number of critical issues will affect decisions to use technology and determine its role in the policy process. And while most managers and researchers generally argue that computers and the technology must be appropriately tailored to the political setting, there has been little systematic examination of this process (Danziger et al. 1982). Consequently, government information policy continues to be sporadic and, in many instances, a reaction to gross mismanagement. For example, since 1974 the U.S. General Accounting Office has estimated that it alone has issued 32 reports discussing "inadequate computer-related planning, improper development and modification of systems and software, deficiencies in equipment acquisition and operation, and the failure to provide adequate privacy protection and security for personal records and systems components" (U.S. General Accounting Office 1981b).

Many individuals argue that any attempt to develop uniform standards and operating policy for the use of computers is doomed to failure from the start because the technology is changing so rapidly that the ink will barely have time to dry on the paper before new, more sophisticated systems and software will render any policy useless. We will come back to this point at the end of the chapter and argue that government officials can indeed establish mechanisms and broad parameters for the collection, use, and dissemination of data and information. But before we arrive at that point, it is important to distinguish between information policy and right to privacy.

INFORMATION POLICY

Information policy is concerned, not with the use of information in the traditional policy setting, but rather with the laws, legislation, executive orders, and operating procedures associated with the control of and access to information. While the forefront of efforts to develop a uniform policy approach to the use of information has been at the federal level, there are indications that states and localities, as they move toward integrated data systems, must confront similar concerns about control of access and guarantees of individual rights of privacy (see Chapter 8). Currently, however, little attention is focused on the intergovernmental implications of information systems.

One reason for the piecemeal approach to information policy is that such efforts have tended to coalesce around one of four major areas: computers, freedom of information, privacy, and science information. A staff report of the Domestic Council Committee on the Right to Privacy (U.S. Government 1976) lists the numerous study commissions that have been formed in recent years to examine facets of these information areas:

- National Commission for Review of Federal and State Laws on Wiretapping and Electronic Surveillance, P.L. 90-351, June 19, 1968
- National Commission of Libraries and Information Science, P.L. 91-345, July 20, 1970
- Electronic Funds Transfer Commission, P.L. 93-495, October 28, 1974
- National Study Commission of Records and Documents of Federal Officials, P.L. 93-526, December 19, 1974
- National Historical Publications and Records Commission, P.L. 93-536, December 22, 1974
- Commission on Federal Paperwork, P.L. 93-556, December 27, 1974
- Privacy Protection Study Commission, P.L. 93-579, December 31, 1974
- National Commission of New Technological Uses of Copyrighted Works, P.L. 93-579, December 31, 1974

In addition, such legislation as the Paperwork Control Act of 1980, the Privacy Act of 1974, the Freedom of Information Act (as amended), the Federal Advisory Committee Act, and the Federal Reports Act of 1942 have had a significant impact on information practices and have led to the development of such bodies as the Office of Federal Information Policy in the Office of Management and Budget, the Office of Telecommunications Policy, the Domestic Council Committee on the Right to Privacy, and the former Office of Presidential Science Advisor (U.S. Government 1976).

Even with the plethora of acts, committees, and agencies involved in the issue of information management, it is generally agreed that these efforts have been piecemeal and fragmented and have overlooked governmentwide policy development. The U.S. General Accounting Office (1982), in a recent study of federal information systems, further urged that

> The Office of Management and Budget, which is responsible for Federal information policy, must clarify guidance concerning automated information security and take a stronger oversight role. Executive agencies must establish and maintain cost-effective administrative, physical, and technical controls to protect their automated systems from misuse.

At the state and local levels, a uniform policy approach to information and information systems is equally fragmented. In many cases, this is due to the historical growth pattern of computer operations in which budget and finance offices were the first to convert from manual to automated form. In the late 1960s, funding from such sources as the Law Enforcement Assistance Administration led to the exponential growth of automated systems for police jurisdictions. With each spurt in growth, control over computing and information resources became centered within these defined units. It is only with the trend toward distributed systems that states and localities have realized that policies are necessary to control the issue of information and ensure citizens' rights to privacy as well as access. In most cases, such policies have usually taken the form of executive directives. As legislatures and councils begin to develop their own staff and have an increased understanding of the potential and pitfalls of information systems, this is expected to lead to formal laws and statutes regulating their use.

Before leaving this discussion of information policy, it is worth noting that such policy does not consist solely of laws and regulations governing external use of information. Information policy also involves internal operating principles; this policy is dynamic in nature and is closely linked with external conditions.

At the initial stages of growth and development, the organization's information needs will be heavily oriented toward external developments and events. For public sector organizations, information policy would be governed by such factors as enabling legislation (for new agencies), political norms, and constituent preferences. Organizations at this stage seek to acquire information as a means of fulfilling their charters and building bases of support.

As organizations mature, their information needs and, consequently, their policy requirements will turn inward, focusing on internal maintenance activities. While broader laws and regulations will continue to prescribe the types and amounts of information that they will need, information policy will be more complex and subtle, reflecting management's needs to exercise control. Such policy, in some instances, may be found in operating and procedure manuals; but it usually is a reflection of the organization's leadership. The Federal Bureau of Investigation under J. Edgar Hoover was an example of this transition in information needs and policy. At its outset, the FBI was formally chartered by Congress to investigate domestic criminal organizations and activities. But as it continued to grow in both resources and political clout, it was able, under Hoover, to re-orient its mission and, indeed, determine its own information needs and requirements. This eventually led to such actions as the investigation of "suspected" subversives, illegal wiretaps, and the collection of sensitive information on political figures. Such operating policy was based more on leadership directive than any enabling law or legislation.

While the example of the Federal Bureau of Investigation is unique in many cases, it brings out the last point. Organizations, particularly those in government, may jeopardize their chances of survival by becoming insensitive to external developments. Information policy, to be effective, must be continually monitored (and changed if necessary) to ensure the proper balance between internal and external information needs.

THE ROLE OF INFORMATION SYSTEMS IN POLICY MATTERS

Information systems have been shown to be a strong asset to organizations, whether in regard to their ability to gain data from many sources or their ability to analyze and disseminate data and information in a timely manner. Yet the role of information technology, computers in particular, presents an interesting dilemma for government officials: How can we reconcile what, on the surface, seems to be a fundamental tension between democracy and technology? At issue are such matters as participation in policy decisions, questions of ownership, the role of technical expertise, and community preferences. Dutton (1982) best sums up this dilemma as follows:

> Americans have a somewhat split political culture in that there seems to be a fundamental tension between a faith in both democracy and technology. In some respects, this is a classic tension between democracy and bureaucracy, or rationality, or most broadly, technology. (p. 29)

In a sense, there is no fundamental choice between democracy and technology; rather, technology will always be shaped to the social and political setting. Perhaps another way to view the relationship between democracy and technology is to say that citizens value democracy as the *appropriate end* and technology as a *necessary means*. The difficulty rests in attempting to reconcile the two.

Politics and Computing

Kraemer and Dutton (1979), in a broad survey of computing in local governments, have suggested that technology, such as computers, can have a direct influence on politics. Specifically, they argue that technology can be an instrument of power for interests in the organization. They go on to examine the relationship of technology and power in government and list the following as the most accepted ones in government today:

- Bureaucratic politics: Computing tends to shift power to top managers (city managers, department heads, and the like).
- Technocratic politics: Computing tends to shift power to technicians or a technocratic elite.
- Old-style politics: Computing tends to shift power to top-elected officials.
- Pluralistic politics: Computing tends to benefit all those who influence computing decisions.
- Reinforcement politics: Computing will increase the decision-making effectiveness of those who control the government organization.

These forms are, of course, not mutually exclusive, as pluralistic as well as reinforcement politics may consist of top managers, technicians, or elected officials; but they serve to illustrate alternative political outcomes in using computer systems. What Kraemer and Dutton conclude is that computing, or generally technology, does not in and of itself result in shifts of power or control. Rather, computing tends to reinforce the position of those in power. The extent to which a government organization is dominated by technocrats, professional managers, or elected officials will determine the manner in which the technology is shaped. Danziger et al. (1982) make a similar point:

> Decision-making power over technological resources varies from setting to setting, with the dominance of particular groups contingent on the

local political system and its specific configuration of dominant values, interests, and actors. (p. 226)

It is therefore necessary to understand the full environment of the government organization prior to determining (and implementing) the appropriate technology.

CONTRIBUTIONS OF AUTOMATED INFORMATION SYSTEMS

The discussion thus far has centered on the role of information systems generally in the policy process of public organizations. As we have seen, this role is complex and involves a mix of individual, organizational, and environmental factors. Yet, although the contribution of automated information systems will be conditioned by these same factors, a number of significant inroads have been made in adapting their actual use in the policy setting. Generally, computerized information systems have been found to have potential value in the following areas (Danziger and Kling 1982):

- Problem finding
- Problem definition
- Providing information regarding alternatives
- Selecting among alternatives
- Policy argument

Problem Finding

The problem finding area refers to the ability of computers to search through and signal conditions that are out of the ordinary. Indeed, this particular task is relatively straightforward because it usually requires the ability to match data against a preprogrammed standard. Also referred to as exception reporting, this task can be performed either during sequential processing or triggered by an on-line system, and provides information on only those events requiring action. The other transactions are assumed to be routine, or within tolerable limits, and are processed accordingly.

One example of sequential processing exception reporting is the closing of accounting ledgers at the end of the month. During the process of posting accounts, a report is usually provided to the accounting staff of items that may include account codes that were improperly posted, deficit balances that were incurred, or transactions needing authorization. For small organizations, with a few hundred transactions per month, a sophisticated exception reporting system may not be necessary. Indeed, there are a number of commercially available software spreadsheets for office use (for example, VuCalc and VisiCalc).

For large organizations, which may encounter tens of thousands of transactions, this form of exception reporting is desirable and allows managers to focus their attention on critical areas. A more elaborate example of this same activity is performed each year by the Internal Revenue Service. Data from tax forms are entered into the computer system, first, to check mathematical computations; those returns whose figures may be outside tolerable limits are subsequently flagged for further checking and/or auditing. While we may not appreciate the efficiency with which the IRS may spot errors (particularly if money is owed), it has allowed this organization to concentrate more on enforcement than routine processing.

Another form of exception reporting—by an online system—is becoming more common as information systems are moving away from batch processing. The distinction here is that the exception is noted immediately rather than during subsequent processing; and in many cases, the computer system will then signal a report or will refuse to accept the data until an adjustment is made. Agencies responsible for claims processing are frequent users of this type. The data entry operator enters claimant information on the computer screen, and checks or warrants are issued as a result. If the claim is invalid for any reason, this transaction may be canceled to await further investigation.

An elaborate example is found in the Pennsylvania Department of Transportation case discussed at the end of this book. Here, an exception report is automatically triggered in each of the district headquarters when a change has been made to the automated bid-letting schedule for highway construction. Although there are a number of security and access provisions that determine who can make such changes, the benefit of this form of reporting is that it is timely and oriented to critical areas of attention.

Danziger and Kling (1982) correctly note that in many government organizations, local in particular, problem finding usually results from ad hoc examinations of data rather than from sophisticated exception reporting systems. This does not mean that such reporting systems are not valid, only that each organization will rely on information systems to varying degrees. Perhaps a cursory glance by managers of routine data reports is all that is necessary. For other situations, the nature of the problem may be so ill-structured that computers provide very little assistance at all.

Problem Definition

The problem definition stage is more removed from the routine scanning and processing of data that may signal the need for further action. In this area, the manager or decision maker attempts to determine the nature of the problem: What does it consist of? What are the ramifications of acting quickly or not acting quickly? How does this problem or issue relate to current or prior conditions and events?

Computerized information systems have limited utility in this area because this deals more with the conceptual nature of events and circumstances. But data provided by these systems may have a primary role in shedding light on particular patterns or sequences of events. For example, police officials may notice that at certain times of the month, the incidence of crime increases in their jurisdiction, and that this pattern is fairly constant throughout the year. They may dismiss the factor of seasons because the pattern is consistent in autumn as well as in spring. Upon closer study (or simple speculation), officials find that this higher pattern concides with the distribution of social security checks by the post office at a fixed time of the month. The problem, while not readily evident, was confirmed by the data provided.

Most administrators, when questioned, place the greatest importance on personal experience or intuition for problem-solving situations; the data supplied by information systems are valued to the extent that they support this intuitive sense (McGowan 1983a).

Providing Information Regarding Alternatives

The ability of computerized information systems to provide information regarding policy and program alternatives has been tremendously helped by advancements in the use of database and decision-support systems. Database systems should not be confused with data banks or the data bank approach. Data banks, according to Senn (1982)

> emphasize collecting and maintaining a large bank of very detailed data about all facets of operation and control of an organization. The assumption here is that it is impossible to identify management's information needs. So, the only sure way to meet current and future information requirements is to collect everything that is potentially relevant, provide for shareability, and develop means of access to the databank so that data can be retrieved when needed. (pp. 389-90)

Senn goes on to note that the cost in storage capacity alone is prohibitive for most public organizations. There are, however, organizations that operate and control data banks for the purpose of broader information dissemination to clients or constituents; the U.S. Bureau of the Census is perhaps the best known example.

Database systems, on the other hand, are "an integrated collection of data structured to model the natural relationships in the data" (Senn 1982, p. 509) and are processed by a variety of programs and software. The advantage of database systems is that they allow the user to organize, store, and retrieve data without concern for the technical considerations of record formats and storage structures (a concept referred to as data independence). For example, a manager may wish to know the historical, current, and projected status of a particular project. Rather than laboriously search through sequentially a historical file of all projects and then current and future project status files, the manager can, through the use of a project identification code, access each file simultaneously and bring the data together into one form or report. For purposes of program planning and policy decisions, this capability of readily accessing several sources of data has obvious benefits.

Decision-support systems are usually found at the next level or hierarchy of information use because they deal with the management information and reporting aspects of database management systems. Decision-support systems are those computer-based systems aimed at making strategic types of decisions. Similar to database systems, there is rapid access and use of multiple data files; but it is the manner in which the data are brought together that distinguishes the two. Decision-support systems are traditionally online and are structured to respond to "what if" type of interrogation. An example would be the ability of an executive or administrator to forecast sales volume given a 5 percent cost increase in resources and a slight decrease in transportation costs. Obviously, the need for a sophisticated decision-support system may not be critical (or cost-effective) for those organizations that do not require rapid access and response time. But for others, for instance, air traffic control, the investment far outstrips its liabilities.

Whether we use a database or a decision-support system, the capabilities exist for information systems to supply data to improve the selection of alternatives. One difficulty, however, is what Danziger et al. (1982) refers to as the "policymaker's complaint":

> they [the policymakers] sense that the appropriate and necessary data do exist, and that they are probably in the government's information systems; but they believe that these data are not readily available to them when they must gather information and when they must make a policy decision. (p. 155)

Obviously, information systems, to be useful at this level of decision making, must be integrated with the management and decision process of the particular organization.

Selecting Among Alternatives

The area of selecting appropriate policy or program alternatives parallels the area of problem definition, for, again, there are certain prerogatives that managers or officials reserve for themselves. One is control over the decision selection. Although the technical capabilities exist to perform this function (decision-support systems), this is rarely, if ever, delegated to computerized systems. To some extent, this is an example of the human being's assertion of control over the machine—to relinquish this control is traumatic for many individuals. The NASA space shuttle guidance system is a classic illustration of this phenomenon. While, in fact, five computer systems are programmed to control the entire operation of the shuttle from liftoff to landing, the chief pilot usually switches from automatic to manual on the landing approach—in a sense, exercising his skills as a pilot rather than as a passenger.

For many government organizations, this phenomenon may not be as critical or readily evident; but it illustrates the point that information systems at this stage merely *augment* rather than *supplant* the final decision. The contribution that they can make is one of filtering or narrowing down the field of choices.

Policy Argument

Computerized information systems have had a pronounced impact in the policy argument area; and this is evident at the federal, state, and local levels of government. The contribution here stems from our earlier discussion of the politics of computing and, more specifically, that of reinforcement politics, for the data and information that are furnished are often used to justify the decisions reached. Computers naturally are valued for this instrumental use, as widely evident in such forums as congressional hearings, appropriation meetings, and council debates. Proponents of one side or another will frequently rely on computer-generated reports to back their position as well as to diffuse the arguments of potential adversaries. Conversely, adversaries will marshall their own set of facts and figures to disprove the opposing side's arguments. It is rare that the information, in and of itself, is so compelling as to sway the decision to one side or another. In most cases, the chief executive or powerful elite will incorporate the information provided in the final decision because the very existence of such information cannot be readily dismissed or dispelled.

An encouraging sign is that oversight bodies, such as councils and legislatures, are becoming more receptive to the use of computer-generated information in such public forums. They are sensitive to its potential impact and are asking more probing questions of agency officials and administrators.

To sum up the contributions of automated information systems, it is possible to say that their overall contribution has been limited to date. But there are some positive signs that this is beginning to change. As professionals move into the political foray of policy debate and argument, they are increasingly using computerized information systems to address the many dimensions of policy questions. At the same time, the technology has advanced to more user-friendly systems that can handle nonroutine inquiries without a detailed knowledge of file structures or formats. Yet, as we move in this direction, there still remain some limitations and constraints that also should be addressed.

PROBLEMS WITH AUTOMATED INFORMATION SYSTEMS

As with any change or adjustment in the way decisions are reached or policies adopted, one must consider the broader environment in which these actions take place. The text so far has emphasized that managers, particularly those in government, are influenced by internal and external conditions; and while information technology has progressed through several stages of growth and development, so also has management technology. Unfortunately, these stages of growth and development do not always coincide. It was suggested earlier that technology as such is often molded to the cultural, economic, and political setting of the particular organization or agency—a contingency-based approach if you wish.

Dutton (1982) has characterized computing in local government as being

- Underfinanced and understaffed
- Nonstandardized even though overlapping across jurisdictions
- Dependent on regional communications networks
- Characterized by multiple, fragmented rather than integrated information systems
- Oriented toward administrative support and social control
- Governed by a pluralistic decision-making process
- Troubled by a split political culture

Of particular note, this listing, although directed at units of local government, would also apply to most state and federal efforts toward information management and operation. This is not to say that no inroads are being made—a number of which have been discussed in the text—but, in general, this particular climate still prevails.

Perhaps at the root of a number of critical issues in government today is the level of financial commitment that can be expected, and computerized information systems are quite susceptible here. The late 1960s and early 1970s witnessed a tremendous infusion of revenue-sharing monies and grant assistance to states and localities; and many of these jurisdictions saw fit to centralize their computer operations, usually converting tax and financial records from automated to manual form. At the same time, funds from the Law Enforcement Assistance Administration, in an effort to upgrade state and local criminal justice operations, gave a tremendous boost to the development of automated information systems in police departments. This led to the development of autonomous EDP units that primarily had a free rein on the type of equipment to be purchased, the areas of application, and the support staff to develop the necessary software. Other government units and agencies were, of course, able to benefit from this growth, but usually at a cost of priority over access and staff support.

With the increasing competition for computing resources in the late 1970s and early 1980s, this picture of revenue abundance began to fade. Centralized computing departments became less the domain of finance officers and more the tool of chief administrators. Applications branched out into such areas as planning, building code enforcement, transportation, personnel, and procurement. This pull and tug between applications and available computing resources led to increased concern over the control of information systems and the need for justification of additional expenditures; budget offices as well as legislatures were not as willing to give EDP officials a blank check for their operations. The end result was a redistribution of computing resources to more users. The growth of better database management systems and mini- and microcomputer technology allowed units and smaller agencies to tailor the equipment to their information processing needs.

Yet the critical issue is the level of funding needed to service applications and a heterogeneous group of users. The state of New Jersey, for example, spends eight-tenths of 1 percent of its operating budget on automation, compared to insurance companies and other private firms, which average 17 percent of their operating budget. Clearly, a stronger case needs to be made for thorough needs assessments of information systems and their expected return on the investment. While dollar benefits associated with improved processing of routine claims and transactions can be readily derived, the expected return for managerial reporting and decision-support applications is more elusive. Indeed, this may be a powerful explanation for most organizations' hesitancy to invest in such higher-order uses.

Another difficulty closely associated with the lack of monetary resources is the lack of analytic and support staff. Government organizations are rife with stories of systems analysts and programmers who, once fully trained, immediately go to work in the private sector for a much higher salary. Recommendations for stemming this exodus range from paying competitive salaries to passivity (sustaining a steady turnover of skills and talent). With the growth in commercially available software, this problem is not as severe for routine forms of tasks and functions. As the nature of the tasks become more complex and nonroutine, however, the problem of staff shortages can be severe. Civil service restrictions also limit the ability of managers to transfer individuals out of their job classification. In an area such as policy and program planning, which by its very nature is diffuse and ill-defined, administrators often resort to ad hoc project staffing to service their needs (McGowan and Loveless 1981).

Nonstandardized and fragmented hardware, software, and procedures have been one of the primary sources of problems in the ability of government computer systems to be either cost-effective or time-efficient. One reason for this, according to the U.S. General Accounting Office, is that computer acquisition and operating practices in government are woefully inadequate and in need of dramatic revision (U.S. Government Accounting Office 1981).

In its study of 18 nonfederal organizations, the GAO found that a critical measure of the success of information systems is user-involvement in the acquisition process. Too often, government agencies purchase equipment and services from several hardware and software vendors, each developing computer systems tailored to the specifications (input documents, report formats) of specific units within the agency. With such disjointed, bottom-up development, it is little wonder that agency officials and administrators are amazed when they find out that one system cannot "talk" to the other—even though the nature of the tasks may be quite similar. Another contributing factor noted by the GAO is government's procurement practices, which require several bids on each major contract. This tendency to distribute the computing largess, while firmly rooted in government's role as a broker for various interests, further aggravates the problem.

The role of computers in the policy process will only be effective when these systems involve all potential users in the procurement and implementation phases. Once an EDP plan has been formally articulated, staff can then work on developing the necessary technical specifications to ensure compatibility.

The dependence on regional communication networks is a problem that is particularly acute at the local level. The data bank and data bank approach (previously discussed) was an effort by a number of federal and state agencies to collect large volumes of data and information for the purpose of handling any possible inquiry or issue related to a particular subject area. Prime examples of regional (as well as national) communication networks are the Uniform Fire Incident Reporting System and the Uniform Crime Report System. The purpose of these two systems, which are developed around standard reporting documents and computer data entry/access, is to collect and provide information of potential use to states and localities. This information may range from statistical summaries and analyses of an agency's activities to trend and location data for purposes of planning, scheduling, or allocating resources.

Unfortunately, the contributions of such regional information networks have been far from dramatic:

> While the data have the potential to provide some analysis of trends . . . they have not, to date, been effectively used for adjusting manpower schedules to follow seasonal events nor to redraw district boundaries by rate of incidence. Whether this can be attributed to financial or political factors (e.g., labor-management agreements, entrenched constituent interests) should not be dismissed, but it is clear that a full commitment to the use of these data has not been made. (McGowan 1982, p. 159)

Regional communication networks, therefore, appear to be viewed more as a one-way conduit for channeling data to state and federal levels rather than as a decision or policy tool.

The orientation of automated information systems toward administrative support or social control has been another problem that has constrained and limited its development in the policy area. Essentially, this emphasis reflects the origin of information systems as a tool of central finance and administrative offices. Administrators quickly saw the potential of computers in converting manual systems and files to automated form and, in turn, reducing clerical and staff overhead. Although the large-scale reductions in personnel never materialized as expected, the tendency to use computers for administrative support activities continues. Indeed, it is estimated that nearly 70 to 80 percent of the use of computer systems in government organizations is devoted toward such tasks as routine processing and summary reporting.

As for social control and information systems, this function is not as evident or pervasive in most government organizations; but it still raises some serious policy and equity questions. There is increasing concern over government's access to and use of information concerning citizens. With the advent of sophisticated information technology, certain agencies are now able to develop a full profile on individuals, ranging from tax and income history to employment status to creditworthiness to health data. In Chapter 8 a number of these concerns are further discussed; but it is important to note here that groups such as the American Civil Liberties Union have long expressed concern over government's use of information, more in terms of social control than social benefit. If computerized systems are to have a meaningful contribution to informed policy debate and decisions, then some means must be sought to ensure citizen access. Community information policy boards are one example of efforts to move in this direction.

The last two areas—a pluralistic decision-making process and a split political culture—should not be construed as flaws in the use of automated information systems. Rather, these are products of the American political system, which ensures the exercise of differing points of view and a democratic process. Some would claim that this represents a triumph of democracy over technology. Even so, this means that information systems cannot (and should not) be expected always to operate as highly efficient, neutral machines. Our culture instills a certain element of tolerance for ambiguity and, often, less than optimal results that, if sacrificed, would lead to rule by a technocratic elite. Given this, computers should be valued as a useful *means*, not an end.

Problems associated with information systems are not problems in the purest sense of the word. These systems are often limited in many cases due to poor management practices that have installed redundant or fragmented approaches. In other situations, it is the nature of the democratic process that has had a significant influence on how they are implemented and used. We have seen that the potential is there for information systems to assist the policy process.

FUTURE DEVELOPMENTS AND PROSPECTS
IN THE POLICY PROCESS

Computerized information systems can be a powerful tool in the policy process. Their ability to assimilate and process large bodies of data has permitted managers and agency officials to respond to constituent and other interests in a timely and reliable fashion. At the same time, this expansion in the technology has fueled an insatiable appetite on the part of individuals to gather more data about what is going on around them, not only in the work setting but in leisure activities as well. With the struggle for information comes a subsequent struggle for power and control. In the policy process, information systems often have this instrumental value, serving to reinforce the position of those in power (reinforcement politics). As previously noted, they are used more for administrative support and social control than for rational argumentation and social betterment. It is therefore useful to consider what adjustments can be made to improve the prospects of information systems, overall, in the policy process.

Agency Prospects for Reform

Policies, Procedures, and Guidelines

A corollary to the justification of the need to gather and process data is a uniform information policy for the individual agency. This should be done in coordination with a governmentwide policy that defines the criteria and rules of access to data; but even in the absence of such policy directives, the organization should adopt a long-range information plan. This plan would articulate the basic goals and mission of the organization and the information needs associated with them. Also included in this plan would be the long-term objectives and the key actors who may be involved (agency personnel, support groups, constituents, suppliers). With this plan as a base, short-range plans and specific information routines and activities to fulfill these plans can then be generated and naturally tied to the budget and accounting procedures noted above.

One of the keys to the success of such short- and long-range plans is the participation of key individuals in their development and use. Too often, such plans have become mere window dressing for those in the agency when they fail to acknowledge the limitations of the environment in which they must operate (fixed or declining resources, political considerations, and the like). It is far better to proceed cautiously during these stages than to make grandiose projections that are doomed to failure. Obviously, as the agency gains experience with the use of computerized information systems, it can build this into future plans. The creation of an agency information policy board or committee is one way to improve this process.

Structural Arrangements

Perhaps one of the more controversial subjects in the development and use of automated information systems is the configuration of the data processing system itself. In the area of policymaking and the decision process, this has strong overtones for the control of resources and, ultimately, the exercise of power and influence. Certain groups argue that "radical decentralization" is necessary if democratization is to be achieved (Danziger et al. 1982). Others argue, in marked contrast, that centralization is the answer if we are ever to overcome the fragmentation and redundancy that have continually plagued information systems in government (Kettinger 1980).

The solution is not so simple. Rather, it depends on the stage of growth and development of the particular organization. For those organizations that are in the initial stages of information use (converting from manual to automated form, focusing on operational uses of data and information), a centralized approach is necessary to bring information management into the overall management framework. This may involve establishing a central body responsible for the development of procedures for planning, costing, controlling, budgeting, and evaluating information (Kettinger 1980). In terms of hardware and software configuration, database management systems are quite adept in providing this centralized function, yet can also be tailored to more management and policy-oriented applications.

As the agency gains more exposure to the use of information systems, it can then tolerate a certain degree of decentralization of computing resources. With the advent of distributed systems, users can gain the necessary experience and can structure their individual needs without reliance on a central body. One of the concerns here is that such decentralization should be accompanied by specific guidelines concerning accessibility, privacy, and security of information. As with the development of information policies and procedures, the advice is to proceed in an incremental fashion—agencies should make organizational changes as the management situation, rather than the technology, dictates.

Government Prospects for Reform

Looking beyond the individual agency's environment, the political and social setting of public agencies must also be considered. Unfortunately, the extent to which one group or agency can push for information reform tends to be limited. But, given the increasing level of awareness of the capabilities (and limitations) of computers and information systems, some inroads can be made here as well.

Data Impact Statement and Data Appropriation Committees

Within the last decade, legislators and various oversight committees have grown somewhat cautious in authorizing legislation or appropriating additional funds without a full understanding of its intended impact. This caution has led to the extensive use of environmental impact statements in the areas of housing development, road construction, nuclear reactor licensing, and the like. Lately, legislators have also asked for economic impact statements in new proposals. These impact statements—environmental and economic—are intended to document as much as possible the primary and secondary costs and benefits of a proposed activity.

Governmentwide Policies and Guidelines

Previously mentioned as a necessary procedure for individual agencies, it is important that government—federal, state, and local—develop uniform information policy guidelines. Legislation in the past (Paperwork Reduction Act of 1980, the Privacy Act of 1974, for example) has made some inroads in the area of information management and control; but it has been piecemeal and fragmented, generally applied on an ad hoc basis to specific agencies or classes of activities. What is needed are specific policy directives and guidelines that encompass the broader realm of information management. This should involve a requirement that information standards and criteria be developed and approved prior to purchasing resources and equipment. Further, such standards and criteria should be examined with a view toward integration with other agencies or levels of government as well as industry. In addition, this broad information policy should address the issue of procurement with an eye toward developing compatible systems and information networks.

Finally, a governmentwide information policy board should be established. The purpose of this board would be to assist in the development and oversight of information standards, the assessment of information value/burden costs, and review of agency information plans. Whether they are established at the federal, state, or local level, such boards should be responsible for long-term information planning and should also serve as a type of appeals court whereby individual or group concerns over government information collection, use, or dissemination can be aired. Naturally, the effectiveness of such policy boards will be determined by the resources that are allocated for their operation, the board membership, and the extent to which they are able to influence the mainstream of policy decisions and practices. While the means are there, such boards must still engage in the pull and tug of politics.

Citizen Input and Citizen-Oriented Applications

One final recommendation is a call for more citizen-oriented applications of information systems, away from the traditional focus on administrative support or social control. With the concern for greater decentralization and democratization of the political process comes a similar concern over the control of the existing technology as a means of increasing citizen participation in the policy generation process. The technology can be readily adapted to this need; individuals now have the capability to tie into a variety of databases and information networks using a moderate-sized home computer. Unfortunately, this also brings in the issue of class distinctions; those who can afford a reasonably sized home computer have this capability.

It is therefore important that government organizations proceed cautiously in this area to avoid disfranchising certain groups or individuals. One means of preventing this is to include citizen representatives on information policy boards. Another step is to communicate openly the process by which computerized information systems are procured and implemented. Too often, this process is shrouded in a veil of mystery or secrecy; and citizens learn of the system long after it is in place. This communication process should emphasize the anticipated benefits as well as costs to the community and should take place in an open hearing format to allow various points of view to be expressed.

Finally, public officials and agency managers should begin to give serious consideration to citizen-oriented applications of computer systems. With the growth of database and distributed process systems, a number of activities that once required cutting through several layers of bureaucracy may be drastically altered. From motor vehicles to tax records to building construction, a system can be developed that allows citizen inquiries and streamlined processing. The cost of building in the necessary security protection and inquiry charges will be more than offset by the benefit of diminished frustration with traditional bureaucratic procedures. But it is this last point, bureaucratic procedures and the reluctance of individual agencies to pool information resources, that has plagued most efforts in this area. The impetus for this change will, of course, depend on the particular government setting and its leadership. With the rising tide of technology and citizen awareness, this barrier, too, will erode.

SUMMARY

The development of policy-oriented uses of information has been relatively slow and fragmented. The reason for this is that the technology will always be shaped to the social and political setting of the government; citizens value democracy as the appropriate end and technology as a necessary means. In addition, the environment of each government agency is unique, encompassing professional, administrative, and structural attributes that, together, determine how policy and program decisions are derived.

Automated information systems can greatly aid the policy process by facilitating the finding of problems, providing information regarding alternatives, and supporting particular policy positions. As professionals enter government, they are increasingly using computerized information systems to address the many dimensions of policy questions. At the same time, the technology has advanced to more user-friendly systems that can handle nonroutine inquiries without a detailed knowledge of file structures or formats.

Yet the use of information systems in the policy process is not without its difficulties. Most of these difficulties result, not from the technology itself, but from poor management practices that have installed redundant or fragmented approaches. At the same time, the nature of our democratic policy process has had a significant influence on how these systems are implemented and used.

Future developments and prospects for information systems involve a mix of agency-specific and broader governmental steps. These range from improved education and training of managers to uniform information policies and guidelines to more citizen-oriented applications of computer systems. The chances for the success of any of these recommended steps will depend on the impetus for change in the social and political setting.

8

Societal, Security, and Privacy Considerations in the Use of Information Systems

Information can be a powerful tool in the policy process of governmental decision making. So, too, is information an important resource for social control. This raises such questions as which groups or individuals have access to information, and for what ends is the information intended. While most of us today have not been involved in situations where this question is directly asked, we can undoubtedly recall times in which we have speculated over *who else* has seen my file, how did the bank or finance agency learn my credit history so quickly, or what are my chances of not paying a parking ticket and getting caught. In each case, data and information are collected, processed, and used to serve a particular objective, and in each, the result will affect us personally.

For government organizations, the issue of control over information takes on added significance because it deals with such concerns as the guarantee of individual liberties, the right of access to public records and documents, and, most importantly, the public interest. Obviously, a number of cross-cutting issues must be addressed. This chapter will attempt to delineate what many of these issues are. In addition, it will touch on the management and operational concerns involved in collecting and using information in an environment of administrative, legal, and statutory constraints. Finally, it will provide a series of recommendations to guide public managers in structuring information systems that are sensitive to the need to protect individual and group rights.

INFLUENCE OF INFORMATION ON
SOCIETY AND INDIVIDUALS

Information abounds in our society, whether it be about ourselves or groups and organizations to which we belong. This information can take a variety of forms. It can be contained in a personnel folder, in banking records, in agency reports, or in the daily newspaper. It can also take on a less formal nature, such as a memorandum, a face-to-face conversation, or our own speculative thoughts and reactions. In other words, limitless sources and types of information are available for a variety of purposes.

As our society grows more complex and the use of technology increases, the demand for information also increases, often at an exponential rate. We are becoming "information-hungry." This is dramatically seen in the use of computers in the work setting and at home. A decade ago, computers were often associated with the notion of "Big Brother," to borrow from George Orwell. They were seen as instruments by which government as well as industry sought to gain data and information on us—often with little concern for our welfare or ultimate benefit.

The 1960s and 1970s saw a rising concern for the rights of individuals vis-a-vis government and industry. While the technology, largely television, allowed us to experience firsthand the dramatic events of the Vietnam War and Watergate, it also raised serious questions about government's ability to act in our regard. This culminated in a series of laws and actions intended to correct the perceived imbalance (such as the Privacy Act of 1974). At the same time, individals sought to gain increasing control over their own events. The advent of smaller, affordable computers is a natural expression of this behavior; and it is a trend that is expected to increase. Of particular interest, we are not witnessing a new variation of this earlier phenomenon—individuals want to gain more information in the hopes of increasing individual control. So we now have agencies competing against one another for control over information resources. Using home computers individuals can tie into larger database systems and perform a variety of tasks that were impossible to perform five years ago. What this means is that the influence of information and information systems is much more pervasive; unfortunately, the concerns over security, privacy, and rights of access have not been adequately addressed. To do so properly, it is best to examine the various levels of influence that information can have.

Social Influences

The social influences of information will be largely determined by the particular mix of norms, values, and culture of the state or nation. What this means is that developing or third world societies must grapple with a set of issues that may, indeed, separate them from the more developed or industrialized nations. This is not to say that there are no predominant or superordinate concerns that are found in both. Rather, the particular ends (as well as means) involved in collecting and using information frequently differ.

The twentieth century was a wellspring of developments in the social structure of the United States. The Industrial Revolution led to the ascendancy of the formal organization and all of the management and control activities associated with business enterprise. At the same time, the actions of government relative to individuals began to encompass a larger sphere of events—the registration of births and deaths and the issuing of passports, marriage certificates, and drivers licenses. But three particular events stand out in terms of their impact on the social influences of information.

The first is the emergence of consumer credit and insurance. It is estimated that the amount of consumer credit grew from approximately $1 billion in 1900 to nearly $218 billion by 1976 (Rule et al. 1980). With the growth of consumer confidence and use of credit, a genuine cottage industry of credit reporting soon followed, leading to a sophisticated (and some claim intrusive) information network:

> The computer system of TRW Credit Data, one of the largest on-line computer systems in the country, in 1977 held information on an estimated 70 million consumers, and was capable of generating more than 200,000 credit reports daily. TRW Credit Data sold over 22 million credit reports in 1977. (Rule et al. 1980, p. 38)

Similarly, the record-keeping system associated with insurance and insurance reporting blossomed as well. Ranging from individual health and life claims to auto, home, and corporate insurance (malpractice, liability), the insurance industry was another avenue in which data and information were rapidly exchanged and scrutinized.

The second major influence on information collection and use was income tax reporting. But, as Rule et al. (1980) note, this is a relatively recent phenomenon—growing at an exponential rate since World War II. While the complexity and subtleties of the tax code often precluded rapid automation, by 1975 the IRS had 3,200 data retrieval terminals in use in its service centers and field offices. With current efforts to simplify the form and nature of tax reporting, this capacity can be expected to increase. At the same time, the IRS is attempting to strengthen its surveillance of returns by gaining access to bank and other records; this will obviously lead to stronger calls for the protection of individual rights and liberties.

Finally, the implementation of social security in 1936 has had perhaps the most dramatic impact on the collection and transfer of information:

> Today the (Social Security) system maintains records on some 140 million living Americans. Contents of these files obviously vary greatly. But most files maintain data on basic matters such as name, data of birth, sex, race, yearly earnings, work history, and benefit history. Under certain circumstances, Social Security files may also include data on circumstances surrounding eligibility for benefits, alcoholism or drug addiction, financial resources other than earned income, etc. (Rule et al. 1980, p. 41)

The social security number has taken on the form of a universal identifier. Indeed, it is rare when a person does not fill out a form or application without automatically listing his or her social security number. The benefit of this identifier is that it allows government and industry to scrutinize several sources about an individual in a fairly efficient manner; the concern, of course, is that this further heightens the anxiety over "Big Brotherism." Critics further charge that surveillance by social security number is a misdirected effort because it fails to track illegal aliens and businesses—those that profit most by not being so readily identified.

Another event worthy of mention was the development of the National Crime Information Center in 1967. Under the direction of the Federal Bureau of Investigation, this center is a data bank of information on crime and criminal activities that is available for use by law enforcement agencies throughout the United States and Canada. While most law enforcement agencies tend to use the system to inquire about specific instances of criminal behavior, the capabilities exist for large comparative analysis with other jurisdictions or performance over time.

By the 1960s and 1970s, as previously discussed, the concern over access to individual records and subsequent uses of information from them came to a climax. Most of this concern was focused on federal information activities. This is not to say that the states and localities were not involved but rather that these jurisdictions tended to orient their information systems to licensing and revenue collection.

In 1970, the Fair Credit Reporting Act was passed:

> The intent of the . . . Act was, first, to create mechanisms for the public to understand credit-reporting practices and monitor the effect of these practices on their lives. Second, it was to establish ways of resolving differences over credit information. . . . Third, it was to create legal responsibilities on the part of bureaus to maintain certain minimum standards of care and competence in their reporting practices. (Rule et al. 1980, p. 89)

Some have hailed this act as a victory for individual consumers in their battle with industry, and, to some extent, this is true. It has focused the spotlight on credit-reporting practices and the possibilities for abuse. But others argue the reverse. Rather, the Fair Credit Reporting Act simply legitimated the practices of collecting and selling personal data, with little if any restrictions on the industry.

The Privacy Act of 1974 was largely a result of the publication in 1973 of the Report to the Secretary of the Department of Health, Education, and Welfare by its Advisory Committee on Automated Personal Data Systems. The impact of the Privacy Act on agency information activities will be examined in more detail in a later section; here it is sufficient to note that the act set out certain guidelines for the disclosure of personal data files to other agencies or individuals. In addition, it provided for individual access to one's records and the ability to dispute their contents. As with the Fair Credit Reporting Act, there are mixed opinions as to the effectiveness in ensuring individual liberties. But there can be little argument that it has changed the nature of government information collection and use.

Finally, the Paperwork Control Act of 1980, also known as the Brooks Act, is the latest effort to control a number of the problems associated with the collection and use of information. While the Privacy Act was aimed at ensuring the rights of access to personal information, the Paper Control Act was intended to correct a number of deficiencies in information *management*. Specifically, it attempted to reduce the burden of information processing on the public and private industry by implementing standards for collecting information (for example, prior approval by the Office of Management and Budget of agency forms). In addition, it established an Office of Federal Information Policy in the OMB to monitor and direct, if necessary, information practices by government agencies. One concern that has been expressed is that the establishment of a central oversight body in the Office of Management and Budget will still make information policies and practices subject to political influences. Whether the Paperwork Control Act is living up to these expectations remains to be seen; but there is little argument that some reform of federal information practices was indeed necessary.

To summarize, the social influences of information systems undergo change as society itself becomes more complex, mobile, and heterogeneous. In those societies with a strong, centralized government, information practices may tend to emphasize control and standardization. Individual rights or recourse to dispute the type or form of information collected may be severely constrained. In some nations, a divisive population or fragmented government may impose its own limitations—unable or unwilling to generate or collect data on the health, economic status, and demographics of its populace. In the United States, we have witnessed a transformation from a society in which little personal data and information were asked for and obtained to one in which extensive profiles of each citizen are available for ready access and scrutiny. As societies become more information-intensive, the need for provisions to protect individual liberties and rights to privacy becomes greater. Although laws and statutes become the basic foundation on which to build such protection, they alone do not provide the sole guarantee.

Individual Influences

By individual influences on information, we are referring to the character or operating style of individual managers in government that may have a direct, as well as indirect, bearing on how information is collected and used. The discussion here is framed around a particularly insightful work by Elliott Morss and Robert Rich, *Government Information Management* (1980). While these authors take a close look at those information practices that place an undue and costly burden on citizens and industry, they also note that bureaucratic power—the desire of bureaucrats to seek and maintain control—is a fundamental factor that influences how information is collected and used.

Bureaucratic power may be traced back to the beginnings of formal organizations themselves. With the desire to standardize production and deliver goods and services in the most efficient manner, an impetus to gain necessary technical expertise grew as well; information and knowledge associated with such expertise became as much of a critical resource as revenue and material goods and supplies. Society today, with its emphasis on professionalism, accreditation, and technical know-how, has made such knowledge even more critical. This is particularly evident in legal hearings or committee sessions where "expert witnesses" are used by one side or the other to lend an aura of credibility to the proceedings. The purpose of this advice is to shed additional light on what otherwise would be a confused or subjective debate. Unfortunately, this usually adds further confusion when expert witnesses counter other expert witnesses.

The point here is that information is power for individuals, bureaucrats in particular. Morss and Rich take this notion a step farther and discuss "bureaucratic pathologies" that are associated with the collection and use of information. Such pathologies, they argue, have frequently resulted in excessive burdens for industry as well as individuals.

Briefly, Morss and Rich categorize the pathologies into two classes: those that are *directly related* and *indirectly related* to excessive information requirements/production. The following constitute pathologies that are directly related to such practices: (1) the inability to specify clear objectives, (2) protecting bureaucratic interests through secrecy, and (3) protecting bureaucratic interests by avoiding embarrassment and risk.

The first pathology, the inability to specify clear objectives, has already been extensively treated in Chapter 7. It relates to the nature of the policymaking process that promotes vagueness and the lack of specificity. Often bureaucrats encourage this lack of detail, particularly with regard to enabling legislation, because it lets them broadly interpret legislative intent and thereby increases their bases of power. The expected results are programs and activities that necessitate the collection of additional information. The Environmental Protection

Agency, when it was implementing the Clean Air Act, interpreted this to mean that it was responsible for developing national standards that defined the amount of pollution allowable. This later evolved into the implementation and enforcement of such standards and the development of a rigorous system for monitoring and inspection. Critics have charged that the EPA has done little to address the original problem of air standards and that its enforcement has been selective and lax.

The protection of bureaucratic interests through secrecy, the second pathology having a direct influence, is deeply rooted in the concept of organizational survival. One means of maintaining power is controlling the flow of information to others. The role of secrecy has a viable role in the protection of national interests and has been rigorously enforced in such agencies as the Departments of Defense and State, the Federal Bureau of Investigation, the National Security Agency, and the Central Intelligence Agency. It is when secrecy is used to serve individual interests that it becomes dysfunctional, resulting in a lack of cooperation, the development of redundant or fragmented information systems, and the like. The General Accounting Office has issued numerous reports on this one phenomenon—claiming that coordinated information practices at the federal level are constrained, not by the technology, but by the reluctance of agencies to share information.

Finally, protecting bureaucratic interests by avoiding embarrassment and risk also leads to inefficient information management. Morss and Rich refer to this as "protecting oneself and one's turf" through such practices as establishing a study commission or committee to investigate a particular issue or engaging in numerous studies or analyses merely as a means of forestalling external review or scrutiny. The end result, naturally, is a great deal of activity that consumes time and resources.

All three actions, the authors conclude, serve neither the public nor industry and simply increase the amount of information that must be collected and processed.

CONTROL OF INFORMATION SYSTEMS IN SOCIETY

Having looked at the types of social, individual, and government influences that have been exercised in collecting and using information, the reader undoubtedly has come to the conclusion that information has been used to further narrow interests rather than broad societal goals. To a large degree, this is true. Because of the pluralistic nature of our governmental system in which various positions and viewpoints are tolerated and accepted, the competition over data and information as a political resource will continue to be fierce. As agencies and bureaucrats vie over program and budgetary control, so, too, will they treat information systems in a similar manner. Unfortunately, the avenues of recourse for the average citizen are limited at best. The following listing, provided by the Commission on Federal Paperwork, highlights a number of citizen complaints concerning government information activities (Horton and Marchand 1982):

- Forms/reports are difficult or complex.
- Costs are excessive.
- Regulations are too complex.
- There is too much overregulation.
- Reporting is too frequent.
- Reporting periods are irregular.
- Filing dates not staggered.
- There is continuous/intensive reporting in lieu of sampling.
- The time frames are unrealistic.
- The review times are unrealistic.
- Audits are excessive.
- There are excessive number of copies.
- There is no data interchange.
- Data are duplicated.
- Little intergovernmental cooperation exists.
- There is a lack of centralized control.
- No central data files exist.
- Forms are not standardized.
- There is a lack of coordination between forms and regulations.
- Forms are the same length regardless of respondent size and capability.
- Programs, systems, and policies are not standard.
- Retention/storage of dated records.
- Form sizes and other specifications are irregular.
- Invasions of privacy occur.
- Confidential information is disclosed.
- Laws, rules, regulations, or administrative procedures are discriminatory.

- Public servants' behavior and attitudes are unhelpful.
- Public servants have inadequate training and skills.
- Information is misused.

This listing provides a serious indictment of government information practices and the ultimate burden that it places on citizens, first, in terms of the direct cost of information collection and use, and second, in terms of the psychological burden. Not only are direct costs passed to the citizen through federal, state, and local taxes but they are absorbed by the individual consumer in product or service prices. As for psychological burdens, they can assume a variety of forms.

The invasion of privacy, an action that engenders a great deal of debate and controversy, has become a paramount concern of citizens today. Individuals are increasingly anxious over government's right to require as well as use personal data and information. Some argue that the right to individual privacy must, in certain cases, be subordinated to broader societal interests and that this is a small price to pay, given issues of national security and the preservation of laws and other legal safeguards. Others, however, counter that in no cases does the individual forgo this basic right, and when government fails to protect individual privacy, it violates its social contract.

All of us have encountered the psychological burden of dehumanization in one form or another, whether we receive our bills on computer punch cards or are asked for our social security number rather than our name. Again, this is a price that is being paid by our changing society; but there is little argument that it tends to break down the personal interaction of individuals and groups. For government organizations, this tendency to dehumanize is often the form of bureaucracy itself in which procedure and process transcend other values or concerns. Unfortunately, this leads to a paradoxical situation: Public agencies that tend to personalize, or humanize, transactions may be guilty of appealing to individual exceptions rather than common standards. In either case, a flavor for individual spirit is lost, often resulting in passiveness and apathy.

The potential for the misuse of information will lead to increasing anxiety on the part of individual citizens. The politicization of the Internal Revenue Service under the Nixon administration is a vivid example of an excepted government practice (income tax reporting) that was used for less than honorable purposes. As these cases come to light, citizens begin to question the primary reason for supplying information and, wisely, call for adequate safeguards before doing so.

Finally, the legitimacy of an individual, institution, or political system becomes an important issue. With the tendency to seek additional control and influence, the question arises of where the role of government ends and that of the individual begins. Unfortunately, this fine line of distinction is becoming increasingly blurred, leading to questions of sovereignty versus individual liberty.

These four psychological burdens have raised the more fundamental issue of what safeguards can be built into information systems to ensure that individual rights will not be trampled upon in the name of government efficiency or control. To examine possible safeguards, it is best to look at the following levels of application: disclosure requirements and legal approaches and administrative guidelines.

Disclosure Requirements

Disclosure requirements refer to those policies and guidelines that govern the disclosure of information—whether on persons, groups, or organizations—from government agencies. With the advent of the Freedom of Information Act of 1966 and the Privacy Act of 1974, there has been an increasing tendency for legislators, often acting in response to citizen concerns, to directly proscribe procedures by which information shall be made available. The criteria for disclosure have been hotly contested in the courts, as clamor by the media for various government papers bear testimony; and there is also a growing concern that the release of too much information will paralyze government officials out of fear of disclosure. One characteristic response, particularly in Washington, is to label most material sensitive or in the national interest. This places an undue burden on the courts to decide; and in most cases, they have tended to use a "balance of interests" test in which the interest to the individual versus the nation as a whole is applied. Unfortunately, this does little to remedy the situation and forces a case-by-case judgment rather than a broad policy prescription.

Disclosure requirements, as they currently stand, follow two complementary paths: those prohibiting the release of information and those outlining the release of information. The first avenue is best exemplified in the Freedom of Information Act (1966), which lists nine categories of information that are *exempted* from disclosure (Kraemer and King 1977, p. 245):

1. Information on national defense or foreign policy, as required by executive order
2. Internal personnel rules and practices of an agency
3. Information exempted from disclosure by statute
4. Trade secrets and commercial or financial information obtained as privileged or confidential
5. Interagency and intraagency memoranda or letters, which would not otherwise be available by law
6. Personnel and medical files and similar files the disclosure of which would constitute a clearly unwarranted invasion of personal privacy
7. Investigatory files compiled for law enforcement purposes except to the extent available by law
8. Examination, operating, or condition reports for the regulation or supervision of financial institutions
9. Geological and geophysical information and data concerning wells

As can be seen from this list, the intent of the Freedom of Information Act was to establish boundaries around certain classes of information deemed sensitive in nature. At the same time, there is a great deal of information that is transferred within and among federal government agencies that remain protected (item 5 in the list).

States and localities vary on the extent to which data and information can be made available, but most, largely through sunshine legislation, have paralleled the federal effort in this area. One interesting point to note is that the Freedom of Information Act does not differentiate in terms of the form of information that is protected; thus computers and automated information systems are governed to the extent that they are used for such purposes as collecting confidential or personal data.

The second avenue of disclosure—that which outlines the release of information—again is not directed solely at the use of computers and information. The Privacy Act of 1974 exemplifies this form. The Privacy Act outlines procedures by which individual files and records are maintained by government agencies. In addition, it ensures individual access and the annual reporting by the agency of the "character" of its record system. Finally, and most significantly, this act provides for civil remedies and criminal penalties in the event of violation. But, as Rule et al. (1980) correctly note, this last action appears to be rarely invoked.

The Freedom of Information Act and the Privacy Act clearly provide a framework by which government agencies can or cannot disclose information. However, they have been open to broad interpretation by the agencies themselves and, in some cases, subject to flagrant disregard. The recent example of the failure of the director of the Environmental Protection Agency to release information on the use of federal funds to clean up hazardous waste sites is a case in point. The director invoked the right of executive privilege under orders from the White House, and the information was secured only after sufficient legislative and public pressure was exercised. Similarly, the General Accounting Office has strongly criticized the Office of Management and Budget for failing to live up to the intent of the Paperwork Reduction Act of 1980 in which the OMB was charged with developing uniform and consistent information policies and practices.

If one were to sum up the issue of disclosure requirements, it might best be labeled as one that is in a continual state of flux. Government officials—at the federal, state, and local levels—rest more on the principle of executive privilege. To release information and data is often to release control over this resource. The result, as expected, is a continuing pitched battle among executive agencies, legislators, the judiciary, and individual citizens over who will exercise such control.

Administrative Guidelines

The use of administrative guidelines to control abuse offers perhaps greater promise than legal or statutory prohibitions. One reason for this is that it recognizes the need for some discretionary use on the part of agency officials, allowing them to tailor information activities to the specific organizational setting. At the same time, administrative guidelines and procedures place the onus on the agencies themselves, rather than relying on the courts or the legislatures to exercise control.

Kraemer and King (1977), in a discussion of possible administrative and professional approaches, suggest that administrative guidelines, in the form of specific steps that should be taken to safeguard data and information systems, usually do not go far enough. At best, they frequently lay out basic principles on what constitutes proper conduct. An example they cite are the guidelines issued by the Council of the Association for Computing Machinery (ACM) in 1966:

1. An ACM member will have proper regard for the health, privacy, safety and general welfare of the public in performance of his professional duties.
2. An ACM member will act in professional matters as a faithful agent or trustee for each employer or client and will not disclose private information belonging to any present or former employer or client without his consent. (Kraemer and King 1977, p. 278)

One alternative is the development of codes of ethics or professional standards. The benefit of this type of an approach—distinct from the use of broad guidelines—is that it is a self-policing action by professionals in the field of information systems. Such groups as the National Association of State Information Systems have attempted to endorse a code of ethics for the use of government data systems. The International City Management Association has also promulgated suggested procedures for improving information systems acquisition and use.

The inherent difficulty with the use of codes of ethics or professional standards is that the "profession" of information systems is ill-defined and embraces a variety of backgrounds and technical orientations. The technology is changing so rapidly, and individuals are entering and exiting the field in such great numbers, that the notion of self-regulation is impractical. A more telling point, according to Kraemer and King (1977), is that the issue here is really one of organizational self-interest and survival rather than professional values. Given this, it is best to begin with the management systems in organizations themselves as a means of building in the necessary protection of individual, organizational, and societal interests.

MAKING INFORMATION SYSTEMS SECURE

In order to make government information systems secure, one must reconsider the nature of government organizations themselves. Obviously, they are faced with a number of day-to-day routine problems and issues that are characteristic of all organizations, both public and private. This involves meeting payroll and expenditure requirements, monitoring the use of resources, and accounting for results. Beyond this, these organizations must also address a broader range of political, economic, and social issues—defending programs before council or legislators, handling complaints and requests from vocal citizenry or constituent groups, and coordinating service delivery with other units or levels of government.

In this complex and varied environment of government activity, several layers of information control must be considered as well. Marchand and Stucker (1977) suggest that the following layers are of particular significance:

- Layer I: controls built into data processing system
- Layer II: physical security
- Layer III: administrative controls
- Layer IV: legal and societal controls

It is interesting to note that, as you proceed from layer I to layer IV, the greater the difficulty in providing security and the greater the costs. But each layer is nested in the one below it, so that system controls, physical security, and administrative controls—if properly constructed and implemented—should satisfy legal and social controls.

Legal and Social Controls

As previously noted, legislation will often prescribe the broad parameters within which data and information can be collected, processed, and utilized. Unfortunately, many managers and those working quite closely with information systems are often unaware of the direct implications for their agency or organizational unit. Therefore, in constructing and implementing such systems, it is important that legislative safeguards be adequately addressed. Kettinger (1980, pp. 147-48), in his work on implementing information systems, stresses that the following questions be examined by evaluators:

- Does the jurisdiction operate under a confidentiality statute? If so, what kind of information is covered by such legislation and to what extent are limitations imposed on its disclosure?

- How is "confidential" information described? Is the material to be withheld from disclosure specifically described in a statute or are particular criteria listed for determining confidentiality?
- If criteria are listed in the legislation, who determines whether the information satisfies these criteria?
- Does the jurisdiction's regulations and policies conform to other information laws or do they provide for withholding more information than is legally justifiable?
- Does the jurisdiction provide pledges of confidentiality for information that it may be required to disclose under Freedom of Information legislation? If the information is contained in a document that includes both privileged and non-privileged information, is the pledge of confidentiality limited to the privileged portions?
- Do the jurisdiction's regulations provide procedures whereby the providers of information may be notified before the agency decides to release the information?

The emphasis here is on a careful scrutiny by agency personnel of existing laws and statutes to ensure that the intent of such legislation is incorporated into information management practice. While this must be done at the federal, state, and local levels, it also requires an understanding of state and federal reporting requirements that may be imposed on the agency. In certain cases, organizations that receive federal or state support must obtain prior approval of information collection activities—whether it be a survey instrument or an affirmative action report. Managers should therefore allocate sufficient time in which these legislative and statutory requirements are fully inventoried and built into the system design.

In addition to the formal legal and statutory framework, this level of safeguards should consider broad agency policies toward the collection, use, and dissemination of information. In a sense, these policies are a formal statement of how legal and statutory pronouncements are defined by the agency and should be evaluated on this basis. If differences emerge on the validity of these policies, this will force the debate (and hopeful resolution) into the proper forum—the legislative/executive arena—thereby obviating the need to rely on judicial interpretation of legislative intent.

Kettinger (1980, pp. 148–49) again provides some useful guidelines for managers to follow in developing needed information policies:

- Collection of information—Is there some definition of who will put what information into the system, and under what circumstances?

- Public and restricted records—Is there an analysis of what records should be restricted, and at what level should access be permitted?
- Classes of sensitivity—Are records and information broken down into different types of sensitivities?
- Sensitivity transience—Is an assessment made to determine if information maintains its sensitivity only for a particular time period?
- Data environment—Does the policy spell out the type of environment in which information should be maintained?
- Dedicated systems—Do the sensitivity requirements of the information mandate an information system solely dedicated to one functional purpose?
- Accuracy of information—Does the policy require periodic checks to ensure that information is being processed accurately?
- System flexibility—Is the policy flexible enough to allow for efficient and effective use of government information resources?

The form that such policies will take obviously will vary from agency to agency and over time; but it is important that the issues be fully addressed. In certain agencies, policies and procedures manuals will often specify the types of information collected and rights of access, whereas in others an information master plan will serve as the appropriate vehicle. The latter type is generally preferred as it offers a convenient focal point for all information-related matters; at the same time, such plans can be readily modified to accommodate changes in information technology or collection procedures. A critical component of such master plans is a built-in mechanism for periodic review and evaluation. This should be done relative to the broader legal environment to which the agency is accountable.

Administrative Controls

Administrative controls, as mentioned, evolve from the prior articulation of legal and social controls and are concerned with safeguarding the management routines associated with the collection, use, and dissemination of data and information. Individuals involved in this stage tend to be more technical in nature; and they must be capable of understanding the capabilities and limitations of both the organization and the information systems involved. Database managers and database administrators are examples of this type of individual. (We should note, however, that this does not and should not preclude their involvement in establishing broad information policies.)

Specific actions involved at this level include

- Marking of confidential information;
- Accountability assigned for handling confidential information;
- Accountability assigned for disposal of information;
- Specific procedures developed for storage of information and computer programs;
- Specific procedures developed to control the reproduction of confidential information;
- Reviews and purging of information;
- Development of emergency procedures in response to possible emergency situations, such as: bomb threats, civil disturbances, earthquakes, fire or explosion, or power failure; and
- Development of contingency operating plans. (Kettinger 1980, pp. 149-50)

Classifying of confidential information is a key step to ensuring that privacy rights, disclosure requirements, and security are maintained. With the advent of distributed and database systems, managers should be able to determine information that is of a sensitive nature and label it appropriately. Ways of doing this may range from partitioning off portions of the database where this information is contained, thereby controlling access, to the use of extensive prefix codes to signal confidential information. The development of automated personnel systems is a good example of this process. Agencies would like to have the capability of generating and reviewing data from personnel files to allow them to forecast future work force needs, attrition rates, progress toward affirmative action goals and timetables, and the like. At the same time, they must ensure that sensitive personnel data are not used or become readily available. Systems can be established in such a way that data elements from each file are retrieved and reported in summary fashion without violating the integrity of the system.

Similarly, accountability must be assigned to individuals for the handling of sensitive information as well as the disposal (purging) of information. As a safeguard for handling information, administrative controls should incorporate some form of routine performance appraisal of such individuals. Indeed, a number of states, and the federal government, have established ethics statutes in which individuals handling funds, procurement awards, and grant awards must routinely furnish financial disclosure statements as a control check. In addition to these actions, an agency should also consider the following points:

- Bonding and insurance requirements
- Background checks
- Periodic security indoctrination
- Thorough training in operating and administrative procedures
- Information access level restrictions

The disposal of information, a particularly sensitive area, is often prescribed by law. Again, agency officials must incorporate these standards into administrative controls. For automated systems, disposal and purging of information usually take the form of "dumping" the data to an offline storage device (tape or disk). The benefit of this approach is that the data are never truly eliminated and can be readily retrieved if needed. Another benefit is that large volumes of data can be archived at relatively low cost and not entail extensive storage space.

9

Future Needs for
Public Information Systems

The purpose of this chapter is really twofold. First, it is integrative—to tie together a number of the loose ends and avenues concerning information systems as a function in public organizations. Second, it is speculative—to look ahead at a number of events that will take place and how they will potentially influence the manner in which information is collected and used in the public setting. But to look at these two areas as separate and distinct is shortsighted. Often it is how we—as individuals and members of organizations—have operated in the past that will determine our ability to cope and adapt to future circumstances or events.

INFORMATION SYSTEMS AND
PUBLIC MANAGEMENT RECONSIDERED

At the outset, one of the predominant themes has been that information systems should be sensitive to, and support, the relevant decision-making requirements of the organization—in this case, public agencies. Rather than trying to develop or model management processes around whatever technology or hardware and software is currently available or in place, agency officials and managers should first determine the organization's needs and objectives. From this, information systems should be subsequently molded.

At the same time, officials and managers should consider the various levels of decision making and operating styles within the organization. It is rare indeed to find an organization that makes only operational decisions—decisions on how many claims must be processed daily or vouchers cleared. In most cases, we witness a hierarchy of decision types, ranging from the operational to the managerial and the strategic. Information systems, therefore, must be capable of addressing these various needs to be truly effective. Unfortunately, as we have seen, such efforts have not always been successful; and many systems are incapable of providing managers with critical data and information.

Beyond the internal needs of the organization are key environmental influences; and they are often quite pronounced for public agencies. These range from the political arena in which the agency's supporters or competitors vie for the control of programs and resources to the legal, technological, and cultural settings. Chapter 2 prescribed a manner in which information systems can be (and should be) sensitive to internal as well as external forces. The argument is made that each agency or organization must develop an information management approach that is sensitive to its particular set of needs; the effort to impose a standardized approach to information and information management for public organizations is doomed to failure for this reason alone.

This does not mean that there are not certain fundamentals of computers and their operation that managers should learn; and Chapter 3 looked at the technical side of this subject. Beginning with a discussion of how data and information are stored, processed, and disseminated, we traced the movement from large scale, standalone computer systems to database management and distributed systems. The technology is advancing at such a rate that decentralized office systems in which managers are capable of structuring their own data processing needs and reports will soon be the norm. What this will mean for traditional organizations such as public bureaucracies will be closely watched in the next several years.

In Chapter 4 we took a closer look at the recent history and current status of information systems at the federal, state, and local levels. At the federal level, concern has been expressed that the information collection activities of agencies, while enormous in scale, have emerged piecemeal and lack a coordinated focus. The Paperwork Reduction and Control Act of 1978 has been one effort to address this problem and vests increased control in the Office of Management and Budget. Whether this will succeed in the future remains to be seen.

At the state level, similar concerns over coordination have emerged and have led to the establishment of centralized information systems for state agencies. Agencies, however, have been reluctant to relinquish such control; and state legislatures are hurrying to establish similar systems for monitoring state actions.

Finally, at the local level, the role of information systems has taken on added importance for, if developed and implemented correctly, they hold the promise of improving service delivery and offsetting revenue losses (computerized property assessments, tax billing, fine collections). One concern here is the ramification of information systems in the area of intergovernmental relations. As each government level—federal, state, local—seems to standardize its information collection procedures, attention should also be devoted to the capabilities of transferring data and information from one level to another. Presently, it is done in a piecemeal fashion and tends to be confined to vertical relations within particular program areas (transportation agencies, social service agencies, and the like).

Properly designing and implementing information systems, the subject of Chapter 5, require public officials and managers to participate in the process actively. This involves several steps. First, systems design and analysis attempt to trace information flow for the organization from the inputs to the information system (government documents, vouchers, reports) to expected outputs. From this, requirement analysis and system documentation follow; and an effort is made to examine intra- and interorganizational linkages of information collection and use. Too often systems have been designed around a specific task or program needs. The advent of database management has allowed organizations to develop systems sensitive to organizationwide needs and flexible to change.

A necessary corollary to designing and implementing information systems is a systematic evaluation of their use (Chapter 6). For public organizations, this evaluation is critical because data and information can have instrumental value for the public as well as the individual organization. Evaluating information systems and their use involves much more than tabulating the dollars invested in hardware and software. Rather, it should be sufficiently broad in scope to determine the benefit of the system relative to the organization's primary goals and activities.

In Chapter 6 an information study approach was presented. Involving the analysis of organizational cost centers, information requirements, lifetime costs, and alternative information management procedures, this study approach can greatly assist managers faced with making changes or modifications to their present information system. More importantly, it can serve as a communication tool to agency support or oversight groups—an area of increasing significance as we move toward the intergovernmental sharing of information.

Chapters 7 and 8 place the role of information and information systems in the broader context of political and societal influences, areas that often separate private sector information practices from those in the public sector. In Chapter 7 we found that the development of information systems for making policy decisions has been slow and fragmented at best. One reason is that computers traditionally have been designed and implemented to address routine operational tasks, tasks in which information collection, use, and processing are fairly standardized (payroll processing, billing, revenue collection, incident reporting). At the same time, implementation in such areas has usually offered the highest return on investment—a fact not overlooked by vendors wishing to establish a foothold in an agency or firm.

Yet, as the technology has advanced to more integrated systems, users are beginning to see the benefits of automated systems for finding problems and supporting particular policy positions. As this trend takes place, information systems will be viewed for their political power, and who controls such resources will be an important variable in the policy process. We see signs of this today as legislatures are implementing information systems to counter a real (and perceived) imbalance in their ability to monitor executive agency programs and activities. Finally, a number of government jurisdictions have instituted uniform information policy guidelines. This is a tacit recognition of the greater value that information systems have in contemporary society, as well as the need to provide some structure to an area that heretofore has been largely unchecked.

To complete the picture of the environment of public management, we treat a number of the security and privacy concerns in Chapter 8. Similar to other developments that took place in the 1960s and 1970s, the rights of individual citizens in the collection and use of information by government agencies have been expressed, leading to such legislation as the Freedom of Information Act and the Privacy Act. Although such acts serve notice to agencies that individuals have a basic right to review data and information about themselves or government actions in general, they have not been uniformly successful. In some cases, agencies themselves have deliberately thwarted their intent. One suggestion here is that administrative control procedures for guaranteeing the integrity and security of agency data be formally stated and subject to third-party review. Beyond this, individuals or firms supplying data and information to public agencies should be informed about the manner in which such data are to be processed and ultimately used.

RECOMMENDED ACTIONS

In a book of this kind, it soon becomes a herculean task to treat all the subtleties and nuances associated with the management of information among government agencies. But we would be remiss if we failed to provide a few recommendations to assist individuals who are currently involved, or expect to be, with information systems in the public sector. The following points are provided to suggest steps that managers can take to make their information system more sensitive to individual, organizational, and technological factors treated throughout this work. While not intended to be exhaustive, it should illustrate that many actions are well within the manager's area of control.

1. *Participate in discussions on automation—procurement and implementation.* Historically, decisions on whether to automate agency activities and the timetable for such implementation have been relegated to EDP officials, select administrators, and outside consultants. Fortunately, this is beginning to change as government organizations find that successful use of automated equipment involves participation by managers at several stages. A recent report by the General Accounting Office bears this out. After reviewing the practices of 18 industrial organizations in acquiring computer equipment, the GAO found that such decisions involved "an integrated set of management control, planning, accountability, and specific procurement practices working together as a whole" (U.S. General Accounting Office 1981a, p. 24). It is incumbent upon managers that they understand the entire process; this will undoubtedly lead to improved organizational communication and a greater appreciation of the system's overall cost implications.

2. *Ensure that data collected are analyzed and interpreted.* While data in any information system go through several stages—from the

collection of basic or raw data to organized output—managers should periodically review the data to determine their current utility. This process should begin with a critical study of input forms. Is the data being collected still compatible with the organization's or unit's intended purpose or goals? Do substantive changes need to be made and portions deleted or added? Finally, and perhaps most important, individuals who are responsible for collecting and supplying the data should understand the uses of this information. Subsequent stages of this study should concentrate on the types of analyses that are being performed to determine whether changes in the format of the data may indeed be necessary and whether other units within the agency have a direct or secondary need for such information.

3. *Engage in training and periodic retraining.* Perhaps one of the more overlooked areas in the information management process, training has traditionally been viewed as a fringe item, often directed at the more technical education of systems analysts and programmers. This recommendation is, in fact, a companion to the previous one because ensuring that individuals understand the uses to which information is put implies education. Training and periodic retraining should be included as a direct item of expenditure in the user's operating budget and should entail a mix of technical instruction for nontechnical individuals, a discussion of organizational communication implications, and the interface between the technology and the individual agency's political environment. To treat each of these as separate and distinct simply ignores the pervasiveness of information technology in current government operation.

4. *Establish quality control procedures.* As with any program entailing the use of human and other resources, it is frequently necessary to monitor and conduct periodic appraisals of operating performance. In doing so, the manager builds into the evaluation process tolerable limits and benchmarks, and this should also be the case for information systems. From the completion of entry forms to computer-generated output, limits for percentage of acceptable error rates or variances should be clearly prescribed by the managers involved. Any deviation beyond these acceptable ranges should be flagged for exception reports that require immediate response or attention. This serves two purposes: First, it allows managers to concentrate on nonroutine matters, and second, it should provide additional data for studies of trends (as a potential justification for committing resources to critical areas).

5. *Collect data with a view toward larger comparisons.* One of the difficulties of working within highly structured, complex organizations is the gradual development of a narrow frame of reference. While educational background and training attempts to orient the student toward a generalist view of the particular field of study, organizational or agency reward systems are often based on allegiance to the unit's norms and accepted patterns of behavior. This is not to say that unit or departmental allegiance should be set aside in favor of some broader, higher level value system. Rather, individual managers can satisfy immediate data or information utilization needs while bearing in mind other uses, such as analyses with comparable jurisdictions or an aggregate study of several organizations. The benefits of this approach are that it often provides insights not evident at the unit level and can also be used to disseminate findings of interest to the general public, research institutions, and other sectors of public and private industry.

6. *Individuals in data analysis should be accessible to senior administrators and managers.* Although this point might appear commonsensical, too many organizations, both public and private, suffer from the class distinction that was previously mentioned. This is due to a number of factors, but the primary reason is one of technical versus nontechnical orientation. Analysts and programmers find comfort in the technology and its constantly changing nature. In addition, they find it extremely difficult (and also unwise) to reduce complex and intricate matters to simple language for others' consumption. Add to this a certain degree of computer phobia on the part of most managers, and one finds a strong chasm that eventually deepens within organizations. It is therefore important that not only do managers seek to understand the technical nature of information systems but that individuals involved in data analysis should be accessible to administrators and managers and should make an effort to understand the organizational and political context within which they must operate. While a certain portion of this awareness can be taught through combinations of formalized and seminar training, the larger part comes from active participation in the agency's decision-making process—understanding the intricate and varied interests that are involved in any decision. Finally, a certain degree of patience with the slow but deliberate process of government is a skill that must be continually honed.

Beyond those actions that individual managers or agency officials should consider are those that involve the broader sphere of policy and intergovernmental concerns:

7. *Develop uniform information policy guidelines.* A number of government jurisdictions have lobbied hard for and have implemented laws and directives that govern the use of data and information systems by public agencies. In some cases, they are quite specific and spell out the responsibilities of agencies in obtaining prior approval of data collection instruments, as well as enduring rights of individual access. However, most have been generally worded and continue to be wearily enforced. There should be a clear expression of legislative intent with respect to government information practices and an effort made to evaluate the costs, both to the agency and to the provider of data and information. Such costs should be weighed against the value of such information (both real and expected). Naturally, this places increased responsibility on the shoulders of legislative bodies to exercise such oversight as well as on executive agencies to justify their information practices; but such debate should be brought out into the public forum as a necessary control.

8. *Coordinate agency information practices.* A necessary corollary of the prior suggestions is that public information policy, once determined, should be operationalized. The Paperwork Control Act, which vests operational control in the U.S. Office of Management and Budget, is a prime example. The General Accounting Office has, in recent years, issued a number of reports to improve on this effort; but there has been little questioning of the necessity to centralize control of agency information practices. Such coordination among executive agencies will serve to minimize reporting and handling burdens, not only between agencies but also with legislative groups and other units of government, industry, and the general public. At the same time, this coordinating body should look at ongoing computing practices to flag areas of possible redundancy and overlap, should disseminate uniform procurement practices, and should ensure the integrity of the data that are collected. By this last point, we mean the levels of security within agency information systems and the protection of data concerning individuals, firms, and the like.

9. *Implement standards for the intergovernmental sharing of information.* This final suggestion touches on one of the more neglected areas of public information systems. In most cases, the trans-

fer of data and information between levels of government has tended to follow functional lines and agency reporting relationships, due in large part to the intergovernmental grants-in-aid process. Termed "picket-fence" federalism by such people as Deil Wright of the University of North Carolina, this process has undergone some new twists today as Washington is attempting to shift program control and oversight back to the states and, in turn, localities.

This shifting of grants, programs, and revenues has had a direct impact on the information activities of government jurisdictions, as it usually entails extensive reporting to ensure compliance with federal (and state) intent. In some cases, this is an extension of having different computing systems that cannot "talk" to one another; for often one jurisdiction may not have sufficient or comparable resources to transfer effectively information to another level or jurisdiction. The result is miscommunications, delay, and invariably, frustration on both sides. Government agencies should therefore give serious consideration to developing information policies that are consistent with their needs to receive and transmit data and information to their levels of government, be it federal, state, or local.

In conjunction with this effort, there should be a formal tally or inventory of the types and amount of information that are being transferred (and expected to be transferred in the future). Frequently, government officials do not really know the scope of this activity alone. It is only in recent years that state legislatures have been able to fully account for the volume and types of grants-in-aid that agencies are receiving.

The federal government as well should play a major role in implementing uniform intergovernmental information practices. One possible means of doing so is building incentives into the receipt of monies that require states and localities to coordinate information transfer—along the lines of the now defunct A–95 clearinghouse process. At the same time, federal support for regional information networks should be explored. The establishment of state centers that are responsible for U.S. Census data sharing is now in place and could be extended to such areas as environmental resources, health, and transportation. Perhaps the most serious impediment to this process is, not one that is technical in nature, but rather the tendency by managers and officials to use information resources as tools to maintain control (and power).

PUBLIC SECTOR CASES FOR INFORMATION
SYSTEMS AND PUBLIC MANAGEMENT*

The three cases that address different levels of government have been included in this book to provide views of and approaches to management of information systems. The cases can be used to develop further the governmental, technical, economic, design, and other issues discussed in the text. They can also be used as mechanisms to demonstrate various practical and conceptual matters that govern use of information systems.

The cases have been selected to help the student or practitioner appreciate the pressures of real organizations, the decisions related to use of information systems, and the messy or ill-defined character of many problems that may be embedded in the bureaucratic, political, statutory, or economic context. The cases are unique because they have been commissioned by the authors from practitioners at the federal, state, and local levels of government. The cases have been structured with a consistent format to allow for an examination of both common and different elements in information systems. In this sense, they provide a valuable tool for integrating organizational, hardware, software, managerial, behavioral, political, procedural, theoretical, and practical perspectives covered in various parts of the book to correspond with classroom or other needs.

Through the governmental processes, organizations and elements of the systems design process were documented at different times in the recent past, with programs such as CETA falling on hard times recently, the cases were designed to illustrate consistent information system principles at various levels of government. Most information systems in government are dynamic in that they undergo continuous scrutiny and are constantly in need of modification; however, the basic approach to information systems design and analysis should remain systematic and manager oriented.

The cases can be used in conjunction with specific instructor-based questions to amplify certain design, managerial, or substantive

---

*Though these cases are comprehensive in nature, they are not intended to illustrate either effective or ineffective information system management. However, they do illustrate the complex array of variables that influence the design and use of public sector information systems.

points or as devices to demonstrate phases in the whole information system life cycle design process across different managerial and organizational contexts. A brief description of each case is presented below.

1. *Local sector*—"CETA: Management Information Systems." Somewhat distinct from the other cases, this case will examine the local and intergovernment aspects of information reporting from the perspective of a county agency. It traces the feasibility, design, and implementation phases of the reporting system and presents the key issues involved in providing critical information on the CETA (Comprehensive Employment and Training Act) program. As a program that was both pervasive and quite visible, the case raises some important points for managers to consider, especially in a climate of resource constraints, increased needs for accountability, and interactions with higher levels of government.

2. *Federal sector*—"Veterans Administration Insurance Management Information System (VAIMIS)." This case examines the following phases of the life cycle design process and the insurance reporting system currently operating within the Veterans Administration: feasibility study, gross and detail systems design, implementation, and evaluation. The case deals with such issues as incorporated fiscal and accounting controls within the reporting systems, as well as the significant issue of access to individual records and rights of privacy.

3. *State sector*—"Programmed Project Management in Pennsylvania: Statewide Data Access." The Project Management System (PMS) is a computerized project information management system that integrates project-related data from the engineering and planning communities within a state department of transportation with the accounting data from the financial managers. The case examines the use of this system in the Pennsylvania Transportation Department and anticipated savings in automating previously manual processes such as tracking activities, developing schedules, and scheduling fund obligations.

APPENDIX A:

Case: Management Information Systems and a County Training and Employment Program: A Case of Conflicting Priorities

The mission of the Comprehensive Employment and Training Act (CETA) of 1973 is to "provide job training and employment opportunities for economically disadvantaged, unemployed, and underemployed persons, and to assure that training and other services lead to maximum employment opportunities and enhance self-sufficiency by establishing a flexible and decentralized system of Federal, State and local programs."[1]

The manpower system for the previous 15 years had experienced a proliferation of categorical grants and a variety of attempts to co-ordinate the manpower programs. The proliferation of programs, each with different authorizations, guidelines, clients, and delivery systems, had resulted in duplication and gaps in service and generally inefficient, ineffective systems.

The political philosophies of the early 1970s emphasized the con-cepts of decentralization, revenue sharing, and Nixon's "New Fed-eralism." The New Federalism doctrine placed administration of locally oriented social and economic programs in the hands of those closest to the area needs and the individual needs. It assumed that local administrators could best respond to community desires. With less federal control, flexibility and innovations would be encouraged.

Yin declares that the "decentralization of government, whether municipal or federal, usually begins with similar motives, i.e., to provide greater control and a sense of participation to those served by government. And it may also be claimed that, for federal govern-ments, decentralization represents one of the few common options for trying to alter governmental behavior."[2] The Comprehensive Employment and Training Act was created, as Yin has suggested, in response to both a need to coordinate and integrate the manpower services and to make the system more responsive to the needs of the individual and the local job market.

The years following CETA's enactment were highly controversial. Critics observed blatant misuse of funds and at best ineffective, inefficient programs. The criticisms and the resulting changes in the CETA legislation were predictable, according to Kaufman: "Decentralization will soon be followed by disparities in practice among the numerous small units, brought on by differences in human and financial resources, that will engender demands for central intervention to restore equality and balance and concerted action."[3]

A major underlying theme of the 1978 CETA amendments and the regulations that followed was improved management systems, not only to meet fiscal and audit requirements, but also to improve the delivery of services to participants. Both the amendments and the regulations emphasized the need for improved management control to ensure the integrity and efficiency of the program, to avoid fraud, and to assist effectively participants in the CETA system.

ORGANIZATIONAL HISTORY

CETA, administered by the Department of Labor, Employment and Training Administration, is implemented through block grants, a consolidation of the previous categorical grants, to state and local governments. The operating government units, known as prime sponsors, include states, cities, and counties of over 100,000 population, and combinations of such government units. There were 473 prime sponsors in fiscal year 1980. The prime sponsor must apply for a grant based on local unemployment trends, labor market conditions, population characteristics, political strategies, available resources, and any other local factors that will contribute to an effective operation of a training and employment program.

HIGHLAND COUNTY

The prime sponsor studied, Highland County, is a suburban county located near a major city in the Northeast. Geographically,

Highland County consists of 480 square miles. There are 62 townships and boroughs within this area, ranging in size from 23 square miles to 0.31 square mile.

The county is classified as a 2–A class county, denoting a population range of 500,000 to 800,000. Based on the 1980 census, the county population is 690,000. It is the third largest county in the state and is also one of the wealthiest. The estimated number of economically disadvantaged within the county is 15,400, or 2.5 percent of the total estimated population, and the nonwhite population is estimated at 27,200, or 4.3 percent. Although Highland is a wealthy county, pockets of economically disadvantaged have begun to emerge, mainly in two boroughs.

The political nature of the county has historically been Republican and conservative. The county CETA directorship is a political appointment by the county commissioners, and the current director was appointed in 1974. The CETA director reports directly to the chief clerk of the county.

The current CETA director's management style is best described as McGregor's Theory X view of workers. The basis of Theory X is that workers are perceived as unable to accept responsibility, wanting to work as little as possible. Workers do not hold the organizational goals as a priority in their daily work, therefore, the worker must be controlled and directed. As such, the director maintains control of critical information. Although the formal organization chart (Figure A.1) shows several levels and degrees of authority, it differs in practice. Authority remains centralized with the director and deputy director.

The composition of the prime sponsor staff is 80 professional and 30 nonprofessional employees. Upon its initiation as a prime sponsor, the staff size was 20, the rapid increase in staff occurring in the years of the countercyclical employment stimulus amendments of 1976. Until the 1978 amendments, the staff were Public Service Employment Program employees. Under this structure, the staff did not receive fringe benefits or comparable county wages. The result was a staff turnover of more than 100 percent. In fiscal year 1979, all prime sponsor employees became county employees, alleviating, to some degree, this discrepancy in wages and fringe benefits and stabilizing the staff. None of the prime sponsor staff has data processing experience.

FIGURE A.1. Highland County Training and Employment Program Organizational Chart

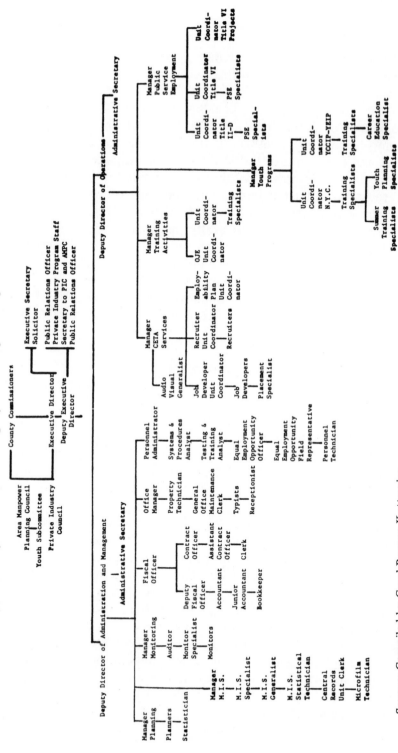

Source: Compiled by Carol Benson Kottmeier.

Organizational Structure

The organizational structure of CETA in Highland County consists of operational departments and administrative departments. The operational departments are the Manpower Services Department, the Training Department, the Public Service Employment Department, the Youth Programs Department, and the Private Sector Initiatives Department. These departments are further divided into functional activities units. The Manpower Services Department manages the activities of outreach/recruiting, eligibility/intaking, employability development planning/counseling, job development/job placement. The Training Department manages the activities of skill training, nonskill training, on-the-job training, and work experience. The Public Service Employment Department manages the structural and counter-cyclical public service employment programs. The Youth Programs Department operates the in-school and summer youth work experiences and the transitional and career work experiences for out-of-school youth. The Private Sector Initiatives Department supports activities of skill and nonskill training and upgrading and retraining of individuals about to be laid off. All programs sponsored by Highland County are subcontracted. The Highland County CETA staff does not provide direct services, but functions as liaisons to the subcontractors and CETA participants.

The operational departments are structured around their respective titles in CETA. The number of participants served are presented in the following table:

Program Activity and Title		FY '80	FY '81 1st Quarter	Planned FY '81
In-school youth, Training activities				
Manpower Services II B/C		2,541	1,132	2,700
PSE	IID	835	364	620
Youth Program	IV YCCIP	171	40	90
	YETP	450	206	325
	SYEP	1,023	N/A	N/A
PSE Program	VI	1,419	145	460
PSIP Program	VII	255	221	450
Total		6,694	2,108	4,645

The eligibility/intake subsystem of the county is geographically dispersed, with eligibility being determined at the five offices throughout the county. Applicant reports, providing a demand analysis, for the first quarter of fiscal year 1981 show a projection of approximately 5,000 applicants per year:

Office 1	408
2	153
3	406
4	127
5	57
Total	1,151

The administrative departments are planning, fiscal, MIS, personnel, and monitoring.

Central Issues

The CETA amendments of 1978 mandate the prime sponsors to monitor, audit, and manage their programs properly. The record-keeping and reporting requirements for prime sponsors were expanded and grew more complex. To assist prime sponsors in the development of improved management capability, an advisory group, composed of prime sponsors and federal representatives, designed specifications for the minimal informational needs of prime sponsors. This report is termed the Functional Management Information System (FMIS). The FMIS is the recommended standard that all prime sponsors must meet for Department of Labor approval and certification of their management information system.

A 1980 evaluation of the existing prime sponsors' management systems ability to conform to the FMIS indicated "that approximately 50 percent of CETA prime sponsors continue to maintain manual MIS's, 30 percent have automated systems, and 20 percent are automated in part. Thirty-nine percent of prime sponsors in the sample met the functional MIS specifications and thus have certified systems, while 50 percent were conditionally certified. (Conditional certification means that a prime sponsor has plans in place and that efforts are underway to meet the FY 1980 MIS specifications)."[4] A prime sponsor receiving conditional certification is eligible for Department of Labor technical assistance.

The program of technical assistance, provided by the Department of Labor, consists of 50 percent matching funds to implement an automated prototype MIS system. The prototype systems have been selected from existing operational systems capable of meeting the FMIS specifications and suitable for exportation and implementation in other sites. Complete systems documentation is available for each prototype MIS. The prototype systems are available for various kinds of hardware and for programs of varying sizes and administrative structures. The prototype systems are public domain, therefore, there is no software cost. The Department of Labor's guideline for an automated prototype system is a participant population of more than 3,000.

Highland County received conditional certification in its MIS evaluation and had a participant population of 6,694 in fiscal year 1980. The county has requested technical assistance for automation of a prototype system.

SYSTEMS FACTORS

Management Philosophy

The basic management philosophy and goals can be evaluated at three management levels. The Department of Labor is, in reality, the major institutional/strategic planning level. Although the CETA legislation proposed policy decision making to be centered at the local level, the categorical nature of CETA has placed this level of management at the Department of Labor. The Heritage Foundation, in preparing an analysis of the 13 cabinet-level departments for President Reagan, found the "Employment and Training Administration one of the most confused and directionless agencies in government . . . charging that the agency tries to pursue three separate functions— economic, social and political—that are sometimes contradictory, depending on which way congressional winds are blowing."[5] The report goes on to say: "Because there are no clear-cut goals, statutes are not clearly conceived."[6]

The second level of management is the prime sponsor's director and deputy director. At this level, strategic planning and coordination of operations are combined. The management style, and therefore respective goals, are best described as traditional. "The two basic elements of the traditional community problem-solving approach are . . . first, a strong tendency to postpone decisions as long as possible in hopes that the problem will either disappear or solve itself. If that does not work, local officials take the next step: They devise a course of action that appears to alleviate the problem but runs as little risk of opposition as possible."[7] As a result, the director and deputy director must react to the demands of the Department of Labor and the local county environment. As mentioned earlier, they control all critical information.

The third level of management, the operational line managers, are suboptimized. Anthony and Herzlinger state: "It is important to emphasize that line managers are the focal points in management control. They are persons whose judgments are incorporated in the approved plans, and they are the persons who must influence others and whose performance is measured. Staff people collect, summarize and present information that is useful in the process, and they make calculations that translate judgments into the format of the system."[8] Line managers' judgments are clouded with suboptimization, the goals being enrollment in their particular programs rather than the appropriate program for the client.

Operational Methods

In Highland County, the CETA programs and services are subcontracted, incorporating recruitment, eligibility determination, employability planning, training programs, and work programs. Because the goals/objectives of the organization are unclear and shifting, individual program goals are unclear and shifting and frequently modified. The goal of quantity, measured by the number of enrollments, is gradually being replaced by a goal of quality, measured by the number of participants obtaining employment.

The major work flows in the present system are between the program departments and the services departments. There is interaction between the program departments, but it is fragmented, all departments fighting for the same client. To initiate an enrollment, the applicant completes an eligibility determination with a recruiter and job service interviewer (Manpower Services Department). If eligible, the applicant is referred to Employability Development Planning, where a counselor and the applicant develop a goal-structured action plan to assist in obtaining unsubsidized employment (Manpower Services Department). The applicant is then referred to a training site or back to the Job Service interviewer for referral to a work site. If not accepted at a training site/work site, the referral process is repeated until placement. If a participant is placed and requests a transfer to another work site/training site, or completes a program and is not placed in the unsubsidized market, the participant returns to the Employability Development Planning Unit and repeats the referral process. When a participant completes the training/work site program, a termination notice is sent to the Highland County program coordinator. If the termination is not unsubsidized employment, the Job Placement Department of Manpower Services is notified to assist the participant in locating a job.

Figures A.2 and A.3 provide the basic outline of this process.

The present operating system, with its fragmentation, provides minimal management control. The applicants are frequently confused by the numerous physical steps required for enrollment in a CETA program activity. There is no clear responsibility for the participant's progress, the responsibility shifting from activity to activity. The system is dependent on subcontractors' accuracy and timeliness in reporting on participant status.

The present management information system within Highland County is centralized. All participant information is sent from subcontractors to the county's operating departments and then to MIS. A central records unit is maintained by the MIS department, and all required reports are generated by MIS. An additional operating problem is the composition of the MIS staff. Staffing is at the entry-level, minimum wage clerical positions. The complex cross-tabulated reports required in the MIS has placed a heavy burden on staff not qualified to perform such duties.

The MIS system has never been documented. The input formats were developed in an ad hoc manner, with no systems approach being utilized. The theme of fragmentation and suboptimization is observable in the use of different systems for each department and/ or program activity. In addition, the input formats have not been updated to include the informational requirements of the FMIS.

Information Requirements

The database is determined by the requirements of the FMIS. The FMIS handbook states several key factors determine the design

FIGURE A.2. Enrollment MIS Information Flow

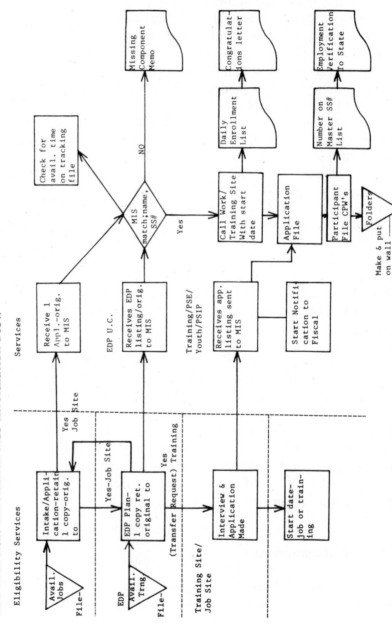

Source: Compiled by Carol Benson Kottmeier.

FIGURE A.3. MCTEP Termination Information Flow

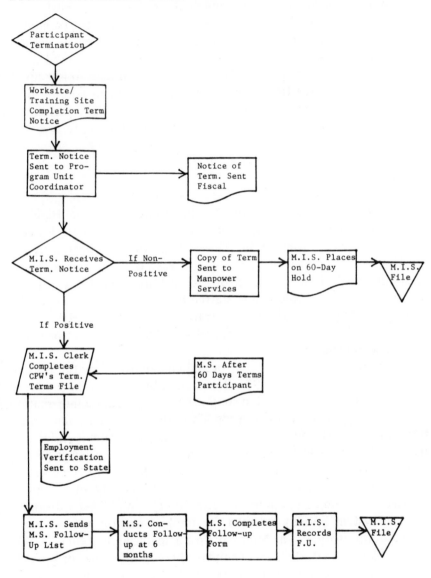

Source: Compiled by Carole Benson Kottmeier.

of the information system, the first being management control. It further states: ". . . prime sponsors must rely on access to a wide variety of information on CETA applicants, participants and programs. . . . Because informational needs for management and compliance monitoring are typically immediate or short term and Federal reporting requirements change, information systems must be modifiable, flexible and responsive. From the perspective of evaluating service delivery, data collected must be extensive and structured to reflect a complete participant profile from intake through follow-up."[9]

In addition to the FMIS requirements, management requires both specific and aggregate weekly reports on applicant and participant status. As quoted previously, the database for CETA is extensive.

Alternative Approaches

The first approach to solving the problems of the Highland County MIS Department was initiated by the director. He leased a word processor in June 1980. This alternative was selected by the director for its perceived low cost and ease of implementation. A feasibility analysis was not performed. Additionally, the word processor was to be located in and staffed by the office manager, yet 90 percent of its functioning was to be for the needs of the MIS department. This alternative was unacceptable to the Department of Labor and the MIS manager.

A feasibility analysis was performed and approved by the Department of Labor in January 1981. The major objectives in the proposed conversion to an automated system are timely, accurate information to facilitate program control, program evaluations, and communications among subsystems. A priority in system selection is an integration of MIS and fiscal data to obtain more accurate costs per participant and participant tracking data (following the client from entry to exit in CETA). In addition, it is considered politically advantageous to select a system compatible with the county's available hardware.

The system initially selected for implementation was the Rural Minnesota prototype. The Minnesota participant population is 10,000 larger than that of Highland County, thereby allowing for growth. The Minnesota system is a geographically dispersed, subcontracted operating system, with a centralized MIS, the same as Highland County. The program activities are the same, with reports generated by title, activity, and subcontractor. The system is mixed, allowing for both online and batch processing. The system provides for ad hoc reporting online and batch and has a search capability. Fiscal and MIS data are integrated. Eligibility determination is automated, with Roledex cards and lists generated for subcontracted agencies use. The system is written in RPGII and installed on IBM System 34 hardware.

The Minnesota system was also selected for the perceived availability, within the county, of an underutilized IBM System 34. As stated earlier, the director controls all critical information and intracounty relations. It was understood that preliminary negotiations to utilize the hardware had been initiated by the director. An on-site investigation of technical capabilities by Department of Labor representatives found no negotiations had been initiated and the hardware was, in fact, a fully utilized IBM System 32.

The second choice for prototype implementation was the Colorado system. As the Minnesota system, the Colorado system is similar in operating structure and size. An additional feature is report generation by counselor, thereby encouraging a case management operating structure. The fiscal component also requires development, design, and completion. The language is FORTRAN and the system is installed on Honeywell Series 60 hardware. This is compatable with the Highland County data processing system.

The CETA MIS manager, having solicited the support of the county data processing department, developed a cost proposal for conversion to the Colorado system. The current manual system's budget is $116,544 per year, the majority of costs in salaries. The proposed annual budget for the system would be $122,878. The conversion costs would be $16,422, for which the Department of Labor would provide 50 percent funding.

The cost proposal and implementation plans have received informal approval from the county's data processing department and the Department of Labor. The proposal was presented in May 1981, one week prior to the director taking a medical leave of absence. It appears that there will be no decision made until the director returns.

Implementation

The feasibility analysis was completed in January 1981 and submitted to the Department of Labor for approval. However, by the end of February, the county's CETA program was in a state of total confusion. Public Service Employment funding was to be frozen March 2, 1981. Communications from the Regional Department of Labor regarding funding levels were contradictory and unclear. All program enrollments were frozen on March 12, and all Title VI Public Service Employment programs were to be closed on March 31. A gradual phase down of Title IID Public Service Employment was scheduled for May through September. As of March 31, DOL indicated a full funding for other titles, and the freeze on program enrollments was lifted. The prime sponsor staff has been reduced from 110 to 84, a staff reduction of 26, and the MIS department has been reduced from 13 to 10. During DOL's on-site evaluation in March, the director was not supportive of a conversion to an automated system. He stated that there were no funds available for such an effort, and the project would proceed only if the Department of Labor totally funded the project. At this time it appears that any conversion to an automated system will have to be initiated through external pressures. This confirms a Regional Department of Labor manager's statement that prime sponsor directors do not view information systems as either a priority or as a management tool.

IMPLICATIONS FOR THE FUTURE

Earlier, expert opinions on the lack of goal-objective setting by the Department of Labor was cited. A "functional MIS" was designed in a confused, directionless, and conflicting environment. The FMIS only begins to address the important questions of impact.

Goodrich, writing on CETA's effectiveness, states:

> The major federal role is guarding against financial mismanagement and ensuring that jobs are properly targeted on groups and geographic areas called for by the policy. The problem with this approach is that the performance indicators don't help in evaluating the merits of various types of programs being funded. This kind of monitoring does very little in estimating the impact of programs being run by prime sponsors. Overall, there is little evidence that the performance measures being used in CETA reports to the Regional Department of Labor relate to favorable outcome placement in good jobs, better earnings, or increased proportion of time in employment. In support of this, an extensive follow-up study of CETA program participants recently concluded that: "Most of

the present set of (indicators) are poor predictors of program impact. Many of the measures presently being used bear little relation to the program's outcomes. Their continued use will yield allocation decisions that are little (if any) better than decisions made by flipping a coin."[10]

The FMIS is a major step toward answering the question of impact. Although the FMIS is all-encompassing in the accumulation of data, the political environment dictates comprehensive flexible reporting to satisfy the questions of compliance, mismanagement, and impact.

As this case study shows, management in the public sector is fraught with conflicting goals and priorities. CETA, by 1978, had come full circle in the decentralization cycle. 1982 forecasts the decentralization cycle beginning again. The CETA experience offers excellent lessons for the future design of block grants, and MIS must play an important role in these designs if management is to ensure the effective, efficient utilization of resources. If not, we will continue to "flip coins."

NOTES

1. Comprehensive Employment and Training Act of 1973, P.L. 93–203, Statutes at Large 87, 1974.

2. Robert K. Yin, "Decentralization of Government Agencies—What Does It Accomplish?" *American Behavioral Scientist* 22, no. 5 (May/June 1979): 525.

3. Herbert Kaufman, "Administrative Decentralization and Political Power," *Public Administration Review* 29 (January/February 1969): 11.

4. "Employment and Training Reporter" (Bureau of National Affairs), 12, no. 16 (1980): 441.

5. Ibid., p. 437.

6. Ibid., p. 438.

7. David R. Morgan, *Managing Urban America: The Politics and Administration of America's Cities* (North Scituate, Mass.: Duxbury Press, 1979), p. 74.

8. Robert R. Anthony and Regina E. Herzlinger, *Management Control in Nonprofit Organizations* (Homewood, Ill.: Richard D. Irwin, 1980), p. 20.

9. *CETA: Management Information System Program*, ET Handbook No. 378 (Washington, D.C.: Department of Labor, 1980), p. 3.

10. James A. Goodrich, "Increasing CETA's Effectiveness: Federal Designs, Implementation Problems and Local Perspectives," *Journal of Health and Human Resources Administration* 3, no. 3 (February 1981): 354.

APPENDIX B:

Case: The Redesign of the Veterans Administration Insurance Program: Information System Development in Progress

The Veterans Administration was established by Executive Order 5398 as an independent agency on July 21, 1930. This action was an outgrowth of an act of Congress (46 Stat. 1016) that became law on July 3, 1930, authorizing the president to consolidate and coordinate federal agencies especially created for or concerned with the administration of laws providing benefits to veterans. It has grown to become the third largest executive agency in the federal government with an appropriation in excess of $22 billion for fiscal year 1981.[1]

Life insurance protection for military personnel and veterans is provided under nine separate programs. Five of these programs (or funds) are totally administered by the Veterans Administration. Three are supervised through contractual agreements with private insurance companies. The ninth fund, Veterans Insurance and Indemnities, is a direct appropriation that supports the costs of insuring disabled veterans at standard insurance rates.[2]

The first insurance policies were issued toward the end of the First World War. Today there are approximately 4.6 million active accounts serviced by two insurance offices, in Philadelphia and St. Paul. If the insurance activity were an independent concern, it would be the fourth largest life insurance company in the nation, with accounts valued in excess of $32 billion under its direct control. Beginning with renewable term policies and expanding into a full range of permanent plans, including whole life, limited payment life and endowment policies, total disability income riders and annuities, the programs have grown in both scope and complexity over the years.

The Veterans Administration is organized into three major subdivisions: the Department of Veterans Benefits, the Department of Medicine and Surgery, and the Department of Memorial Affairs. The Department of Veterans Benefits contains the insurance activity. The assistant director for insurance has overall responsibility for the insurance program. He oversees four separate units—the Insurance Actuarial Staff, the Insurance Program Management Division, and two Insurance Operations divisions.

The Actuarial Staff is responsible for the general financial planning and viability of the insurance funds under the VA's control. The staff determines the amount of cash to be kept onhand for claims against the funds, provides financial projections on investments, and determines dividend rates.

The Insurance Program Management Division formulates and evaluates policy, plans, regulations, procedures, and standards affecting the insurance programs on a nationwide basis and makes recommendations to the assistant director for insurance. It also reviews and analyzes proposed and enacted legislation that would impact on the insurance activity. Both the Actuarial Staff and Program Management Division are located in Philadelphia.

The two Insurance Operations divisions have five subunits or sections.

The Policy Service Section is responsible for the general maintenance of the active insurance accounts, including updating records, converting term policies to permanent plans, associating unassociated or misapplied remittances, processing certain changes of plan and reinstatements, registering beneficiary and optional settlement changes, granting loans and cash surrenders, paying dividends, and making refunds.

The Medical Determination Section performs standard underwriting functions. This section issues new policies, total disability income riders, and processes changes of plan and reinstatements requiring medical evidence. It also processes many items similar to those done in the Policy Service Section connected with its particular areas of responsibility.

Claims on policies in force are the responsibility of either the Death Claims or Insurance Claims Section. When notice of death is received, the Death Claims Section determines the proper beneficiary and secures a claim for payment. The beneficiary(ies) must be properly identified and the appropriate type of settlement determined.

Any complex or contested issues regarding a death claim are resolved by this unit. Disability claims by or on behalf of an insured veteran for benefits under the Waiver of Premiums clause and/or a Total Disability Income Provision (TDIP) of the contract are handled by the Insurance Claims Section. This section has responsibility for determining if the requirements for such benefits are met or continue to be met where they have already been granted. In addition, the section conducts clerical actions and correspondence related to claims actions.

As in the Death Claims Section, Insurance Claims must resolve any complex or contested issues regarding the awarding or denial of benefits. In both sections, this procedure is the first step in an appellate process that can go to the federal courts. This section also has jurisdiction in questions of fraud in the procurement or reinstatement of insurance or the Total Disability Income Provision, conversion to an endowment policy, and a change of plan to one with lower reserve value.

These four main sections are supported by personnel in the Insurance Files Section, who maintain the insurance folders, associate record printouts with folders, forms, and correspondence, and route them to the proper section. The entire operation and various subsystems are overseen and coordinated by the chief of the Insurance Operations Division.

Functions such as receiving and delivering mail and supplies, typing and transcription, and dispatching correspondence are performed by the Administrative Division. Receiving and processing remittances, releasing disbursements, accounting, and auditing are done in the Finance Division. Both of these divisions are independent of the insurance activity. Data processing for insurance is performed by one of three VA regional data processing centers that come under the control of the Office of Data Management and Telecommunications in Washington (See Figure B.1).

The Insurance Program is largely a mail-order activity with some direct contact with clients through telephone inquiries. Mail is classified as remittance-bearing, that is, correspondence, forms, and applications with money attached, and nonremittance-bearing. The latter is scanned by the Receipt and Dispatch Unit (Administrative Division) for a file number, which is used to request a record printout (RPO) of the insurance policy, and hand-coded by category and destination (see Figure B.2). If no file number is included, the mail is referred to

FIGURE B.1. Target Computer System Support

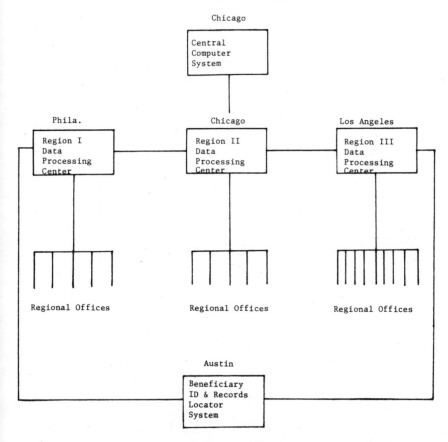

Source: Veteran's Administration 1979. The Target System, Part XXV, Supplement No. 1.1, mp–6. Washington, D.C.

an index unit for identification of the file number. Indexing can be done by means of a card file or through the Beneficiary Identification and Records Locator System. The BIRLS system was developed to identify and locate veterans records for a database work processing system used for compensation and pension and education awards called TARGET. A summary screen containing such information as a VA claims number, social security number, dates of birth and death, dates of service and discharge, insurance file number, and location of records can be requested with as little as two items of information.

FIGURE B.2. Non-Remittance Bearing Flow Chart

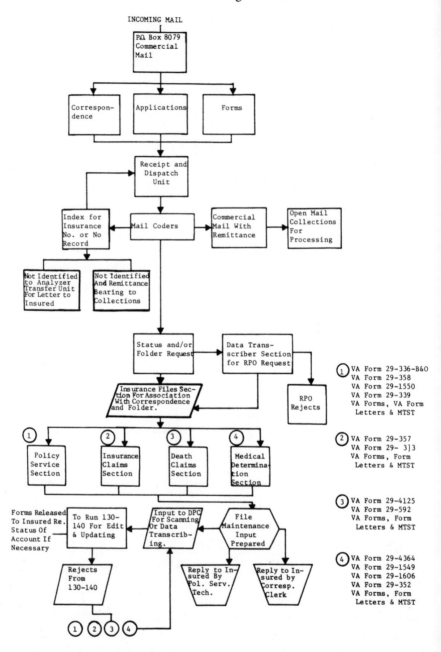

Source: Veteran's Administration 1980. Insurance Preliminary Study, Volumes 1–14. Washington, D.C.: Office of Data Management and Telecommunications and the Department of Veterans Benefits.

BIRLS does not show any insurance policy numbers, which may differ from the file number, but the database contains this information and will use it to identify records if it is input. Both BIRLS and TARGET use cathode ray tubes and a Honeywell 6600 series computer system.

The RPOs are output overnight in batches and associated with the correspondence and/or insurance folder the following day by the Insurance Files Section. They are then routed to the appropriate section for processing. If correspondence cannot be identified, it is returned to the sender with a form letter asking for more information.

Remittance-bearing mail is handled separately from other mail (see Figure B.3). Envelopes bearing the special post office box designation for remittances and checks erroneously sent to the other address go to the Collections Section of the Finance Division where the payment information is entered into the Remittance Processing System (Bell & Howell). At the same time, the checks are photocopied, microfilmed, and cancelled. The cancelled checks are packaged and shipped to the Federal Reserve Bank. The Remittance Processing System enters the type and amount of payment on a magnetic tape that is later transferred to the main computer master records. The reason for the remittance is identified by means of preprogrammed transaction codes. RPOs are generated the next morning if correspondence requires clerical action. The matching of the RPOs with the correspondence is done by data processing personnel and sent to the insurance activity. If the system is unable to apply the money, IBM cards identifying the information fed to the computer are produced. A special unit in the Policy Service Section then attempts to identify and apply the remittance clerically.

Until December 1980 Philadelphia's data processing was principally performed on an IBM 7080 computer. Additional hardware included an IBM 360/40 and an IBM 1401. The St. Paul office used an IBM 1401, an IBM 360/20, and an IBM 360/40. The IBM 7080 broke down in December 1980 and was replaced by an IBM 360/65, which emulates the 7080's programs.

Programs are maintained on card, tape, and disk. Input is accomplished through batch processing of optical character reader documents, which are hand-prepared, and cards, which are keypunched onto magnetic tape by the Inforex unit in the DPC. Processing of a day's work is done overnight. Some of St. Paul's data processing is also done in Philadelphia. The data are transmitted over telephone

FIGURE B.3. Remittance Bearing Flow Chart

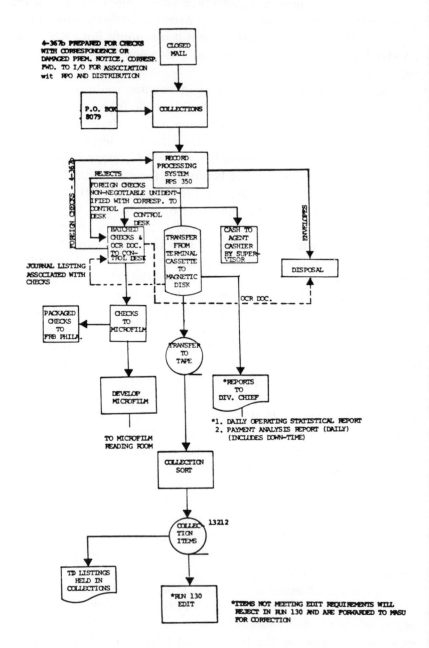

Source: Veteran's Administration 1980. Insurance Preliminary Study, Volumes 1–14. Washington, D.C.: Office of Data Management and Telecommunications and the Department of Veterans Benefits.

lines to magnetic tape. When transmission is complete, the tapes are then sent to other machines for processing. The completed work is then retransmitted to St. Paul. Certain OCR documents and cards are also sent to Philadelphia for processing. Any rejects resulting from these inputs are corrected in the Philadelphia insurance office and re-input. Heavy cyclical output such as billing is deferred to weekends rather than being produced on a level and more timely basis on week-days.

Looked at from a purely data processing standpoint, the prob-lems of the existing system are primarily hardware related. The sys-tem is highly dependent on interaction with human elements, thus making its effectiveness reflective of the operators' attentiveness. This has caused considerable problems in the past. The response time for error correction is becoming more difficult due to the lack of available computer language expertise. This expertise is currently limited and steadily decreasing. The present insurance system has five separate master records—inforce, awards, liability/miscellaneous transactions control, general ledger, and deduction. Of these, the inforce subsystem processes the total file in two separate operations using two master files, one for St. Paul and the other for Philadelphia.

In addition to the loss of the IBM 7080, it was decided in early 1981 for economy reasons to close down the small data processing facility in St. Paul. How the data processing needs of the Insurance Operations Division in St. Paul will be met and how this action will affect the Philadelphia DPC is not known at this writing. Yet another decision is in the works that could further complicate the problems of the insurance program and its support elements. In an effort to slow the flow of money into the economy, the Office of Manage-ment and the Budget and the VA central office in Washington are considering an increase in the interest rate for loans against VA in-surance policies. The present interest rate is 5 percent per year. A new rate has not been set yet; however, this pending regulatory change will serve to illustrate a problem with the existing data pro-cessing system.

Permanent plans of insurance accumulate what is referred to as reserve or cash value. The amount of the reserve value varies, depend-ing on the type of plan and the length of time it has been in effect. Under VA regulations, an insured may borrow up to 94 percent of the reserve. Repayment of the policy loan is not mandatory; however, it is possible, with the annual capitalization of interest to the principal, that the outstanding loan balance will at some future date exceed the cash value of the policy. When this happens, the policy is automatically cancelled and may not be reinstated. Currently, there are two separate loan interest rates—the 5 percent already mentioned and an older 4 percent rate. When the 5 percent rate became effective in January 1971, the preexisting 4 percent loans were left intact. Therefore, it is possible for a policyholder to have two outstanding loans. Should a new loan rate be instituted, the possibility exists for a policy to carry three loans. The problem is that the master record cannot accommodate more than two loan segments.

The amount of the new interest rate is not important for the purpose of this case study. Let us assume that a policyholder who already has two outstanding loans applies for a new one after the rate increase. Since the DPC will require six months to reprogram the computers, all new loans will have to be processed and maintained "off tape," that is, manually. It now takes a clerk an average of seven and one-half minutes to prepare the input for a computer-processed loan. Until the new rate is programmed, it will take the same clerk approximately 75 minutes to process the loan manually.

Without going into more technical detail, 12 other functions will be affected and at least 3 organizational elements in Insurance Operations and the Finance Divisions. After the program changes have been made, the new loans will be inserted on to the master records and any existing 4 percent loan will be removed and manually maintained. This situation will continue until the off-tape loan is satisfied or the master record is expanded.

In line with the general policy of the Veterans Administration, a new Honeywell 6600 series computer system was purchased in 1977. This system is currently handling compensation, pension, and education programs for the VA nationwide. It also provides a national information network to all VA regional offices and centers and to the VA central office in Washington. This new system, called TARGET, became operational in late 1979. Data are processed online using cathode ray tubes. The two primary performance constraints on the redesign of Insurance, then, are that the new programs must operate on a Honeywell 66/80 computer, or at least a compatible central processing unit, and they must be able to process simultaneously with the existing programs.

Because the present data processing system worked so well for so long, the need to plan for future requirements in this area was slow to be perceived. Problems began to emerge in 1975 and became increasingly more serious as time went on. Finally, in 1978 the need for a new system was recognized. Several factors may have contributed to this realization.

The second half of the decade witnessed the loans of experienced personnel in the insurance program. This was particularly true in the Policy Service Section. Much of the VA's work force were World War II veterans who were reaching retirement age during the late 1970s. New employees were largely Vietnam era veterans; however, these new employees were not always able to take advantage of their predecessors' experience and historical knowledge.

The advancing average age of the largest group of policyholders, World War II veterans, which was approaching 60 in 1981, places new demands on the insurance activity. Their insurance is becoming more important to many of them, and they are requesting more assistance and sophisticated information for financial planning purposes.

While the number of active policies is decreasing by about 2.4 percent per year, the available personnel to service the contracts has decreased at a faster rate. A modern data processing system would enable the insurance activity to handle the work load while improving service to its clients without increasing staff. A new system would also enable the DPC to reprogram for legal and regulatory changes more quickly without the need to revert, at least temporarily, to manual processing.

Finally, the fact that Philadelphia was used as a pilot station for the TARGET system provided the program's management with the opportunity to see a modern database system in operation.

In November 1979, a team was set up to conduct a preliminary study as the first phase of the Insurance Redesign Project. The team members included individuals from the Insurance Program Management Division representing the users, the Philadelphia DPC, and the Office of Data Management and Telecommunications representing the suppliers. The approach selected for the project is called Systems Development Methodology/70 (SDM/70) developed and patented by Katch and Associates and Atlantic Software.[3]

As part of this first phase of the Insurance Redesign Project, 85 individuals were interviewed about all aspects of the insurance system and support activities. Personnel at all levels of the units concerned had input. In addition, flowcharts of major information processes were drawn and current system outputs were carefully evaluated. The results of the preliminary study identified 14 problems and needs related to the current system. Among the most important were:

1. The inflexibility of the master records and the inability to expand them to meet current and future requirements
2. The inadequacy of the system in the management reports necessary for proper management and control of the program
3. The inability of the current insurance system to provide immediate access to veterans' records for timely response to direct veteran inquiries
4. The inability of the present system to provide for the automation of many insurance procedures now being manually performed
5. The need for the actuarial system to be expanded to capture additional information automatically in order to eliminate the manual calculations now required

The current insurance ADP system produces a large number of reports, and, with the modifications done over the years, these are sufficient for monitoring the programs. However, the reporting requirements for management control have not kept pace with modern management techniques. Consequently, the following additional information output is required:

1. Work measurement reports by operational section
2. Work measurement reports by individual clerks and by transaction type
3. Reject listings by individual clerk and by transaction type
4. Studies containing mortality figures and other actuarial data relative to the subprograms and funds
5. One-time, user-actuated special reports such as geographical concentration or individual policy financial projections

The documentation for the preliminary study was extensive, filling 14 volumes of varying length and topically organized.

As a result of the preliminary study, the design team was able to develop three viable alternative designs. Two of the three could have two different machine or software configurations. Common to all three alternatives were batch processing of inputs, overnight updating of the master records, and use of Honeywell hardware. Under each alternative, changes in the programs could be accomplished in six weeks or less rather than the current six months.

Alternative 1 would provide a redesigned system written in COBOL. The master record would be expanded to include all the desired data elements, both existing and new. Additional processing functions would be provided and additional automated correspondence would be generated. The software could be either tape file or database.

With this alternative, retraining of insurance personnel would be minimal, since the way work is presently done would not change significantly. Some transaction codes would be modified to enable the clerks to read output more easily. However, there would probably be little or no financial savings under this alternative. This is important because of continued reductions in staffing. Due to the condition of the current DPS, alternative 1 is generally considered as a given. Implementation of this alternative could take place as early as October 1983.

The second alternative differs from the first in that it provides online inquiry capability through CRTs. The input media and format would remain the same (OCR documents and keypunch). The software configuration in this design would have to be database. The benefits to be derived from alternative 2 would be faster service on telephone inquiries, which now have a minimum 24-hour turnaround time, and a reduction or elimination of the RPO currently required for almost all incoming work. Since the RPO is often used as a turnaround document for making inputs to the master record, the processing time for work items may be lengthened due to the loss of precoded identifying information. This additional time would not, however, be significant in most cases.

Alternative 3 is by far the most radical and costly departure from the current system. In addition to the features of the first two alternatives, this design would permit online processing of the work. The data would be edited and stored for overnight updating of the master file. Through the use of front-end editing programmed into the system, clerical rejects are expected to be reduced from the present 15 percent to between 1 and 3 percent. In addition, auditing and award functions now done by the Finance Division would be done by the system with random selection of cases for postaudits.

Among the benefits to be derived from the third alternative would be a significant reduction in paper flow, a reduction in personnel required to process the work, faster processing of work, and the virtual elimination of redundancy caused by the high reject rate. Additional costs would be incurred in purchasing cathode ray tubes and printers, training of personnel, and the possible purchase of an additional central processing unit.

Currently, the Philadelphia VADPC has two CPUs to handle TARGET with approximately 70 percent of their core capacity available to insurance. This excess capacity is now used as backup for the TARGET system should it be needed. There are three regional data processing centers for the VA throughout the United States. The central computer system is in Chicago, as is one of the regional centers. The other two are in Philadelphia and Los Angeles. The centers are also linked to the BIRLS system in Austin, Texas. If one center has problems, the other two can assume some of the traffic. Should the insurance programs be added to Philadelphia's existing CPUs, they could be taken offline if problems develop with TARGET. If the downtime lasted for several hours, it would become impossible to process work under alternative 3. Therefore, a third CPU at Philadelphia may be necessary. This would add about $1.3 million to the cost of that alternative.

Regardless of which alternative is finally chosen, several benefits will be realized from the redesign: reduction of administrative costs by automation of manual procedures, elimination of multiple inputs caused by existing hardware limitations, and automation of correspondence. Among the intangible benefits anticipated will be reduced training time for new employees, better service to clients, accountability at the individual level for errors and pending cases, and a computer system that is more easily maintained and more responsive to the user's needs.

In the spring of 1981, the second phase of the redesign began. Identification of the viable alternatives actually initiated the feasibility study. The general functional specifications were completed in April and work began on "fleshing out" each of the alternatives. Three areas are being closely examined under each alternative: organizational structure, work flow, and anticipated costs and benefits. Based on the information developed in the preliminary study, the team is reviewing the structure of all affected units in insurance and the support elements to see how each alternative will affect them. The same is being done with the work flow. Once this task has been completed, the costs and benefits of each alternative should be more easily identifiable. Simultaneously, work began on the initial steps of the cost-benefit analysis. Base year data were developed (fiscal year 1980 is being used) and work load projections for the system life cycle (through fiscal year 1992) were made.

NOTES

1. *1982 Congressional Budget Summary (revised), Volumes III and IV* (Washington, D.C.: Veterans Administration, Office of the Controller, March 1981).

2. Ibid.

3. *SDM/70: Systems Development Methodology* (Philadelphia: Katch & Associates and Atlantic Software, Inc., n.d.).

APPENDIX C:

Case: Programmed Project Management in Pennsylvania: Statewide Data Access

This case study deals with the design and implementation of the Project Management System (PMS) in the Pennsylvania Department of Transportation. One of the significant points concerning the PMS is that it was developed under some of the most difficult circumstances that can be faced by any public agency; the department was fighting for its very existence. The specific causes of this crisis situation will be detailed later. In spite of these adverse conditions, the PMS was successfully implemented and is making significant contributions in the area of planning and scheduling the use of dwindling resources that must be efficiently used to maintain and restore an extremely large highway system.

The Project Management System is a computerized information management system that integrates project-related data from the engineering and planning communities with the accounting data from the financial community. The data are stored in a common database and are accessed by users located both in the department's central office and the 11 engineering districts. The PMS has enabled people in the various branches of the department to obtain consistent information on all projects because everyone is accessing the same database.

The PMS was developed using department personnel and computer facilities. It employs online updating to make changes to project data. It therefore also serves as a powerful communication tool, because any change made anywhere in the state is instantaneously available to all other systems users.

The types of project-related and accounting-related data in the PMS enable it to track the physical and fiscal progress of the projects on the department's program. The use of standard report-generating packages in conjunction with the data has resulted in significant time savings by automating previously manual processes. Examples in this area include tracking preconstruction activities, developing the letting schedule, scheduling the obligation of federal funds, and cash flow projections.

DEPARTMENT BACKGROUND AND COMPUTER FACILITIES

The Pennsylvania State Highway Department, Department of Transportation, was created by legislative act on 1 July 1970. The bill combined a variety of transportation-related areas, including mass transportation, hazardous substances transportation, high-speed transportation, the Bureau of Motor Vehicles, the Bureau of Traffic Safety, and the Department of Highways. Also included was responsibility for waterways and aviation. To manage this myriad of activities, the department instituted a management structure divided into five major areas of responsibility.

- Highway Administration is responsible for the design, services, construction, and maintenance of the state highway system.
- Planning is responsible for developing the economic analyses and plans for future highway networks, their maintenance, and their accompanying service.
- Administration manages the department's administrative services, which include Personnel, Fiscal and Systems Management, Equal Opportunity, and Office Services.
- Local and Area Transportation deals with a variety of functions, which include aiding municipal highway and transit services, rail, aviation, and goods movement.
- Safety Administration includes the motor vehicle registration and driver license operations, safety programming, planning and analysis, and traffic safety.

One aspect of the department's efforts to meet these responsibilities is the operation of a large computer system. In addition to internal needs, the department also provides support to the governor's office, Pennsylvania State Police, and the departments of General Services, Environmental Resources, Justice, and Revenue.

The computer system is an IBM 370/168 multiprocessor (MP) with 14 million characters of main memory. This is supplemented by 20 billion characters of data stored online on 96 3330 Mod 11 disk drives and an additional 10 billion characters stored online on a 3851 mass storage facility.

The large online data requirements result from the need to provide continuous availability of records on approximately 10 million vehicles and 8 million vehicle operators for the Safety Administration and State Police support responsibilities. Other major applications include the Project Management System (PMS), Project Inventory System (PI), maintenance management, construction contracts, accounting, payroll, inventory management, traffic safety, right of way, and the state road log. These applications are implemented in an information management system (IMS) database environment and process approximately 135,000 transactions each day. Computer operations are scheduled 24 hours per day, 365 days per year.

Another major part of the computer system is the statewide communication network. In addition to the approximately 600 computer terminals in the department's central office, approximately 100 are located in the 11 engineering districts and 67 county offices. The state police also perform inquiries from a remote terminal. The communication network provides around-the-clock availability of the department's applications systems to the field offices.

The Fiscal and Systems Management Center (FSMC) is responsible for the design, implementation, and maintenance of the major application systems. The department has also experienced success in encouraging individual bureaus to utilize a standard report-generating software package to prepare special reports. This has been beneficial for all concerned. The FSMC personnel have more time to devote to new development activities and the bureaus find that they can obtain reports quite rapidly and tailor them to their own needs.

THE NEED FOR A PROJECT MANAGEMENT SYSTEM

At the beginning of the current administration (1979), Pennsylvania's transportation program was so far behind that of other states that gaining control of program management required extraordinary measures. Pennsylvania's 45,000 miles of state-owned highway rank fourth in the nation in total miles in a state system. Since the three larger states (Texas, Virginia, North Carolina) do not have to contend with severe winters, Pennsylvania's highway system is among the most difficult in the nation to maintain. Deferred maintenance and lack of good management controls had resulted in a crisis situation that threatened the department's existence.

Prior administrations saw few financial constraints in the transportation area. For some years, highway construction was largely bond financed, so that any time additional funds were required, more bonds were sold. That practice resulted in a current annual debt service in excess of $200 million and total aggregate debt service of over $2 billion through 2006. The department's capital program was essentially recorded in the legally mandated 12-year program, a "wish list" of projects to be built in the next 12 years. The basis for financing the state share of these projects was again primarily the sale of bonds. The department now does all its project work on a "pay as you go" cash basis to avoid the problems previously created by bond financing.

The financial environment is now characterized by tight fiscal constraints. At the federal level, ceilings are placed on the amount of federal funds available for construction and maintenance projects, and at the state level, the department has seen its revenues and buying power severely cut by the combined effect of inflation and reduced fuel consumption. The current emphasis on maintenance and restoration of existing roads requires examination of the entire 45,000-mile system and equitable allocation of the limited resources available to accomplish the work.

To meet this challenge, the department is, for the first time, following explicitly stated and measurable objectives. Monthly reports are prepared for each level of the department's management that compare estimated with actual achievement of the stated objectives. Central to defining and monitoring the department's direction is the newly formed Program Management Committee (PMC). The committee, chaired by Transportation Secretary Thomas Larson, is composed of high-level managers who work with the extended 12-year program (based on operating cash resources), a four-year program, and a one-year obligation plan to ensure that the department's long- and short-range projects are planned and scheduled in accordance with available resources. The PMC's members, inadvertently but beneficially, represent the major geographical areas of the state since their backgrounds or homes are in these areas. As a result of this even geographical distribution and of the committee members' extensive travel to project sites, most projects brought to the PMC for approval have been viewed by at least one committee member. To support the PMC, a Center for Program Development and Management has been created to serve as the staff clearinghouse for all PMC actions and information requests.

The state is divided into 11 engineering districts, and the district engineers have been given a greater role and responsibility in implementing the department's program. This decentralized operation has enabled the department to be more responsive to the transportation needs of highway users because the district engineers are closer to and better able to understand local concerns.

Still another departmental initiative resulted from the realization that an information system was needed to monitor its program's progress. This need was translated into the development of the computerized Project Management System, the subject of this case study. The PMS is essentially an "electronic filing cabinet" that contains the equivalent of an "electronic manila folder" for each project on the state's program. Computer terminals provide access to the system in each engineering district office and in the central office bureaus so each organization inputs and extracts project-related data into the same "folder" whenever it adds/extracts data for a given project.

The storage of project data in a common database for the entire state has, for the first time, enabled people in various branches of the department to obtain consistent information on all projects. The classic problem of getting different answers to the same question from a number of branches of the same department has been virtually eliminated.

SYSTEMS OBJECTIVES AND CONCEPTS

Objectives

The Project Management System is a computerized information management system with the following objectives:

- Identify projects on the department's program and monitor the status of their federal funding.

- Track the physical and fiscal progress of each project by maintaining information concerning previous activity, current status, and future estimates.
- Eliminate confusion that could result from multiple lists of project-related information by maintaining a common database for statewide use.
- Provide a communication tool that will provide instantaneous transmission of project information to all system users.
- Enable information requests to be met by inquiring into the database (maintained as part of daily operations) instead of short-fuse telephone inquiries to the engineering district offices.

Systems Concepts

The "programmed project" managed by the PMS is the aggregate of all phases (design, utilities, right of way, and construction) and incorporates all federal agreements that are used across the phases. The relationship between a project and federal agreements for its phases is depicted in Figure C.1. At the state level, the federal agreements are essentially charge numbers in the department's accounting system. The preparation of management-level information on any particular project required the PMS to "reach" into the entire population of accounting charge numbers, extract only those relating to the project in question, summarize the detailed information (costs incurred, future cost estimates) contained with each of these charge numbers, and report the aggregated information.

In accomplishing this summary function, the PMS integrates data that historically have been separate: that maintained by the engineering and planning communities and that maintained by the financial community. This integration is demonstrated in Figure C.2. Figure C.2 emphasizes the importance of the links between the programmed project and the federal agreements (accounting charge numbers, which will accrue the costs and show estimated future expenditures). It is the ability to traverse the links in either direction and move, selectively, from detail to aggregate or aggregate to detail, which gives the PMS its power as an extremely useful management tool.

Any single project can have many related accounting charge numbers (federal agreements) across its phases. To accommodate this one-to-many situation, the PMS employs two separate databases: one

FIGURE C.1. Relationship Between Projects and Federal Agreements

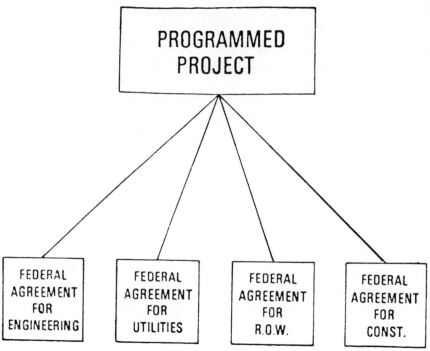

FIGURE C.2. Project Data/Accounting Data Integration

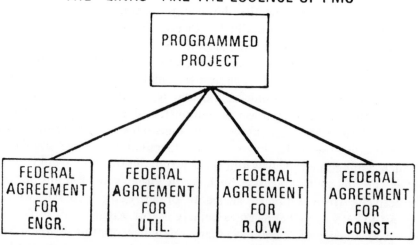

Source: Department of Transportation. *Project Management System* (PMS), Commonwealth of Pennsylvania, N.D.

for programmed projects and one for accounting charge numbers. As explained earlier, the PMS is driven by the links between the elements of the two databases.

The general data categories for programmed projects are listed below:

- Basic information (federal funding category, functional class, federal aid system, length, ADT)
- Narrative, including a project description and status information
- Project location (route and stationing)
- Related accounting charge numbers (links)
- Overall project costs for the engineering, right of way, and construction phases broken into federal, state, and other (local) shares
- Milestone achievement dates (physical progress)
- Senatorial and legislative districts

The general categories for accounting charge numbers are as follows:

- Basic information (federal project number, participation percentage)
- Narrative description of the work being performed
- Related programmed projects (links)
- Prior costs, current costs, and estimated future costs broken into the following shares: federal, state used to match the federal, state used for nonparticipating costs, and other (local).

The two separate databases are for programmed project data and accounting charge number (SPN) data. The upper portion of Figure C.3 shows that data enter the database either through online data entry from systems users or from an interface with the department's accounting system. The lower portion of the flowchart shows that reports are extracted either directly from the database or from fixed-length records written to a separate storage device. These records contain merged data from both databases and were created to meet special reporting requirements. The significant point is that while some data manipulation is accomplished with conventional programming languages (PL/I), all reports generated for systems users are created using a standard report generating package. One of the

FIGURE C.3. PMS Operational Flowchart

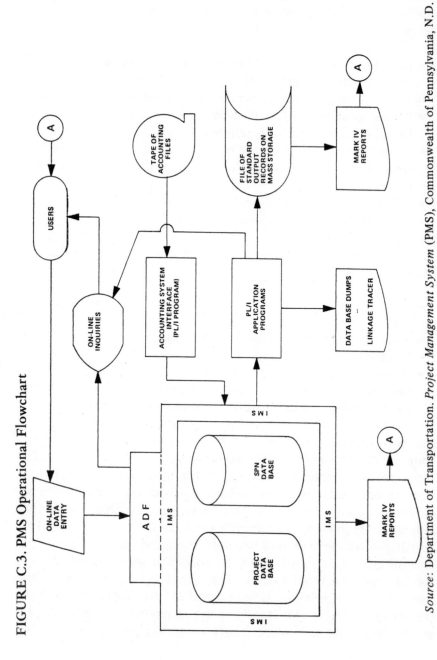

Source: Department of Transportation. *Project Management System* (PMS), Commonwealth of Pennsylvania, N.D.

main selling points for the PMS is that it is flexible enough to meet almost any reporting need (within the limitation of available data). Seldom will two users need exactly the same report (differences would occur in selection criteria, sort sequences, output formats, time period covered). Literally hundreds of different reports have been prepared in response to user requests. The PMS staff consists of five people, none of whom exists solely for the purpose of generating reports. However, armed with a knowledge of the databases and a good report-generating package, they can take a few notes from a telephone call, develop the reporting code, run the report, and return to their previous tasks. Obviously, some report requests take longer to develop but the bulk of them can be met relatively quickly. Another advantage to using a report-generating package is that it is easy to learn so that other bureaus can generate their own reports, freeing the system staff to spend more time on development and system maintenance.

Systems Users

The Project Management System is a lot of things; it is databases, reports, computers, display terminals, printers, and telephone lines. But most of all it is people. The computerized information system is not an end in itself but, rather, it is what the people using the system can do with the information it stores that determines the success or failure of the system. Producing a user-oriented system has been a continuing goal throughout the PMS development.

Most of the more than 260 users had never encountered a computerized system before and, as might be expected, many of them felt a great deal of apprehension about getting started. The PMS was designed for easy use, and this, combined with hands-on training and a comprehensive user's manual, has enabled most people to become proficient without a great deal of difficulty. The list of users includes the secretary, the district engineers, most of the executive staff, fiscal personnel, engineering and programming personnel, and support personnel.

It has been encouraging to observe the transition of the user perception of the PMS. Initially, "the system was winning," that is, many users felt somewhat enslaved to simply entering data into a computer terminal. Now, however, as the users become more knowledgeable and the system's capabilities increase, they are able to see ways to make the system work for them and provide them with the types of management information they need for their day-to-day work. This management information usually is in the form of a report extracted from the databases. The PMS staff has been extremely sensitive to turn these report requests around overnight for all but the more complicated reports. The users are the "customers," and it is imperative that the PMS provide them rapid and reliable service.

Security

With the commitment the department has made to the PMS in terms of personnel, time, and resources, security of the system is a major consideration. This includes both physical security of the data and necessary security measures to prevent invalid data from entering the database.

In the area of physical security, daily database backup copies are made and stored on computer tape. These copies can be used to restore the database should any problems develop. The tape copies are first stored in a fireproof vault and eventually to an off-site storage location (one of the department's county offices) to ensure that there will always be a means of recovering the databases.

Protection of the databases during normal operation involves controlling system access and data quality. Each user has a unique identification code that must be used to gain access to the PMS. Within that authorization, each user has been given a "profile" that defines his or her capabilities (retrieve, update, add, or delete) for each data entry screen (transaction). Each engineering district has access only to its own projects for update. Additionally, individual data fields are checked for validity. Invalid data are rejected and must be corrected before being accepted by the system.

Automatic Message Sending

One of the PMS objectives is to serve as a communication tool. A typical problem is that a change in a project schedule or estimated cost occurs but only a few people ever find out about it. Automatic message sending facilitates the dissemination of this critical information.

Any change in specified data fields causes a message automatically to be sent to any number of users on the message's "mailing list." Typically, these messages are used for notification of project additions or changes in a project's schedule or estimated costs. Users may access their messages through the computer terminals and are also given a daily printed listing of these messages for a permanent record.

Online Inquiry Capabilities

There are more than 3,700 individual programmed projects in the PMS and any single district office has between 250 and 650 projects. It would be difficult and time consuming to search sequentially through all the projects every time a list of projects with some common characteristics was needed. The PMS Inquiry System was developed to permit users to interrogate selectively their portions of the database. The inquiry capabilities are in three areas:

- Select all projects that meet criteria specified by the user.
- Select all projects that will achieve a certain milestone date (physical progress) within a specified time frame.
- Select all projects that have "missed" specified milestone dates by more than a tolerance specified by the user.

The PMS Inquiry System has proved to be an effective tool for enabling managers to focus their attention on a subset of the projects within their responsibility instead of having to contend with large listings of projects. A hard copy of the inquiry results can be obtained on printers located with the computer terminals. In this regard, the system also functions as an online report generator.

PMS APPLICATIONS

The discussion below reviews some of the applications using PMS data, which are in addition to preparing selective project listings. These applications represent a significant savings in time and personnel compared to manual document preparation.

Scheduling the Obligation of Federal Funds

The Highway Trust Fund, authorized and maintained by the federal government, is a major source of funding for many highway and bridge projects. Depending on the nature and location of the work, the federal government will fund, on a cost reimbursement basis, various percentages (up to 100 percent) of the project costs. Each state is apportioned or allocated an amount of money for which it may apply each fiscal year. An early step in the complicated process of obtaining this federal aid is the preparation of a schedule that lists the individual projects for which the department plans to obtain federal obligation within the fiscal year. This plan must identify the month in which a particular project will have its federal funds obligated because the federal procedures often place limits on the amount of funds that may be obligated to certain points within the fiscal year as well as on the annual total.

For each project, the PMS stores the dates associated with the federal obligation for the engineering, right of way, and construction phases. It also contains project cost data (broken down into federal, state, and other shares). With this available data, the PMS accesses the estimated costs and estimated federal obligation dates simultaneously to place the federal fund requirements into the appropriate month (based on the federal obligation date). These data, summarized across all projects, result in a menu of projects available for obligation consideration. On the "first cut," the dollar value of the candidate projects typically exceeds the obligational authority available to the department. The department's management then must make decisions at the program and/or project level to mold the menu of projects into an obligation plan. The obligations are totaled by county, engineering district, and statewide.

Tracking Preconstruction Activities

Figure C.4 shows a sample project status chart, which is primarily a collection of preconstruction milestone dates that are posted as either estimated, actual, or not applicable for a particular project. A few milestones are also captured that track the construction phase from an overall viewpoint. The milestones provide data on the physical progress of each project. The achievement of various approvals is also recorded since these items are often required to qualify for the federal funding described above.

For the most part, engineering district offices enter the estimated dates, but many of the actual dates may only be entered by central office bureaus. The prime concern is to capture a data element at its source and have it input there. For example, all interaction with the Federal Highway Administration for obtaining federal funding is co-ordinated through the Bureau of Highway Design. Personnel in that bureau are the first to be notified when federal approval is granted for a given project. These same personnel enter the actual approval date into the PMS.

Developing the Letting Schedule

An important document prepared by the department is the letting schedule, which shows the bid dates for various projects. The ability to accomplish the required administrative tasks in time to actually accept bids on the dates estimated on the letting schedule has a sig-nificant impact on the department's ability to manage its cash flow and accomplish the needed physical work on the highway system. Using a processing mode similar to that described above for the obligation plan, projects available for letting in a specified time frame are evaluated in light of established criteria (approvals) and, if all criteria are met, placed on the schedule for letting within a specified month. The major data provided include the project location and description, the month during which the project is to be let, and an indication of the cost range for the project.

The letting schedule is prepared once every three months for the following six-month period. The department distributes the schedule to the contracting industry. This has worked out well for both the department and the contractors. The contractors are able to plan the use of their own resources more efficiently, and the department has found that, in most cases, this increased awareness has resulted in lower bid prices.

The preparation of the letting schedule originally was a com-pletely manual process. The PMS has automated the production pro-cess so that the entire schedule can be generated overnight. This has freed people in the engineering, planning, and financial communities from worrying about physically producing the schedule and has en-

FIGURE C.4. Preconstruction Activities

DATE REPORT PREPARED: 81 03 23
SHORT TITLE: HACKETT RD BRIDGE
GROUP TITLE:

COUNTY: WASHINGTON DISTRICT: 12 IDEN: PIPER
L.R.: 62034 SECTION: A01
T.R.: SPUR:

| PROJECT STATUS CHART |
| PMS REF NBR: 124C032 |

(CATEGORY) GENERAL	(LAST UPDATE) (PIPER)	(LAST DATE) (81 01 21)	ACT FLG	EST DATE (YY MM DD)	ACTUAL DATE (YY MM DD)
DATE APPROVED BY PMC FOR DESIGN---FROM PR SEG = = >					
FM 4232 & 21 (DES & UTIL) SUB TO CO				79 11 16	81 03 16
FORM 4232 SUBMITTED TO FHWA				80 02 01	
FHWA APPROVAL OF FORM 4232				80 03 01	
COMPTROLLER APPROVAL OF FORM 21				80 03 20	80 03 10
SCOPING MEETING AND FIELD VIEW			X		
SECTION 105 APPROVAL					
CONSULTANT AGRMT EXECUTED -DESIGN			X		
PUBLIC HEARING DATE			X		80 08 08
N.E.P.A. APPROVAL					80 08 19
TSP OR DESIGN APPROVAL					80 08 19
ACT 120 AND PA BULLETIN ADV					80 09 03
DESIGN FIELD VIEW (STEP 9 APPRV)				81 02 01	80 11 13

(CATEGORY) STRUCTURES	(LAST UPDATE) (PIPER)	(LAST DATE) (80 11 13)	ACT FLG	EST DATE (YY MM DD)	ACTUAL DATE (YY MM DD)
SUBMIT TS & L				81 04 01	
DIST C. O. REVIEW TS & L				81 06 01	
COMPLETE STRUCTURE DESIGN				82 02 01	
C. O. REVIEW AND APP STR DES				82 04 01	

(CATEGORY) DESIGN	(LAST UPDATE) (PIPER)	(LAST DATE) (80 11 13)	ACT FLG	EST DATE (YY MM DD)	ACTUAL DATE (YY MM DD)
COMPLETE SOILS REPORT				81 09 01	
TYPICAL SECTIONS APPROVED				81 04 01	
PAVEMENT DESIGN APPROVED				81 04 01	
INTERCHANGE-CONTOUR GRAD & DRAINAGE			X		
PIPE HYDRAULIC COMPUTATIONS APPRVD				81 06 01	
SERVICE ROADS APPROVED			X		
REQUEST FOR D. E. R. PERMIT				81 02 01	
WATERWAY APPROVAL				81 03 15	
CORPS OF ENGINEERS PERMIT			X		
PRELIMINARY LIGHTING PLANS			X		
FINAL LIGHTING PLANS			X		
DEVEL PLANS FOR SIGNS AND SIGN STRT			X		
FINAL TRAF SIGNAL PLAN AND PERMIT			X		
COMPLETE PROJ UTIL RELOC EST (4171B)				81 08 01	
MAINT & PROTECTION OF TRAFFIC PLAN				82 04 01	
SAFETY REVIEW COMMITTEE MEETING				82 04 01	
FINAL DESIGN OFFICE MEETING			X	81 11 01	
DISTRICT REVIEW PS & E				82 04 01	
FINAL PLAN REVIEW				82 05 01	

R.O.W.

(PIPER)	(80 11 13)	FLG	(YY MM DD)
R.O.W. PLAN COMPLETED -------			81 07 01
COMPLETE R/W PROJ DAMAGE ESTIM-----			81 08 01
FINAL APPRAISALS AND PRE-APPROVALS---			82 02 01
FM 4232.21 & 46 SUBMITTED TO C.O. -----			81 08 01
FORM 4232 SUBMITTED TO FHWA --------			81 06 01
FHWA APPROVAL OF FORM 4232----------			81 07 01
COMPT. APPROVAL OF FORMS 21 AND 46 ----			81 11 01

BID/LET

(ORAGE)	(81 02 23)	FLG (YY MM DD)	(YY MM DD)
PS & E IN C.O. --ON TIME?	(N = NO)--		
SUBMISSION OF 4232 TO C.O. -------------		82 06 01	80 12 11
SUBMISSION OF 4232 TO FHWA -------------		82 03 01	81 01 27
FHWA APPROVAL OF 4232 -----------------			
FINAL R.O.W. CLEARANCE ---------------		82 05 01	
FINAL UTILITY CLEARANCE --------------		82 05 01	
ADVERTISE-------------------------		82 08 01	
AVAILABLE FOR LETTING ---------------		82 10 01	
CURRENTLY SCHEDULED LETTING = = = = =>			
(DATE LETTING WAS SCHEDULED) ------			
FIRST PREVIOUS SCHEDULED LETTING -----			
(DATE 1ST PREVIOUS WAS SCHEDULED) ----			
SECOND PREVIOUS SCHEDULED LETTING----			
(DATE 2ND PREVIOUS WAS SCHEDULED) ----			
SCHEDULED LET (PMSMIL INQUIRY) -------			TYPE:

CON CONTRACT

(PIPER)	(80 11 13)	FLG (YY MM DD)	(YY MM DD)
AWARD CONTRACT ----------------		82 11 01	
AGREEMENT EXECUTED --CONSTRUCTION ---		82 11 01	
NOTICE TO PROCEED --------------		82 12 01	
FINAL INSPECTION (PHYSICAL COMPL)----		83 12 01	
REQUEST FINAL FHWA INSPECT/ACCEPT ---		83 11 01	
FHWA FINAL INSPECTION/ACCEPTANCE ----		84 02 01	
ISSUE ACCEPTANCE CERTIFICATE --------		84 02 01	

P.U.C.

(PIPER)	(80 11 13)	FLG	(YY MM DD)
HOLD P. U. C. FIELD CONFERENCE-------			81 09 01
HOLD P. U. C. FORMAL HEARING-------			82 02 01
P. U. C. PREPARE AND PUB ORDER-------			82 05 01

Source: Department of Transportation. Project Management System (PMS), Commonwealth of Pennsylvania, N. D.

abled them to concentrate their efforts on identifying (by entries in the appropriate data fields) the projects that should appear on the letting schedule. A series of "trial" letting schedules is generated over the course of the three months between the preparation of the "final" schedules. District and central office personnel review the trial schedules, effect coordination to iron out any confusion regarding the department's intentions for particular projects, and make any database updates that may be necessary to move a project onto or off the letting schedule.

This coordination permits the generation of a letting schedule that is both accurate and timely.

Planned Applications

Several other applications can be implemented from PMS data. The department is developing techniques for producing a 12-month forecast of cash needs for payments to contractors for both construction and maintenance projects. Plans are also underway for using estimated future expenditure data to identify those projects for which the required amount of federal aid exceeds that currently obligated by the Federal Highway Administration. Early identification will permit timely corrective action. Another tedious process that can be aided by the PMS is the development of the federally mandated 105 program. This program requires submission of the individual phases of federal aid projects for which federal obligation will be requested within a given fiscal year. This can be prepared by combining narrative, cost, and scheduling data for the individual projects.

CONCLUSIONS

In order to address the difficulties created by the current tight fiscal constraints, the effects of past poor management, and the pressing maintenance needs on one of the largest highway systems in the nation, the Pennsylvania Department of Transportation has implemented a number of new concepts for administering the state's transportation program. These include

- Performance objectives
- A Program Management Committee

- A Center for Program Development and Management
- "Pay as you go" cash financing for all projects
- A decentralized organization with more program implementation responsibilities for the District Engineers
- A Project Management System

The PMS is a computerized information management system that integrates project-related data from the engineering and planning communities with accounting data from the financial community. It employs a centralized database with online data updating by users located throughout the state. Now that it has survived the initial resistance most new systems encounter, the PMS is proving itself to be a useful communication and management tool.

If an announcement that the PMS was being discontinued had been made one month after systems implementation, it would almost certainly have drawn a standing ovation from the users. That is no longer the case. The painful initial data loading is complete. Useful management reports are being prepared, and, although there is still a great deal of work to be done, there is definitely a light at the end of the tunnel. In the online information management system tunnel, the light at the end does not signify the end of the work but rather a point of stability where the user can get away from bulk data entry and spend more time on data maintenance for individual projects.

This data maintenance mode provides the opportunity for more frequent updating of the critical data items (estimated costs, milestone dates, project status) and still requires less time than users had to spend getting the basic project data entered (route, stationing, funding categories). The more frequent updating of the critical data items gives the PMS additional power to generate reports that reflect these more current estimates made by department managers in the field.

These capabilities enable the PMS to make major contributions in the area of scheduling the efficient use of dwindling resources. It is a key systems solution to assist in program management in the Pennsylvania Department of Transportation.

Bibliography

Ackoff, R. L. 1967. "Management Misinformation Systems." *Management Science* 14, 4 (December): B140–B156.

Aldrich, Howard E. 1979. *Organizations and Environment.* Englewood Cliffs, N.J.: Prentice-Hall.

Allen, Thomas. 1977. *Managing the Flow of Technology.* Cambridge, Mass.: Massachusetts Institute of Technology.

American National Standards Institute. 1971. *Standard Flowchart Symbols and Their Use in Information Processing.* (New York: American National Standards Institute).

Anthony, Robert N., and Regina E. Herzlinger. 1980. *Management Control in Non-Profit Organizations.* Homewood, Ill.: Richard D. Irwin.

Bozeman, Barry, and E. Cole. 1982. "Scientific and Technical Information in Public Management." *R & D Management* 13, 4: 479–93.

Buffa, Frank P., and George C. Fowler. 1981. "Information Systems for Cost Control—Models to Municipal Users." College Station: College of Business Administration, Texas A&M University.

Chartrand, Robert. 1977. *The Legislator as User of Information Technology.* Report No. 80–11 SPR. Washington, D.C.: Congressional Research Service, Library of Congress.

Cleland, David I., and William R. King. 1983. *Systems Analysis and Project Management.* New York: McGraw-Hill.

Chi, Keon S. 1982. "Computer Reporting Network for Welfare Administration: The Wisconsin Experience." *Innovations* (July): 1–7.

Colton, Kent W., (ed). *Police Computer Technology.* (Lexington, MA: Lexington Books, 1978).

Colton, Kent W. 1980. "Police Computer Technology." *Public Productivity Review,* March. pp. 21–42.

Danziger, James N. and Rob Kling. 1982. "Computers in the Policy Process," in James N. Danziger, William H. Dutton, Rob Kling and Kenneth Kraemer, *Computers and Politics* (New York: Columbia University Press), pp. 136-168.

Danziger, James N. 1977. "Computers, Local Governments, and the Litany to EDP." *Public Administration Review* 37, 1 (January/February): 28-37.

——, William H. Dutton, Rob Kling, and Kenneth L. Kraemer. 1982. *Computers and Politics: High Technology in American Local Governments.* New York: Columbia University Press.

Danziger, J. N., K. L. Kraemer, and J. L. King. 1978. "An Assessment of Computer Technology in Local Governments." 1978. *Urban Systems* 3: 21-37.

David, E. E., Jr. 1980. "Industrial Reserach in America: Challenge of a New Synthesis." *Science* 209 (July 4): 133-38.

Davidson, William H. 1984. *The Amazing Race: Winning the Technorivalry with Japan* (New York: John Wiley and Sons).

Davis, G. B. 1978. *Computers and Information Processing.* New York: McGraw-Hill.

——. 1974. *Management Information Systems: Conceptual Foundations, Structure and Development.* New York: McGraw-Hill.

——, and G. C. Everest. 1976. *Readings in Management Information Systems.* New York: McGraw-Hill.

Davis, R. M. 1977. "Evolution of Computers and Computing." *Science* (March 18): 1096-101.

Dutton, William H. 1982. "Eighty Thousand Information Systems: The Utilization of Computing in American Local Governments." *Computers, Environment and Urban Systems* 7: 21-33.

Edelson, B. I., and R. S. Cooper. 1982. "Business Uses of Satellite Communications." *Science* 215 (February 12): 837-42.

Galbraith, Jay. 1974. "Organization Design: An Information Processing View." *Interfaces* 4 (May): 28-36.

Ginzberg, Michael J. 1981. "Steps Toward More Effective Implementation of MS and MIS." In *Management Information Systems*, edited by M. J. Riley. San Francisco: Holden-Day.

Goldstein, Robert C., and Richard Nolan. 1982. "Personal Privacy Versus the Corporate Computer." In *Managing the Data Resource Function.* Edited by Richard Nolan. St. Paul, Minn.: West.

Hall, R. H. 1977. *Organizations, Structure and Process.* Englewood Cliffs, N.J.: Prentice-Hall.

Harrell, R. D. 1980. *Developing a Financial Management Information System for Local Governments: The Key Issues.* Chicago: Municipal Finance Officers Association, Government Finance Research Center.

Harrell, Rhett D., ed. 1981. *Developing a Financial Management Information System for Local Governments: The Key Issues Proceedings Document.* Washington, D.C.: Government Finance Research Center.

Hayes, Frederick O'R., David A. Grossman, Jerry E. Mechling, John S. Thomas, and Steven J. Rosenbloom. 1982. *Linkages—Improving Financial Management in Local Government.* Washington, D.C.: Urban Institute Press.

Hicks, James O. 1985. *Management Information Systems* (St. Paul, MN: West Publishing Co.).

Hodges, P. 1981. "Technologies to Get You Through the Eighties." *Output* (August): 22–39.

Horton, Forest W., Jr. 1979. *Information Resources Management: Concept and Cases.* Cleveland: Association for Systems Management.

——, and D. A. Marchand, eds. 1982. *Information Management in Public Administration.* Arlington, Va.: Information Resources Press.

Kast, F. E., and J. E. Rosenzweig. 1979. *Organization and Management, A Systems and Contingency Approach.* New York: McGraw-Hill.

Katz, Daniel, and Robert L. Kahn. 1966. *The Social Psychology of Organizations.* New York: Wiley.

Kelly, Frank. 1978. "Computerization of Budgetary Processes in the States." *Public Administration Review* 38, 4: 381–86.

Kettinger, William J. 1980. *Developing an Information Resource Management Activity in Local Government: An Implementation Guide.* No. 2. Columbia: Bureau of Governmental Research and Service, University of South Carolina.

Kettinger, William J. 1983. *Implementing Integrated Office Systems: Ten Lessons Learned from S.O.A.P.S.* Institute of Information Management, Technology and Policy, College of Business Administration, University of South Carolina.

Kling, Rob, and Kenneth Kraemer. 1982. "Computing and Urban Services." In *Computers and Politics: High Technology in American Local Governments.* Edited by James N. Danziger, William H. Dutton, Rob Kling, and Kenneth L. Kraemer. New York: Columbia University Press.

Knight, K. E., and R. R. McDaniel, Jr. 1979. *Organizations: An Information Systems Perspective.* Belmont, Calif.: Wadsworth.

Kraemer, K. L., and W. H. Dutton. 1979. "The Interests Served by Technological Reform: The Case of Computing." *Administration and Society* 11, 1: 80–106.

Kraemer, K. L., W. H. Dutton, and J. R. Matthews. 1974. "Municipal Computers: Growth, Usage and Management." *Urban Data Service Report* 7, 11 (November): 1–15.

Kraemer, K. L., and J. L. King. 1977. *Computers and Local Government. A Manager's Guide.* Vol. 2. New York: Praeger.

Kraemer, K. L., and J. L. Perry. 1979. *The Federal Push to Bring Technology to Local Governments: The Case of Computers.* Irvine, Calif.: Public Policy Research Organization, University of California.

Lawrence, Paul R. and Jay W. Lorsch. 1967. *Organization and Environment.* (Boston, MA: Graduate School of Business Administration, Harvard University.)

Lucas, H. C., Jr. 1978. *Information Systems Concepts for Management.* New York: McGraw-Hill.

McGowan, Robert. 1983a. "Patterns of Information Acquisition by Public Managers: A Study of State Agencies." *American Review of Public Administration* (March).

———. 1983b. "The Professional in Public Organizations: Lessons from the Private Sector?" *American Review of Public Administration* (March).

———. 1982. "The Use of Computers in Government: A Look at Municipal Fire Services." *Computers, Environment and Urban Systems* 7: 159.

——, and S. Loveless. 1982. "Strategies for Information Management: The Administrator's Perspective." *Public Administration Review* 41 (May/June): 331-39.

Madnick, S. E. 1977. "Trends in Computers and Computing: The Information Utility." *Science* 195 (March 18): 1191-198.

Marchand, Donald, and John Stucker. 1977. *Information Systems in Local Government: Management Strategies and Technical Assistance for Obtaining Low Cost Data Processing Services.* Columbia: University of South Carolina.

Martin, James. 1976. *Principles of Data-Base Management.* Englewood Cliffs, N.J.: Prentice-Hall.

Mason, Richard O., and Ian I. Mitroff. 1973. "A Program for Research on Management Information Systems." *Management Science* 19, 5: 475.

Mayo, J. S. 1982. "Evolution of the Intelligent Telecommunications Network." *Science* 215 (February 12): 831-37.

Meyer, Marshall. 1979. *Change in Public Bureaucracies.* Cambridge: Cambridge University Press.

Morss, Elliot R., and Robert Rich. 1980. *Government Information Management: A Counter-Report of the Commission on Federal Paperwork.* Boulder, Colo.: Westview Press.

Municipal Finance Officers Association of the United States and Canada. 1980. *Governmental Accounting, Auditing, and Financial Reporting.* Chicago.

Murdick, Robert G., and Joel E. Ross. 1979. *Information Systems for Modern Management*, 2nd ed. Englewood Cliffs, N.J.: Prentice-Hall.

Newell, A., and R. F. Sproull. 1982. "Computer Networks: Prospects for Scientists." *Science* 215 (February 12): 843-52.

Nolan, D. A. 1982. "Natural Project Control," in Jack B. Rochester (ed.). *Perspectives on Information Management.* (New York: John Wiley and Sons), pp. 23-40.

Northrop, Ilana, William H. Dutton, and Kenneth L. Kraemer. 1982. "Management of Computer Applications in Local Government." *Public Administration Review* (May/June): 234-43.

Oettinger, A. G. 1980. "Information Resources: Knowledge and Power in the 21st Century." *Science* 209 (July 4): 191+.

Office of Management and Budget, Executive Office of the President, *Memorandum to Associates in Information Technology*, "Subject: Federal Data Processing Resources," Washington, D.C. August 20, 1979.

Office of Management and Budget, Executive Office of the President. *Standards Team Report.* President's Reorganization Project, Washington, D.C. June 13, 1978.

Pennsylvania, Commonwealth of. Office of Budget and Administration. Bureau of EDP Policy and Planning. 1983. *Commonwealth EDP Master Plan 1983.*

Perry, J. L., and K. L. Kraemer. 1979. *Technological Innovation in American Local Governments: The Case of Computing.* New York: Pergamon.

Petersen, John E., Catherine L. Spain, and C. Wayne Stallings. 1983. "From Monitorings to Mandating: State Roles in Local Government Finance." In *Readings in Public Administration—Institutions, Processes, Behavior, Policy*, 4th ed. Edited by Robert T. Golembiewski and Frank Gibson. Boston: Houghton Mifflin.

Pfeffer, Jeffrey. 1978. *Organizational Design.* Arlington Heights, Ill.: AHM.

Pogrow, Stanley. 1979. "Technical and Political Dimensions of Data Rationality in the Implementation of Public Policy." Paper presented at the Annual Meeting, Midwest Political Science Association.

Public Law 89-306. 1965. 89th Congress, H. R. 4845. October 30.

Public Law 96-511. 1980. Chapter 35. Coordination of Federal Information Policy (Paperwork Reduction Act of 1980). December 11.

Quade, E. S. 1975. *Analysis for Public Decisions.* New York: Elsevier.

Radford, K. R. 1977. *Complex Decision Problems: An Integrated Strategy for Resolution.* Reston, Va.: Reston.

Rosenthal, Stephen R. 1982. *Managing Government Operations.* Glenview, Ill.: Scott, Foresman.

Rule, James, D. McAdams, L. Stearns, and D. Uglow. 1980. *The Politics of Privacy: Planning for Personal Data Systems as Powerful Technologies.* New York: Elsevier.

Savas, E. S. 1982. *Privatizing the Public Sector.* (Chatham, N.J.: Chatham House Publishers, Inc.)

Savas, E. S. 1969. "Computers in Public Administration." *Public Administration Review* 29 (March/April): 225.

Senn, James A. 1982. *Information Systems in Management*, 2nd ed. Belmont, Calif.: Wadsworth.

Simon, Herbert A. 1973a. "Applying Information Technology to Organization Design." *Public Administration Review* 37, 1: 268-78.

———. 1973b. "The Structure of Ill-Structured Decision Processes," *Artificial Intelligence* 4: 181-201.

Steiner, George A., and John B. Miner. 1982. *Management Policy and Strategy*, 2nd ed. New York: Macmillan.

Strassman, Paul A. 1980. "The Office of the Future: Information Management for the New Age." *Technology Review* (December/January): 52-65.

Thierauf, Robert J., and George W. Reynolds. 1980. *Systems Analysis and Design: A Case Study Approach.* Columbus, Ohio: Charles E. Merrill.

U.S. Department of Health, Education, and Welfare. 1973. Secretary's Advisory Committee on Automated Personnel Data Systems. *Records, Computers and the Rights of Citizens.* Washington, D.C.: U.S. Government Printing Office.

U.S. Department of Labor. 1980. Employment and Training Administration. *ET Handbook No. 378 Functional Management Information System.* Washington, D.C. July.

U.S. General Accounting Office. 1982. *Federal Information Systems Remain Highly Vulnerable to Fraudulent, Wasteful, Abusive, and Illegal Practices.* Washington, D.C.

———. 1981a. *Non-Federal Computer Acquisition Practices Provide Useful Information for Streamlining Federal Methods.* Washington, D.C. October.

———. 1981b. *Solving Social Security's Computer Problems: Comprehensive Corrective Action Plan and Better Management Needed.* Washington, D.C. December.

——. 1980. Comptroller General. Report to the Congress of the United States. "Wider Use of Better Computer Software Technology Can Improve Management Control and Reduce Costs." Washington, D.C. April 29.

U.S. Government. 1976. Domestic Council Committee on the Right to Privacy. *National Information Policy: Statement of the Problem and Recommendations.* Washington, D.C.: National Commission on Libraries and Information Science.

U.S. Office of Management and Budget, Executive Office of the President. 1978. Acquisition Team Report. "Federal Data Processing Reorganization Study," *President's Reorganization Project.* Washington, D.C. June 20.

——. 1979. Information Systems Policy Divisions. *Computer Security: A List of Policies, Regulations, Reports and Other Reference Documents Pertaining to the Development of Federal Computer Security Programs; to Reduce Fraud and Waste, to Protect Personal, Proprietary and Other Sensitive Information.* Washington, D.C., February.

——. 1978. Operational Management Team Report. "Federal Data Processing Reorganization Study." *President's Reorganization Project*, September.

——. 1978. Personnel Team Report, "Federal Data Processing Reorganization Study." *President's Reorganization Study.* Washington, D.C. September 1.

——. 1978. *President's Reorganization Project. National Security Report.* Federal Data Processing Reorganization Study. Washington, D.C. October.

——. 1978. Report of the General Government Team to the President's Federal Data Processing Reorganization Project, "Information Technology: Challenges for Top Program Management in the General Government Agencies," *President's Reorganization Project.* June.

——. 1978. Report of the Human Resources Team, "The Federal Data Processing Reorganization Study," *President's Reorganization Study.* September.

——. 1978. Small Users Team Report, "Federal Data Processing Reorganization Study." *President's Reorganization Study.* Washington, D.C. July 1.

——. 1979. Summary of the Federal Data Processing Reorganization Project, "Information Technology and Governmental Reorganization," *President's Reorganization Project.* Washington, D.C. April.

Wamsley, Gary L., and Mayer N. Zald. 1976. *The Political Economy of Public Organizations: A Critique and Approach to the Study of Public Administration.* Bloomington: Indiana University Press.

Warwick, D. P., with Marvin Meade, and Theodore Reed. 1975. *A Theory of Public Bureaucracy.* Cambridge, Mass.: Harvard University Press.

Wright, Deil S. 1978. *Understanding Intergovernmental Relations.* North Scituate, Mass.: Duxbury Press.

Index

About the Authors
and Contributors

JACK STEVENS is an Associate Professor of Public Administration at The Pennsylvania State University where he teaches and does research in organization and management strategy, managerial commitment, policy implementation, information systems, financial management, national security administration, business-government relations and human resource management. He has recently published in journals such as the *Academy of Management Journal, Public Administration Review, Policy Studies Review, Journal of Management*, and *Public Productivity Review* among others. Jack is on the editorial board and has twice served as a symposium editor for *Public Productivity Review* as well as an ad-hoc reviewer for the *Academy of Management Review* and *Work and Occupations.* He has been active in the Public Sector Division of the Academy of Management and American Society for Public Administration section on Management Science and Policy Analysis as both a reviewer and presenter. He has also been a consultant to Federal, state and local governments and agencies for the past eight years.

ROBERT P. McGOWAN is an Assistant Professor of Management in the Graduate School of Business and Public Management, University of Denver. He was previously a senior consultant with Deloitte, Haskins, and Sells, C.P.A. where he was responsible for the implementation of automated financial and management control systems in the public sector. He has also worked in the U.S. Department of Commerce and Illinois Department of Transportation. Robert McGowan is currently teaching and consulting on the role of advanced technology industry in local economic development.

CAROLE BENSON KOTTMEIER received an undergraduate degree in Political Science from Cedar Crest College and a Master's Degree in Public Administration from The Pennsylvania State University. She has managed training programs, counseling and assessment services, and the management information system for Comprehensive Employment and Training Act (CETA) programs. Carole continued her work in governmental information systems as a consultant to the Governor's Management Improvement Plan in New Jersey. Ms. Kottmeier is currently consulting to federal, state and local agencies in information and management systems.

SCOTT KUTZ received his Bachelor's and Master's Degrees in Civil Engineering from The Pennsylvania State University. He later designed and implemented the Project Management System (PMS) which is an on-line computer system used by The Pennsylvania Department of Transportation to manage highway and bridge projects. He is currently employed by IBM Corporation as a State Government Industry Specialist where he is concentrating on the application of geoprocessing software to manage the data used in Roadway Management Systems.

MICHAEL J. O'NEIL is currently employed as a management analyst in the Office of Program Planning and Evaluation of the Veterans Administration's Central Office, Washington, D.C. He began working for the VA in 1975 after serving as a military intelligence specialist in the United States Army. He has had several years of experience at all levels of the VA's Insurance Activity and was involved in the planning and development of the redesign of the Insurance ADP System. He earned a bachelor's degree in international relations from St. Joseph's University in Philadelphia and a Master of Public Administration from the Pennsylvania State University.